Coming Soon to a Festival Near You:

Programming Film Festivals

Edited by

Jeffrey Ruoff

First published in Great Britain in 2012 by
St Andrews Film Studies
99 North Street, St Andrews, KY16 9AD
Scotland, United Kingdom
Publisher: Dina Iordanova

Secure on-line ordering:
www.stafs.org

British Library Cataloguing-in-Publication Data
A catalogue record for this book is available from the British Library.

ISBN 978-1-908437-02-0 (paperback)

University of
St Andrews

The book is published with the assistance of the Centre for Film Studies at the University of St Andrews and the Royal Society of Edinburgh.

St Andrews Film Studies promotes greater understanding of, and access to, international cinema and film culture worldwide.

The University of St Andrews is a charity registered in Scotland, No. SC013532

Cover image: Mariola Brillowska sits front and centre at the screening of her film *Des Teufels Kinder* (*Children of the Devil*, 2011, Germany) at the 4th Animator festival in Poznań, Poland, July 2010. © Animator International Festival of Animated Film

Cover design: Duncan Stewart.

Cover and pre-press: University of St Andrews Print & Design.

Printed in Great Britain by Lightning Source.

To Natalie and Glennis,

my alpha and omega

Festivals have multiplied and spread to become the single most important arbiter of taste in cinema — more important than scholars, or critics, more important even than film schools.

— Cameron Bailey, co-director, Toronto International Film Festival, 2009

Contents

Acknowledgements

My understanding of cinema has been shaped by film festivals. They have brought me in touch not only with films, but with international programmers, critics and filmmakers whose comments have contributed directly and indirectly to *Coming Soon to a Festival Near You*.

As a graduate student, I attended the mecca of American independent film, the legendary Flaherty Film Seminar, in 1988, 1989, and 1990 at Wells College in Wells, New York, and many years later in 2003 at Vassar College in Poughkeepsie, New York. In 1990 and 1991, I went to the Margaret Mead Film and Video Festival (then programmed by my friend Elaine Charnov) at the American Museum of Natural History in New York City. In 1993, following the trail of early cinema specialists, I saw a week of films from 1913 at the Pordenone Silent Film Festival in northern Italy. In 1994, thanks to a Fulbright research grant in France, I was able to attend the Göttingen International Ethnographic Film Festival in Germany, the Festival dei Popoli International Documentary Film Festival in Florence, Italy, and the Cinéma du Réel International Documentary Film Festival in Paris. At Cinéma du Réel, a British critic memorably asked veteran director Frederick Wiseman, after a screening of his three-hour-and-twenty-minute *High School II* (U.S., 1994) when Wiseman was going to finish editing the film. In 1995 and 1996, while teaching in the Netherlands, I feasted on the International Documentary Film Festival Amsterdam, and in 1997 Beeld voor Beeld: Documentary Film Festival on Cultural Diversity, also in Amsterdam. In 2000, I attended the French/American Film Workshop in Avignon, a festival, now no longer in existence, that brought together independent filmmakers from the U.S., France and Europe.

Beginning in 2004, I started to attend festivals more systematically and I am grateful to Dartmouth College for funds that made these journeys possible. In 2004, 2006, and 2008, I travelled to the biennial Carthage Film Festival in Tunis, the great festival of Arab and African cinema, where I was enchanted by many films which, unfortunately, will never reach North American shores. In 2005, I attended SilverDocs: American Film Institute/ Discovery Channel Documentary Festival in Washington, D.C., and the International Film Festival Marrakech. Catalogues of the 2006 Telluride Film Festival in Colorado and the 2006 Lisbon International Documentary Film Festival in Portugal used some of my writings on cinema. In 2007, I made a long-anticipated trip to the Pan-African Film Festival of Ouagadougou in Burkina Faso, where I watched movies in open-air theatres under the stars. In

2008, I attended the Edinburgh International Film Festival in Scotland, while programmers at Cinéma du Réel borrowed ideas from my anthology *Virtual Voyages: Cinema and Travel* (2006) for a retrospective section entitled Figures de Tourisme. In 2009, I finally fulfilled my Dartmouth colleague Bill Pence's suggestion that I attend a 'real film festival'; while on a fellowship in Cassis, France, I obtained a festival pass and cruised up the Riviera in a rented car to go to the Cannes International Film Festival. In 2011, the International Istanbul Film Festival offered delights inside and outside its theatres.

Over the years, I have enjoyed discussing film festivals with Bill Pence, Director of Film at the Hopkins Center for the Arts at Dartmouth College and co-founder of the Telluride Film Festival. Bill has contributed in numerous ways to this anthology. My colleagues in the Department of Film and Media Studies at Dartmouth — Jim Brown, Peter Ciardelli, Cheryl Coutermarsh, Mary Desjardins, David Ehrlich, Mary Flanagan, Gerd Gemunden, Amy Lawrence, Jodie Mack, Bill Phillips, and Mark Williams — have created and maintained a wonderful place to teach and do research. Susan Bibeau, Jeffrey Hawkins and Anthony Helm give the kind of timely computer advice that makes scholarship both feasible and enjoyable. I would like to acknowledge my students, too numerous to mention individually, whose comments have contributed to my thinking on film festivals.

My thanks to the Office of the Provost, the Dean of the Faculty, the John Sloan Dickey Center for International Understanding, and the Leslie Center for the Humanities for support for my research. I am grateful to Provost Carol Folt, Associate Dean Kate Conley, Chris Wohlforth, associate director of the Dickey Center, and Adrian Randolph, director of the Leslie Center, for funds to bring two programmers and a film critic to Dartmouth to discuss *Coming Soon to a Festival Near You*. The Leslie Center hosted this event and I am indebted to administrator Isabel Weatherdon for her valuable assistance. At this workshop, Zoë Elton, Gerald Peary and Richard Peña shared their individual chapters and made important contributions to the overall approach of the anthology. Bill Pence joined our discussions and made many crucial comments. Funds left over from the workshop also supported the completion of this manuscript.

My thanks to all the contributors to this volume for completing their work brilliantly, and on time, making my work as editor as pleasurable as possible. I learned a lot. My editor at St Andrews Film Studies, Dina Iordanova, and production editor Alex Marlow-Mann, provided outstanding and expedient help throughout the whole process of manuscript preparation. The references in this anthology to related St Andrews books attest to Iordanova's pivotal contribution to the burgeoning field of film festival studies. My gratitude is also due to Nina Graybill, Esq., for legal assistance. A special thanks goes to Cornelia Waterfall whose pen and inquisitive mind improved this manuscript in innumerable ways. I am grateful to Peter Fong for editing the manuscript and to John Bealle for indexing it.

My final thanks are reserved for my wife Glennis Gold and our daughter Natalie Gold, to whom *Coming Soon to a Festival Near You* is dedicated. As director Guido Anselmi says in Federico Fellini's *8½* (1963, Italy/France), which premiered at Cannes in 1963, 'Life is a festival, let's live it together!'

Contributors

Mahen Bonetti, originally from Sierra Leone, is founder and executive director of the African Film Festival, a non-profit arts organisation established in 1990 in New York City. AFF showcases works of African filmmakers and develops ways to share the vision and culture of African film with American and international audiences.

Marijke de Valck is an assistant professor in the Department of Media Studies at the University of Amsterdam and the author of *Film Festivals: From European Geopolitics to Global Cinephilia* (2007). With Skadi Loist, Marijke founded and runs the Film Festival Research Network, www. filmfestivalresearch.org, that aims to facilitate exchange among researchers, critics and festival professionals. She is also co-editor of *Cinephilia: Movies, Love and Memory* (2005) and has published articles in journals such as *Cinema Journal, International Journal of Cultural Studies* and *New Review of Film and Television Studies*.

Gönül Dönmez-Colin is an independent film scholar and curator. Among her books are *Women, Islam and Cinema* (2004), *Cinemas of the Other: A Personal Journey with Filmmakers from the Middle East and Central Asia* (2006) and *Turkish Cinema: Identity, Distance and Belonging* (2008). She is also an adviser to Kerala International Film Festival, Chennai Women's Film Festival, and Mannheim-Heidelberg International Film Festival.

Zoë Elton works in film and theatre as a curator, writer, director and educator. As long-time director of programming for Mill Valley Film Festival, her initiatives range from pioneering video programmes in the 1980s to the recent Active Cinema programme. She has consulted for the Rwanda Film Festival, is an adviser for the Mendocino Film Festival and Frame of Mind Films, and is film reviewer for KVOT in New Mexico.

Marcin Giżycki is a Polish art historian, critic, filmmaker, and the artistic director of the Animator International Festival of Animated Films in Poznań, Poland, founded in 2008. He was editor-in-chief of *Animafilm* magazine and, since 1988, has taught at the Rhode Island School of Design in Providence, Rhode Island. He has made a number of documentary and animated films, including *The Island of Jan Lenica* (1998), *A Sicilian Flea* (2008), and *Alfred Schreyer from Drohobych* (2011).

Sayoko Kinoshita is an animation producer and director. Her independent documentary animation shorts, including *Made in Japan* (1972), *Japonese* (1977), *Pica Don* (1978), *The Last Air Raid — Kumagaya* (1993) and *Ryuku Okoku — Made in Okinawa* (2004), made with Renzo Kinoshita, have received numerous prizes internationally. Since 1985, she has been the director of the Hiroshima International Animation Festival, which she founded with Renzo. She served as the president of the International Animated Film Association (ASIFA) from 2006 to 2009. She is a visiting professor at the Osaka University of Art.

Sangjoon Lee is a postdoctoral fellow of Screen Arts and Cultures at the University of Michigan-Ann Arbor. He received a PhD in Cinema Studies at New York University. His dissertation is entitled 'The Transnational Asian Studio System: Cinema, Nation-State, and Globalization in Cold War Asia'. Prior to his graduate studies in North America, Lee was an assistant producer, screenwriter, and video journalist in the Korean film and television industry for many years.

Toby Lee is a PhD candidate in Social Anthropology and Film & Visual Studies at Harvard University. Her dissertation, an ethnographic and historical study of the Thessaloniki International Film Festival, examines how public culture and its institutions shape notions of place and cultural citizenship in Greece today. Her research interests include cultural politics, urban studies, and the anthropology of space and visual culture.

Skadi Loist is a PhD candidate and Junior Researcher in the Department of Media and Communications at the University of Hamburg, Germany. With Marijke de Valck, she co-founded and runs the Film Festival Research Network, www.filmfestivalresearch.org. Her PhD project analyses queer film festivals in the U.S. and Germany. She co-edited *Bildschön: 20 Jahre Lesbisch Schwule Filmtage Hamburg* (2009) and, since 2002, has been working with the Hamburg International Queer Film Festival.

Gerald Peary is a professor in the Department of Communications at Suffolk University in Boston, the programmer and curator for the Boston University Cinematheque, and a long-time film critic for *The Boston Phoenix*. He is the author of eight books on cinema and of numerous articles in newspapers, magazines, and scholarly periodicals. He wrote and directed the 2008 feature documentary *For the Love of Movies: The Story of American Film Criticism*.

Richard Peña has been the programme director of the Film Society of Lincoln Center and the director of the New York Film Festival since 1988. He is a professor in the School of the Arts at Columbia University, where he specialises in film theory and international cinema. From 2006 to 2009, he was a visiting professor in Spanish at Princeton University. He is also currently the co-host of Channel 13's weekly *Reel 13*.

Jeffrey Ruoff is a film historian, documentary filmmaker and an associate professor of Film and Media Studies at Dartmouth College. His *An American Family: A Televised Life* (2002) is the definitive study of the documentary series many consider to be the forerunner of reality television. His anthology *Virtual Voyages: Cinema and Travel* was published by Duke University Press in 2006. He is currently producing and directing a documentary about the dance company Pilobolus, *Still Moving: Pilobolus at Forty*.

James Schamus is CEO of Focus Features, the motion picture production, financing, and worldwide distribution company whose films include *Lost in Translation* (2003), *Brokeback Mountain* (2005), and *Coraline* (2009). Schamus is an award-winning screenwriter and producer (*The Ice Storm*, 1997, *Brokeback Mountain*) and a professor at the School of the Arts at Columbia University, where he teaches film history and theory. The University of Washington Press published his *Carl Dreyer's* Gertrud: *The Moving Word* in 2008.

Illustrations

Front cover. Screening, 2010 Animator International Festival of
    Animated Film

Introduction:
Programming Film Festivals

Jeffrey Ruoff

Film festivals are crucial exhibition circuits, because they nurture independent films, showcase national cinemas, and bring international films to ever-increasing audiences. In recent decades, as art cinemas have closed, and as cities have explored new ways to enhance tourism and cultural exchange, more festivals have appeared every year. There are now several thousand throughout the world (figure I.1).

The first ever, the Venice International Film Festival in 1932, put cinema on a par with the other arts at the Venice Biennale. After the Second World War, it was joined by other European festivals, including the Cannes International Film Festival, founded in 1939 but opened only in 1946, and the Edinburgh International Film Festival in 1947. In 1957, the San Francisco International Film Festival opened — the first major festival in the U.S. — followed in 1963 by the New York Film Festival (NYFF). By the mid-1960s, there were dozens of festivals, still mostly in Europe and North America. Then, in the late 1970s, festivals became a global phenomenon with, for example, the Cairo International Film Festival starting in 1976, the Hong Kong International Film Festival in 1977, and the Havana Film Festival in 1979.[1]

As will become apparent throughout *Coming Soon to a Festival Near You*, festivals either celebrate film as an art, affirm different kinds of identity via film, facilitate the marketing of films, or often, indeed, some combination of these. The Telluride Film Festival in Colorado, for example, exhibits the best of world cinema, showcasing film as a medium of artistic expression. The Pan-African Film Festival of Ouagadougou (FESPACO) in Burkina Faso militates for politically engaged cinema as a medium of cultural and national identity (figure I.2). Initially a showcase for award-winning films from other festivals, the Toronto International Film Festival has morphed into the major market-oriented festival in North America, with strong ties to Hollywood studios.

Festivals distinguish themselves in a number of ways, through their

"What this place needs is a film festival."

I.1. Mischa Richter spoofs the globalization of film festivals in this 1984 cartoon published in *The New Yorker*. © Mischa Richter/The New Yorker Collection/ Cartoonbank.com

locations, by awarding prizes, and by providing markets, media exposure, production funds, and other initiatives. They also distinguish themselves through their programming — the films and related events that they schedule. Some specialise in a particular kind of cinema, such as non-fiction at the Cinéma du Réel International Documentary Film Festival in Paris. Some festivals curate a limited number of screenings, whereas other mega-festivals — like the Berlin International Film Festival — seemingly offer something for everyone. Programmers increasingly fulfil

I.2. Among other attractions at FESPACO, memorable evening screenings take place in Ouagadougou's permanent open-air theatres. © Jeffrey Ruoff

the role of cultural gatekeepers, who triage worldwide film production, guiding audiences through the multitudes of movies produced annually. Programming, however, is not a matter of festival directors simply choosing the films they want to show. Even the most powerful festivals — Cannes, Toronto, Venice, Berlin, Sundance — engage in delicate negotiations with filmmakers, distributors, and sales agents to secure the rights to première new works. Furthermore, agents and distributors, not festival programmers, determine in great measure the programming options of secondary festivals (Peranson 2009: 30).

Festivals are celebrations, featuring entertainment and, if effective, transcendental moments of 'time out of time' (Falassi 1987). A film festival is a live event. Successful festivals maximise this live dimension. Programming seeks to highlight the event status, the sense of community, face-to-face contact with audience members, programmers and filmmakers. Festivals also involve showmanship. Programmers are barkers — circus ringmasters, if you will — that recall cinema's origins in fairgrounds. It is one thing to see a gloriously restored 35mm print of the Egyptian classic *Al-Momia* (*The Night of Counting the Years*, Shadi Abdei Salam, 1969). It is quite another to see the same movie introduced at Cannes 2009 by director Martin Scorsese, a special guest of the festival.

I.3. Will the 2011 'Jasmine Revolution' rejuvenate the Carthage Film Festival in Tunis, the pioneering biennial celebration of Arab and African cinema? © Jeffrey Ruoff

Extraordinary events also occur *outside* theatres. That same year, Belgian director Felix van Groeningen, together with four actors from his film *La Merditude des choses* (*The Misfortunates*, Belgium/Netherlands, 2009), bicycled naked along the Riviera in Cannes, cleverly publicising their movie by re-enacting a risqué scene.

There are festive events at most film festivals: dinners, schmoozing, partying, special trips. The International Istanbul Film Festival, for instance, caps a week of screenings of Turkish films by programming an afternoon cruise for festival guests on the Bosphorus, an illuminating experience of sun, sky and water that complements the visions of Turkey in the movies. Skiing provides another way of networking at Sundance in Park City, Utah. And who would fly to the Carthage Film Festival (figure I.3), the biennial festival of Arab and African cinema in Tunis (Ruoff 2008), and not sample the delights of its twelfth-century medina and ancient Phoenician ruins?

Premières and Festival Stature

A fundamental distinction for festival programming is the first-timeness of a film. *Pace* cultural theorist Walter Benjamin, who argued that the advent of photography augured the end of the aura of art in an age of mechanical reproduction (1968 [1936]), a festival première bestows an aura on movies, temporarily conferring on film the status of a unique artwork. Premières attract the most attention from the media; *Variety* magazine has a long-standing policy of reviewing every film at its world première. Festivals compete intensely amongst each other to host these events. The quantity of world premières by established directors helps define the significance of a given festival in the pecking order of the international circuit.[2]

In addition to the main (often competition) screenings, major festivals also typically host opening and closing night premières, gala affairs which bring the full clout of the festival to bear on producing defining media events. These occasions mutually reinforce the prestige of the festivals, their sponsors, patrons, donors, audiences, the films and the filmmakers. Gala screenings are tricky events for programmers, with so many constituencies to please. When working effectively, these galas can brand a film or a festival with a single iconic image, usually that of a star on the red carpet (although a celebrity director is also a distinct possibility), glamorous, sexy, adored, talented, at the top of her or his game.

The aura of the première excites programmers, filmmakers, sponsors, exhibitors, distributors, journalists and audiences alike.[3] If critically and/or commercially successful, both festivals and films are branded together, and breakout movies such as *Sex, Lies, and Videotape* (Steven Soderbergh, U.S., 1989) are forever associated with the festival (in this case Sundance) that premièred them. Although film is ostensibly an art form in which there is no original artefact, the première attains the ephemeral status of an original, one-of-a-kind live event. To have been present at the première of *E.T.: The Extra-Terrestrial* (Steven Spielberg, U.S., 1982), with its standing ovation at the closing gala at Cannes, is to have participated in a privileged collective experience of cinema, the coronation of a commercial auteur (Ebert 1987: 93).

In *Film Festival Yearbook 3: Film Festivals and East Asia*, film scholar and programmer Abé Markus Nornes asks 'which film festivals matter' (2011: 37). Who attends film festivals determines how and for whom they matter. Cannes matters because it is attended by 30,000 film professionals — stars, producers, distributors, exhibitors and thousands of journalists.[4] The audience, not the films, makes the festival. Director Satyajit Ray, recalling his time on the Berlin jury, remarked that 'Film festivals are memorable not so much for the films one sees there as

I.4. The film festival in Marrakech, which takes place at the Palais des Congrès, has succeeded principally in recruiting Anglo-American producers to shoot on location in Morocco. © Jeffrey Ruoff

for the people one meets: directors, producers, critics, actors from all over the world' (Cowie 2010: 123-4). Festivals that would *like* to matter, such as the International Film Festival Marrakech or the Mar del Plata International Film Festival in Argentina recognise this and go so far as to pay for established stars to appear, such as Tom Cruise or Catherine Deneuve (who received $50,000 for two days in Mar del Plata, according to Quintín 2009: 45), thus guaranteeing a certain visibility in the international press. For similar reasons, the Tribeca Film Festival in New York City puts celebrities on its competition juries.

Tribeca, however, offers proof that celebrities alone do not a good festival make. Similarly, despite the presence of directors such as Oliver Stone, Martin Scorsese and Ridley Scott over the past decade, Marrakech has yet to attract the right people in sufficient numbers to rise in the festival firmament (figure I.4). Meanwhile, flush with funding, the Dubai International Film Festival and the Abu Dhabi Film Festival, both in the United Arab Emirates, are spending lots of money to become the premier Arab film festival. But money by itself does not guarantee stature. Lacking programming vision, Dubai and Abu Dhabi — like Marrakech — have yet to establish themselves as influential stops on the international film festival circuit.

Festivals actively cannibalise each other. Programmers attend film festivals and copy each other. They innovate new strategies to distinguish their festivals which, if successful, are then imitated by others. In the case of the New York African Film Festival (NYAFF), founder Mahen Bonetti was inspired by African films she saw at NYFF, at the Locarno Film Festival in Switzerland, and, finally, at the mother of all African film festivals, FESPACO. Bonetti set out to provide audiences at NYAFF with similarly rich images of Africa as seen by African directors themselves. So, festivals beget other festivals. We could create a genealogy of film festivals — to go alongside critic and programmer Quintín's delightful 'festival galaxy' (2009) — Venice begat its rebel son Cannes, Cannes begat its antithesis, the Festival du Film Maudit, and so on.

Festivals also beget filmmakers. On its 30th anniversary, in 2011, the Istanbul film festival published an anthology of essays by filmmakers and critics, *30: 20 Directors from 30 Years of the Istanbul Film Festival*. Here, Turkish directors such as Tayfun Pirselimoğlu and Derviş Zaim recall the IIFF screenings of their youths — the films that influenced their careers as filmmakers — a concrete demonstration of the role festivals play not only in the lives of individual directors, but also in generations and in national cinemas (Alpan 2011). Similarly, the Carthage Film Festival, founded in 1966, nurtured and inspired a generation of filmmakers — Nouri Bouzid, Férid Boughedir, Moufida Tlatli, Nacer Khemir, and others — who formed the Tunisian new wave from 1986 to 1996 and found recognition at international festivals around the globe (Ruoff 2011: 33).

The Programmer as Auteur, Critic, Historian

A successful festival — such as the 2010 Mill Valley Film Festival (MVFF), which presented more than 90 screenings — programmes geographical balance (films from Asia, Africa, Latin America, the Middle East, Europe and North America); films that appeal to different sensibilities, audiences and demographics; commercial movies as well as recondite ones (figure I.5). A prestigious festival (such as MVFF 2010) features high-profile opening night movies (*The King's Speech*, Tom Hooper, UK, 2010 and *Conviction*, Tony Goldwyn, U.S., 2010), an attractive centrepiece screening (*Miral*, Julian Schnabel, UK/Israel/France, 2009, in the presence of Schnabel), and a closing night screening (*The Debt*, John Madden, U.S., 2010) followed by a party with gourmet cuisine and live music. Programming balance also means avoiding duplication, providing distinctive categories (new American films, contemporary documentaries, children's films) and

I.5. The Mill Valley festival in northern California, which observed its 34th anniversary in 2011, celebrates film as a medium of artistic expression. © John Casado

specific emphases (Canada, the 'Body in Balance'). Special events include in-person tributes to illustrious stars (Annette Bening) and in-person spotlights with other major actors (Edward Norton, James Franco) and directors (Alejandro González Iñárritu), film-related live music concerts, and workshops on the 'art, technology and business of filmmaking' (MVFF Catalogue 2010).

Each festival constructs its own ideal spectator. For example, ethnographic film festivals speak to a specialised audience of anthropologists, students, and documentary filmmakers (Ruoff 1994). Or take the Flaherty Film Seminar, a programmer's paradise. Films are not submitted, they are sought out by the programmer. The Flaherty sells passes only to the entire seven-day event, no tickets for individual screenings. It does not publish the programme in advance, so as you sit down in the theatre and the lights go dark for a screening, you never know what to expect. With just one theatre showing one film at a time, all participants watch the same movies together. Debates with filmmakers follow the screenings and then evolve into conversations over shared breakfasts, lunches, and dinners. Over time, films play off one another, a cinematic call-and-response occurs.

Furthermore, the Flaherty typically takes place in a small town, a kind of film camp, with few distractions. By the end, a group of more than 100 people have all seen, debated, and discussed a body of progressive documentaries and experimental film/videos. This community may be divided by age, gender, ethnicity, ideology, aesthetic preferences, and so forth, but it comes together through the communal experience of attending screenings, discussions, dances, and parties (Ruoff 1996). Similarly, NYFF director Richard Peña hopes passionate viewers will be able to take in most of the 25-30 films in his main slate, an important justification for the small number of movies shown. The ideal NYFF spectator is a serious cinéphile, someone who knows the world history of cinema, its most important artists and its emerging ones, bringing a wealth of prior knowledge to each new screening. At the other end of the spectrum is the World Film Festival in Montreal with more than 300 films screened, a forest of films in which no two random spectators would ever see the same collection of movies.

Like the Flaherty, a good festival offers a performance, with opening and closing acts, suspense, detours, and surprises along the way. Thoughtful programming creates a kind of narrative, an unfolding experience of cinema and related events. As programmer, critic and film director Mark Cousins suggests, a film festival should be authored,

> Think of [festivals] as shows being produced on stages (cities, former fishing villages on the Cote d'azur, etc) which, thus, have *mise-en-scene* just as films have *mise-en-scene*. The people who run film festivals must think of themselves as storytellers and stylists. They must ask themselves what the narrative structure of their event is, and its aesthetic. (2006)[5]

Others, such as Telluride co-founder Bill Pence, describe programming as montage, igniting sparks as films rub up against one another, creating surrealist juxtapositions. Pence took inspiration from the Flaherty model and still today, unlike nearly all festivals in the world, the Telluride Film Festival does not announce its programme in advance. In addition, like the Flaherty and the Pordenone Silent Film Festival in northern Italy, Telluride enjoys a largely captive audience, a group that travels to the little resort town in Colorado for the duration of the Labor Day weekend festival in September.

Authored festival programming is itself an act of film criticism, as critic Richard Porton and his colleagues argue persuasively in the anthology *Dekalog 3: On Film Festivals* (2009). Programmers' identification of and support for new trends, new waves, new directors, and new films provide the first cut for critics and academics who will later write the history of cinema. Furthermore, festival screenings of older restored prints and other archival endeavours directly intervene in the discourse of film history. Festival directors themselves, like NYFF's Peña, work in the business of film history. The Busan International Film Festival in South Korea, established in 1996, significantly raised the international profile of South Korean film and has become a principal portal for Asian cinema. Cameron Bailey, co-director of Toronto, goes so far as to claim that festivals have become 'the single most important arbiter of taste in cinema — more important than scholars, or critics, more important even than film schools' (2009: 41).

Through their programming, influential curated festivals, such as NYFF, Telluride, and the International Film Festival Rotterdam, write their own initial version of the history of cinema — which films deserve consideration, which films deserve to be remembered and, ultimately, which films deserve to be shown again and again. Other authored festivals engage directly in the work of film criticism through polemical essays, catalogues, and studies of individual directors. Witness the books and essays produced at the Pesaro Film Festival in the late 1960s (de Valck 2006: 182-3), Edinburgh in the 1970s (Lloyd 2009), at Locarno, at the Amiens International Film Festival, and at the Buenos Aires International Festival of Independent Cinema (Koehler 2009: 93). In this light, the essays in *Coming Soon to a Festival Near You* could be seen as an extension of the work of film festivals themselves.

The Contributions

In this volume, film scholar Marijke de Valck's history of film festival programming opens the contributions because it provides a lucid overview of programming practices from the 1930s to the present. Subsequent chapters, many focussed on individual festivals, will call to mind, and refine, de Valck's thoughtful distinctions. Moreover, these individual festivals themselves have histories, and readers will note how they have evolved in relation to de Valck's suggestive periodisation of programming as 1) platforms for national cinemas, 2) showcases of auteurs, new waves, and cinéphilia, and 3) globalised, professionalised, and institutionalised events with substantial sponsorship, expanding beyond art cinema and reaching out for audiences that justify their funding.

De Valck's first stage of programming — the showcasing of national cinemas — has shifted to become an important function of the leading festivals of *individual* countries. So, the Istanbul film festival, as described in Gönül Dönmez-Colin's chapter, offers an annual review of Turkish films, whereas the Thessaloniki International Film Festival, discussed by Toby Lee, features the best in recent Greek films, and Toronto surveys, naturally, the latest in Canadian cinema, and so on throughout the world. De Valck similarly does well to suggest the symbiotic, but also reactive and competitive relationships that obtain among different festivals, showing that specialised themed and identity-driven festivals often arise as a result of perceived lacunae in major festivals.

Next, we leave the perspective of the historian de Valck for that of festival participant Gerald Peary, a film critic. Peary's essay is in the travel genre of festival writing, of which Kenneth Turan's *Sundance to Sarajevo: Film Festivals and the World They Made* (2002) is a leading exemplar. (My favourite, book-length version of the genre is Roger Ebert's 1987 *Two Weeks in the Midday Sun: A Cannes Notebook*, graced with Ebert's own awkward sketches.) Richard Porton claims that this kind of film criticism is 'inordinately celebratory' (2009: 2), but as much as any essay in this collection, or in Porton's own *On Film Festivals*, Peary's memoir actually stokes the reader's desire to rush to a film festival, to watch movies, and to have fun. This because Peary's essay conveys a strong sense of being there — 'there' meaning, in his case, many different places over the past 30 years. At film festivals, Peary enjoys movies, the company of actors, other cinéphiles, and filmmakers. For Peary, festivals offer a kind of passport to the world, not only the world of cinema, but the real world, too.[6] In chronological order and with a deceptively breezy style, Peary's postcards from film festivals around the world nicely convey shifting geopolitical sands as well as the changing playing field of the global festival circuit from the late 1970s, 1980s, 1990s, and the opening decade of the twenty-first century. Eager to get on the next plane, Peary remains duly sensitive to the allure of location, location, location — a defining feature of festivals since their inception in European spas in the mid-twentieth century.

Film festivals play a major role in sustaining independent animators and animation as an art form. Film scholar and programmer Marcin Giżycki charts the global spread of festivals of animated film as a reaction to a split in the field between independent animators (themselves divided between narratively oriented auteurists and experimental non-narrative filmmakers) and Hollywood film and television industry animators (now, of course, located all over the world, particularly in Asia). Giżycki describes well the interconnections among different animation festivals, how new ones rise up in response to perceived deficiencies in others, how programmers rely on other festivals to network and establish connections that make their own festivals thrive. Now programming a festival he co-founded — the Animator International Festival of Animated Film in Poznań, Poland — Giżycki argues for the broadest and most inclusive possible definition of animation in festivals, a new kind of expanded cinema that embraces live spectacles.

Of course, festivals are not only about film as art. Distributors — such as Kino International's Donald Krim (Kehr 2011) — have long recognised the potential and importance of film festivals for the distribution and exhibition of international cinema. Taking a different tack from other contributors to this volume, distributor, screenwriter and film scholar James Schamus lays out what it costs a studio to stage a gala première at a major international film festival, with an eye to illuminating the place festivals play in the economy of images that position and advertise a motion picture in the build-up to its theatrical release. Nothing is free. Schamus shows the major festivals as a competitive marketplace, increasingly focussed on producing these iconic snapshots to secure a defining image within the festival circuit.

We segue from Schamus' illuminating discussion of publicising films via festivals to Richard Peña's personal history as a programmer. A native New Yorker, now director of the New York Film Festival, Richard Peña writes of coming of age with NYFF in the 1960s (when it was simply 'the Festival') and then taking its reins from the late 1980s to the present. With just a handful of festival directors over the years, NYFF has stayed remarkably consistent in its vision — a commitment to auteurism, modernism and film as an art form — while expanding its embrace of art cinema from Europe to the world as a whole. Covering the past 50 years of NYFF, Peña roots his chapter in the history of cinema and of film criticism. As ever, NYFF remains a curated festival where the director and selection committee choose among thousands of entries and ultimately lay down their critical chips in favour of a tiny selection of what they consider to be the cream of the crop of international cinema. An exemplary cinéphile festival, NYFF has no market. Press coverage is extensive, yet mostly devoted to written reviews of films and emerging trends, with an emphasis on directors rather than stars and fashion. (Positive coverage in the media is obviously a boon for later distribution and exhibition.) At NYFF, there are no awards, the films screen in first-rate theatrical settings and, unlike Cannes, the general public is welcome to attend.

The relative stability of the New York Film Festival contrasts with the recent history of the flagship festival in Greece. Anthropologist and film scholar Toby Lee tracks a disruptive moment in the history of the Thessaloniki film festival, the national and international showcase for Greek cinema, when, on the occasion of its 50th anniversary in 2009, programmers there were faced by a boycott by Greek filmmakers. Imagine a 50-year retrospective of Greek cinema with no Greek films! In such moments of crisis, as occurred at Cannes in May 1968, when the festival was cancelled in response to a countrywide general strike, the underlying political bases and engagements of festivals come to the forefront. Toby Lee suggests that despite our era of globalisation (or perhaps because of it), and despite theoretical claims of the so-called death of the nation as a meaningful category of analysis in film criticism and history, national cinema — like citizenship itself — is still fought over, in play, up for grabs, in the European community as well as in the Middle East, Latin America, Southeast Asia and so on.

National cinema again comes into focus as film scholar Gönül Dönmez-Colin surveys a great variety of festivals in Turkey, showing the role festivals have played in the development of film culture there. Festivals serve important functions in Turkey, nurturing Turkish cinema, developing sophisticated audiences, tutoring new generations of filmmakers and supporting freedom of expression. Even though they might compete with one another for premières and funds, collectively, Turkish film festivals are engaged in a project of national cinema building. Festival programmers showcase a great diversity of cinematic expression in a country susceptible to censorship from both religious authorities and military leaders. The presence of censorship suggests that cinema really matters, that there are genuine issues at stake, that films are especially precious when at risk. While Dönmez-Colin highlights the specific nature of political interference in Turkish festivals (individual films banned, festivals shut down by military rulers), *Coming Soon to a Festival Near You* makes it clear that politics routinely affect programming, and many film festivals — such as Berlin — explicitly embrace political engagement and controversy.

After Dönmez-Colin's countrywide survey of festivals, we turn to a single northern California festival as seen from the inside. Director of programming at Mill Valley since 1991, Zoë Elton has reconstructed a typical day in her life during the festival. As much as any account I have ever read, Elton's chapter captures the perspective of a programmer in the telescoped heat of the moment, bringing us into what she calls the 'maelstrom of festival time'. As in an Alain Resnais film, time expands and the mind flits back and forth among past, present, and future. This whirlwind reminds me of the work of a film director as depicted in François Truffaut's *La nuit américaine* (*Day for Night*, France/Italy, 1973) or — minus the masculine midlife crisis — Federico Fellini's *8½* (Italy/France, 1963), in which the protagonists are bombarded with queries, requests, imploring demands, and obliged to shift gears constantly from professional and personal circumstances, leading a virtual army of co-workers in the collective enterprise of cinema. So here we see a festival programmer at the heart of her festival, following 35mm prints on their transnational voyages, introducing screenings, negotiating with publicists, conversing with attendees, making public pitches for funds, juggling projection formats, briefly enjoying the magical elation of an audience, scrambling for a bite of food, snatching a few hours sleep, crossing paths with celebrity.

Once Mill Valley begins, Elton's programming work is over. As we follow her day, she neatly leaves a trail of crumbs that shows the months of preparation behind the special moments that festivals provide. Quoting animator Chuck Jones, Telluride co-founder Bill Pence says of programming, 'In every major undertaking, there are two key components, hard work and love. But only the love must show' (Calloway 2006). In her first-person account, Elton gracefully shares both. She demonstrates that festival screenings such as those at MVFF — frequently in the presence of directors or actors — are, for the public, one-of-a-kind live events, the communal experience of the screening heightened and magnified. Elton also reveals how festivals produce these unique experiences for audiences and how savvy programmers, successful directors, and stars repeatedly create those moments for different audiences.

Turning to another highly curated American festival, the next chapter features an interview I did with Bill and Stella Pence, co-founders in 1974 of the Telluride film festival in Colorado. Film exhibitors and distributors, the Pences partnered with two archivists — James Card, director of the George Eastman House International Museum of Photography and Film in Rochester, New York, and Tom Luddy, director of the Pacific Film Archive at the University of California-Berkeley — to create the festival. From the beginning, Telluride emphasised revivals of classic films, as well as in-person tributes to filmmakers from earlier eras and to ambitious contemporary directors working inside and outside of Hollywood. The 1979 festival, for example, offered tributes to French director Abel Gance, Hollywood editor/director Robert Wise, and German actor Klaus Kinski. Telluride has always mixed the old and the new, showcasing continuity in the art of motion pictures, connecting the past and present to the future. This chapter emphasizes the synergistic dimension of programming, describing how Telluride creates a hothouse atmosphere in which films echo, refract, and enhance one another. The experience of attending the festival rises, like the Rocky Mountains where it takes place, far above ordinary screenings. For the several thousand who travel there, the festival celebrates cinema through a four-day party and communal conversation; the small town itself becomes the festival. Telluride thrives on the belief that the love of movies can bring people together. The result is a community of cinéphiles — almost a family of them — fiercely devoted to film as an art.

Identity-based festivals also offer communal experiences of cinema, but these are typically organised around cultural politics. Film scholar Skadi Loist surveys the history and current state of gay and lesbian film festivals, focussing on evolving programming strategies for communities intensely engaged in their representations. Whereas the wave of women's film festivals that grew out of the feminist movement of the 1960s and 1970s has now largely dissipated, gay and lesbian festivals continue to grow and proliferate. As Loist notes, gay and lesbian programming has developed in relation to on-going theoretical critiques and evolving self-definitions in the larger community, as successive waves of writing on lesbian, gay, bisexual, and transgender (LGBT) identity dialogue with festival programmes. Queer programming strategies have recently begun to complicate the earlier goal of simple representation of community members. In the end, Loist argues in favour of the queer readings that LGBT festival audiences provide regardless of the content of the films screened. Loist suggests that LGBT audiences are now prepared to go beyond 'by, for and about' identification with characters to encounters with less essentialist programming.

Regional film festivals emphasise national cinemas in transnational contexts. Film scholar Sangjoon Lee's essay offers an important rebuttal to Stephen Teo's contention that the Asia-Pacific Film Festival, founded in 1954, is 'not a film festival' because APFF's programming was not 'free from the influence of the studios, film companies, and their vested interests' (Teo 2009: 121). Here Teo blushes at the notion of festivals as markets. Are there any film festivals in the world free from the influence of studios, companies, and their interests?[7] Like Berlin, APFF, as Sangjoon Lee describes it, was a quintessential Cold War festival, a front in the war against communism. Festivals that travel, particularly from country to country such as APFF, have a hard time maintaining continuity from one event to the next; just the number of acronyms in Sangjoon Lee's essay suggests these difficulties. Younger festivals — such as Busan in South Korea and the Shanghai International Film Festival in the People's Republic of China — have rendered APFF largely irrelevant today, but this should not obscure its pioneering, historic role in programming Asian cinema.

Similarly, festivals have played a major part in the international promotion of African cinema. In the early 1990s, in partnership with the Film Society of Lincoln Center, Mahen Bonetti founded the New York African Film Festival. Bonetti's essay, on her desire to redefine the image of Africa in American media, is a reminder how many festivals are the work of one strong personality, inspired by and collaborating with others. Seen from the outside, the concept of 'African cinema' construes the whole continent as a monolith. Seen from the inside, Africa offers a diverse potpourri of national cinemas, popular indigenous media, and individual artists travelling across national and international borders. Initially setting out to provide new positive images of Africa for U.S. audiences, Bonetti now strives to break down the notion of Africa as one place. She aims to introduce viewers to subtle distinctions among directors, nations, genders, and regions across the vast continent.

As we have seen, some film scholars also programme film festivals. There are also programmers engaged in film history. In addition, there are filmmakers who organise festivals; for example, Sayoko Kinoshita, a Japanese animation filmmaker who became a festival programmer. Since the mid-1980s, Kinoshita has dedicated her life to championing animation as an art form and celebrating the work of other filmmakers. Her chapter tells the story of how she and her husband, Renzo Kinoshita, came to found the Hiroshima International Animation Festival. As with Bonetti at NYAFF, we see again how festivals, including the first animation film festival in Asia, are the product of individuals with strong, clear vision and steadfast determination. If animation is not appreciated as an art form in your country, Kinoshita seems to suggest, you need to create a festival that showcases animation as a medium of artistic expression. In so doing, her example tells us, you will build an audience for animation as an art, and filmmakers who screen their work at your festival will take encouragement from enthusiastic audiences. Kinoshita's essay also shows how festival programmers are indebted to their cohorts, how a successful festival quickly becomes enmeshed in an international web of like-minded filmmakers, programmers and critics.

Although this collection of essays features contributors from the Netherlands, Japan, Poland, the U.S., Korea, Turkey, Sierra Leone, and Germany, and is broadly international in scope, it does not attempt to be comprehensive or encyclopaedic. Nor does Coming Soon to a Festival Near You cover film festivals according to their relative prestige on the international circuit. On the contrary, because there is already a fairly extensive literature on the powerhouse festivals (Cannes, Sundance, Toronto, Venice, Berlin; see the bibliography at www.filmfestivalresearch.org), I have found it worthwhile to shine a light on other festivals. I hope readers will enjoy the richness of festivals discussed here and that this anthology spurs additional writing about the international film festival circuit.

Conclusion

Seeing films at festivals is unlike watching them on home video, streaming on computers or playing on mobile devices; it is also fundamentally different from regular multiplex or theatrical screenings. Programming festivals is as different from year-round programming as night is from day. Film festivals are live, communal affairs. All kinds of special events take place: Q&As with filmmakers, press conferences, tributes, panel discussions, retrospectives, master classes, dinners, concerts, parties, cultural encounters, home stays by visiting filmmakers, salons, school visits. As Coming Soon to a Festival Near You demonstrates, successful programming orchestrates all these events in relation to cinema. The best programming has an inner logic, or narrative structure, that finds audiences for films and films for audiences.

Film festivals provide alternative exhibition venues for independent films and international cinema. Whether celebrations of film as an art, affirmations of cultural identity, or markets, festivals enhance the shared, collective dimensions of cinema. Although on the margins of the commercial industry as a whole, festivals remain important for the circulation and recognition of smaller, specialised films. Festivals nourish less commercial forms of cinema: independent animation, gay and lesbian films, documentary, New Romanian Cinema and the like. Since the advent of the internet in the 1990s and the proliferation of mobile viewing devices in the past decade, film festivals have only grown, in size, in number and in variety. All signs suggest they will continue to do so.

Works Cited

Aftab, Kaleem (2008) 'Due North: The Ballerina Ballroom Cinema of Dreams', *The Independent*, 23 July 2008. On-line. Available HTTP: http://www. independent.co.uk/arts-entertainment/films/features/due-north-the-ballerina-ballroom-cinema-of-dreams-874666.html (27 May 2011).

Alpan, Cem (ed.) (2011) *30: 20 Directors from 30 Years of the Istanbul Film Festival*. Istanbul: Istanbul Foundation for Culture and Arts.

Bailey, Cameron (2009) 'The Festival as Dinner Party', *Schnitt: Das Filmmagzin*, 54, 2, 41.

Benjamin, Walter (1968 [1936]) 'The Work of Art in the Age of Mechanical Reproduction', *Illuminations*. New York: Harcourt Brace Jovanovich, Inc., 217-52.

Bordwell, David (2011) 'Never the Twain Shall Meet: Why Can't Cinephiles and Academics Get Along', *Film Comment*, 47, 3, 38-41.

Calloway, Larry (2006) 'The 33rd Telluride Film Festival and the Sudden End of the Pence Era'. On-line. Available HTTP: http://larrycalloway.com/tride-2006 (25 May 2011).

Clarkson, Wensley (1995) *Quentin Tarantino: Shooting from the Hip*. London: Piatkus Books.

Cowie, Peter (2010) *The Berlinale, The Festival*. Berlin: Bertz + Fischer.

Cousins, Mark (2006) 'Widescreen: On Film Festivals', *Prospect*, December. On-line. Available HTTP: http://www.prospectmagazinec.uk/2006/12/7970-widescreen (25 May 2011).

de Valck, Marijke (2006) *Film Festivals: History and Theory of a European Phenomenon that Became a Global Network*, published PhD thesis, University of Amsterdam.

de Valck, Marijke and Skadi Loist (2009) 'Film Festival Studies: An Overview of a Burgeoning Field', in Dina Iordanova with Ragan Rhyne (eds) *Film Festival Yearbook 1: The Festival Circuit*. St Andrews: St Andrews Film Studies with College Gate Press, 179-215.

Ebert, Roger (1987) *Two Weeks in the Midday Sun: A Cannes Notebook*. Kansas City, MO: Andrews and McMeel.

Iordanova, Dina with Ragan Rhyne (eds) (2009) *Film Festival Yearbook 1: The Festival Circuit*. St Andrews: St Andrews Film Studies with College Gate Press.

Iordanova, Dina with Ruby Cheung (eds) (2010) *Film Festival Yearbook 2: Film Festivals and Imagined Communities*. St Andrews: St Andrews Film Studies.

____ (2011) *Film Festival Yearbook 3: Film Festivals and East Asia*. St Andrews: St Andrews Film Books.

Kehr, Dave (2011) 'Donald Krim, Film Distributor, Dies at 65', *The New York Times*, 22 May. On-line. Available HTTP: http://www.nytimes.com/2011/05/23/movies/donald-krim-film-distributor-dies-at-65.html?_r=1&emc=eta1 (24 May 2011).

Lloyd, Matthew (2009) *How the Movie Brats Took Over Edinburgh: The Impact of Cinephilia on Edinburgh International Film Festival, 1968-1980*. St Andrews: St Andrews Film Studies.

Mill Valley Film Festival Catalogue (2010). Mill Valley: California Film Institute.

Nornes, Abé Markus (2011) 'Asian Film Festivals, Translation and the International Film Festival Short Circuit', in Dina Iordanova with Ruby Cheung (eds) *Film Festival Yearbook 3: Film Festivals and East Asia*. St Andrews: St Andrews Film Studies, 37-9.

Peranson, Mark (2009) 'First You Get the Power, Then You Get the Money: Two Models of Film Festivals', in Richard Porton (ed.) *Dekalog 3: On Film Festivals*. London: Wallflower, 23-37.

Porton, Richard (2009) 'A Director on the Festival Circuit: An Interview with Atom Egoyan', in Richard Porton (ed.) *Dekalog 3: On Film Festivals*. London: Wallflower, 169-81.

Porton, Richard (ed.) (2009) *Dekalog 3: On Film Festivals*, London: Wallflower.

Quintín (2009) 'The Festival Galaxy', in Richard Porton (ed.) *Dekalog 3: On Film Festivals*. London: Wallflower, 38-52.

Ruoff, Jeffrey (1994) 'On the Trail of the Native's Point of View: The Göttingen International Ethnographic Film Festival', *CVA Newsletter*, 2, 15-18.

____ (1996) 'Reminiscences of a Journey to the Flaherty Film Seminar', *Wide Angle*, 17, 1-4, 66-9.

____ (2008) 'Ten Nights in Tunisia: Les Journées Cinématographiques de Carthage', *Film International*, 6, 4, 43-51.

____ (2011) 'The Gulf War, the Iraq War, and Nouri Bouzid's Cinema of Defeat: *It's Scheherazade We're Killing* (1993) and *Making Of* (2006)', *South Central Review*, 28, 1, 18-35.

Stringer, Julian (2003) 'Regarding Film Festivals', unpublished PhD thesis, University of Indiana-Bloomington.
Turan, Kenneth (2002) *Sundance to Sarajevo: Film Festivals and the World They Made*. Berkeley, CA: University of California Press.

Notes

For comments on earlier drafts of this introduction, I am indebted to Gönül Dönmez-Colin, David Ehrlich, Zoë Elton, Gerd Gemunden, Amy Lawrence, and Gerald Peary.

[1]   In a recent essay in *Film Comment*, film scholar David Bordwell calls for a rapprochement between academics and film critics (2011). *Coming Soon to a Festival Near You* accomplishes this goal, featuring contributions by festival programmers, a film critic, an industry professional, and academic film scholars. This broad variety of perspectives provides a rounded view of festivals. I hope this anthology reaches an equally diverse audience and encourages further exchanges among different sectors of the film world. Participating directly in festivals, film critics have long recognized their importance, as have distributors and studios. More recently, academic scholars have acknowledged festivals as a significant dimension of film culture, with doctoral dissertations by Julian Stringer (2003) and Marijke de Valck (2006) leading the way. Since 2009 festivals have become an important arena of film scholarship; see de Valck and Loist 2009, their regularly updated website, www.filmfestivalresearch.org, and the annual *Film Festival Yearbook* series edited by Dina Iordanova.

[2]   Festivals dice premières in ever finer distinctions: world, international ('North American'), national, regional ('New England'), local ('Boston'), and so forth. Of the several thousand film festivals that exist, comparatively few are engaged in the première stakes. Many large audience-oriented ones, such as the Chicago International Film Festival, simply bring interesting films and special events to audiences in their cities.

Film festivals sprout everywhere nowadays. Fifteen minutes from where I live in rural Vermont, the village of White River Junction hosts the annual White River Indie Films (WRIF); 2011 is already its eighth year. With a budget of around $10,000, WRIF 2011 screened 20 films on DVD over a three-day period for around 1,000 audience members. In addition to opening and closing night events, it hosted photo exhibitions, panel discussions with experts and directors, and offered workshops on acting, digital technology and producing. Too modest to register on the international or national festival circuit, WRIF offers a chance for a few independent filmmakers in New England to connect with local audiences. The festival also calls attention to a handful of international movies, connecting viewers with worthwhile films.

3   Obviously most movies still make their way outside the film festival circuit. Others may or may not have one-of-a-kind premières. Presumably there was no première to speak of when Kenneth Branagh's *Thor* (U.S.) opened simultaneously on 3,955 screens in the U.S. on 6 May 2011.

4   Thousands of people who attend Cannes — producers, filmmakers, programmers — spend their time in meetings; is this a *film* festival? Promoting *Felicia's Journey* (Canada/UK, 1999) in competition there, director Atom Egoyan didn't see other films at the festival, 'It's very deforming when you're going through an event like Cannes. You're in a very strange bubble those ten days. You don't see the other films and you're talking endlessly about your own work. So you're divorced from any reality of what the other competition films are like' (Porton 2009: 176).

5   For an example of Mark Cousins' concept of festivals as authored events, see his lively collaboration with actress Tilda Swinton on The Ballerina Ballroom Cinema of Dreams (www.cinemaofdreams.co.uk), a one-time festival which took place in Nairn, Scotland, in August 2008 (Aftab 2008).

6   More than ever, the international film festival circuit is not only for films, but also of course for programmers, actors and, naturally, directors. Quentin Tarantino rode the international festival circuit to stardom. For six months, he traveled the world with his first movie, *Reservoir Dogs* (U.S., 1992), giving an average of two interviews a day, and his presence became as noteworthy as his film (Clarkson 1995: 178).

7   What is and what is not a film festival is an interesting question, though I don't see any a priori definitions. Some would say that White River Indie Films, which screens DVDs for a local audience in small-town Vermont, is not a festival, that simply calling an event a festival does not make it one. Many people would not consider the Flaherty to be a festival and, indeed, the Flaherty has continued to refer to itself as a seminar over the past 55 years. De Valck's essay in this volume shows that most film festivals (Cannes and Berlin in the 1950s etc.) would be excluded by Stephen Teo's narrow definition (2009: 121).

PART I

FINDING AUDIENCES

FOR FILMS

Chapter 1

Finding Audiences for Films: Festival Programming in Historical Perspective

Marijke de Valck

'A film that is not screened is dead.' This quote from the acclaimed head of the Cinémathèque Française, Henri Langlois, can be found at the top of some handwritten notes by Hubert Bals, director and programmer of the International Film Festival Rotterdam from its foundation in 1972 to his untimely death in 1988. Bals scribbled down the annotations in 1982 in preparation for a report in which he would expound his vision of the future of the IFFR. Prompted by a pending reorganisation of the Rotterdam art scene and anticipating a critique of the poor financial management of the umbrella organisation Film International,[1] Bals was compelled to defend the activities and relevance of his beloved organisation. His reply is an example of the idea that the best defence is to attack as, in his customarily stubborn way, he called for an expansion of Film International's activities — starting a desk for promotion and foreign sales as well as an international co-production market — instead of considering cutting down on activities or expenditures.[2] In the context of this volume on programming, the notes, and especially the quote he chose to represent his ideas on the future of the film festival in Rotterdam, are of particular interest because they are emblematic of a distinct philosophy that dominated and defined film festival programming in the 1970s and continues to exercise influence on festivals today. Here I will contextualise what I'd like to call the art of festival programming by providing a historical perspective on programming since the early years.

Until recently there has been little research and even less published work on the programming of films at film festivals. The contemporary increase in attention has manifested itself in debates on curating and programming at conferences, seminars and meetings, as well as some publications.[3] Among these, the anthology you are holding is the only book-length publication to date (that I am aware of) to dedicate itself to the theme of programming for film festivals. While the relevance of such a focus might be obvious to those familiar with the diverging exhibition circuits for audiovisual material (theatres, museums and galleries, DVD or Blu-ray, television channels, Web-based platforms etc.), I will use this opportunity to dwell on the specific context of the film festival and the festival circuit further along in my contribution. To begin, it is worthwhile dedicating some words to the importance of the theme of festival programming and thus also to this volume as a whole.

Programming can be defined as the core activity of film festivals. One of the festival's main functions is to screen films, in particular high-quality ones that do not find exposure elsewhere. Film festivals thus function as cultural gatekeepers for a substantial part of world film production. Festival programmers select films that they consider worthy of being seen — I will return to the topic of selection criteria later — and subsequently present the selected films to a public in a framed context; this is what we call the programme. I understand programming foremost as a *cultural* practice, because programming implies a committed handling of cinema as cultural expression and an evaluation of films as artistic accomplishments. This is what, ultimately, sets film festivals apart from commercial distribution and exhibition networks, for example in theatres and multiplexes, where the activity of programming of films is not driven by artistic or cultural concerns but primarily by the business interests of entrepreneurs. Scheduling would be a more appropriate term here. This is not to say that commerce is irrelevant or that exploitation strategies do not occur at film festivals. Festival markets, for example, attest to the presence and influence of film as business, and festival organisations need to account for their spending and present proof of popularity to the stakeholders that fund and sponsor the events. Still, it is clear that programming at film festivals is not a mere layer of sugar-coating on an otherwise savoury pie. On the contrary, the ideals of programmers, who carefully pick and present films, and the engagement of festival visitors, who flock to watch and discuss these programmes, are key ingredients that determine the rich, sweet taste of the festival cake. Therefore, if one wants to understand or critique film festivals, it is necessary to understand the scope and effects of programming.

Unfortunately, festival programming is a tough cookie when it comes to critical analysis. A central problem is the heterogeneity of the film festival circuit: there are many different festivals, with diverging aims and resources, and consequently also many different programming practices. Because the contemporary situation seems to be a potpourri of sorts, it is virtually impossible to draw a general framework for understanding festival programming. What's more, many choices cannot be understood but in relation to other programming practices. For example, the lack of attention to African cinema at major international 'A-list' film festivals is countered by smaller, themed festivals, networks and initiatives elsewhere that are specifically dedicated to screening and promoting African cinema. One way to clarify these issues is to look back at film festival history and reconstruct how festival programming developed. I will provide such an overview below. More specifically, I will point out consistencies, turning points and foundational notions that still operate in festival programming today. My aim is to better grasp the practice of programming and, ultimately, also to provide (historical) references to those working as festival programmers or directors in order to help them make informed decisions vis-à-vis future transformations of the festival circuit.

Before Programming As We Know It

Those who know my book *Film Festivals: From European Geopolitics to Global Cinephilia* (2007) will be familiar with my periodisation of festival history into three phases. The original categorisation lends itself well for an overview of the development of programming. Phase one runs from 1932, when the Venice International Film Festival was founded, to 1968, the year of the big upheaval at the Cannes International Film Festival. In this early period, film festivals were organised as showcases of national cinemas, which meant that nations were invited to submit one or more films to the competition programme of the festivals, the exact number being determined by factors like the country's annual film production, its size and — less democratically — its political weight. The selection of national submissions resided typically with ministries of culture, national film funds or other government cultural bodies — the exception being the U.S., which left its selection in the hands of the Motion Picture Association of America (MPAA), an association for film producers which served the interests of the motion picture industry rather than acting with a concern for issues of cultural identity and national cinema. Due to this format, programming, as we know it today, was not yet a core activity as film festivals were not responsible for the selection of their flagship competitions.

The early years of film festivals have contributed, however, to one of the most persistent presentation strategies employed by festivals: programming along national lines. Begun as a European phenomenon, festivals could originally be understood as an extension of the tradition of world fairs and expositions, in which technological and cultural achievements were displayed at international platforms as proof of national achievements. At festivals, cinema was regarded as a cultural product that could be considered an expression of a national identity. Government involvement in the selection of festival entries underlined the recognition of film as a national good, while downplaying aesthetic criteria such as formal innovation or stylistic experiment. One particular festival rule from this period required submitted films to respect the 'good relations' between nations, thereby blocking offensive political content (such as different national perspectives on the events of the Second World War). Although the format of festivals as showcases of national cinemas was abandoned in the second phase, the practice of using geographical markers continues today, for example, in the labelling of newly discovered trends. The so-called new waves — such as the recent New Romanian Cinema — are predominantly identified by their country of origin.

Over the years, people involved in festival organisation became increasingly critical of the practice of 'outsourcing' the selection of films to governmental bodies. Various diplomatic disputes seemed to contradict the ideal that 'the best cinematographic works' were screened in competition and limited festivals by acting as forums for international relations and displays of geopolitical power.[4] If cinema as art was the main concern of festivals, would it not be better if they freed themselves from governmental interference? Dissatisfaction with the situation grew throughout the 1960s. People also criticised festivals' preoccupation with stars and glamour and lamented the increasing influence of market activities. Calls were made to reform festival organisations and make film culture their central concern.

The tipping point was reached in 1968, the year of widespread student demonstrations, anti-Vietnam War protests and labour strikes. Jean-Luc Godard, François Truffaut and their followers disrupted Cannes' 21st edition, asking for solidarity with workers and students, protesting against the mistreatment of Henri Langlois as head of the Cinémathèque Française, and, while they were at it, demanding that the festival change course. The result was significant and caused a snowball effect throughout the festival circuit. In the 1970s film festivals were reconceived as independent organisations with professional programmers who picked films and constituted programme sections. This is the beginning of the second phase, a defining period for our contemporary perspectives on programming.

The Age of Programmers

The second and, for programming, most influential phase in film festival history runs until the 1980s. I have called this period the age of programmers, because programming issues became a central concern for festival organisations (de Valck 2007: 167). After the upheavals at major festivals, the road was paved for a new generation of festival events in which a new class of festival directors, who loved cinema and believed in the power of programming, called the shots. Since the old, major festivals had only partly reorganised after 1968, there was still demand for further reformation and thus new 'specialised' or 'themed' (sections at) film festivals could emerge. On the one hand, these new events were reactions against the dominance of glamour and commerce at the old festivals, on the other, they took up the (interventionist) agenda of the pre-war avant-garde. As I argue in *Film Festivals*,

> Programming became an issue of cinéphile passion (recognising new great auteurs and movements) and political sensibility (representing both large social movements or liberation struggles) and personal issues that remained underrepresented in the mainstream public domain, such as those relating to gender, race and ethnicity. (2007: 174)

Ulrich Gregor, head of the International Forum of the Berlin International Film Festival for many years, and Hubert Bals come to mind as emblematic figures of this age.

It is important to note that the new programming practices of the 1970s were preceded by several scattered developments. In Germany the creation of the Forum was prepared by the work of the collective Freunde der Deutsche Kinemathek (Friends of the German Cinematheque), active since 1963 (Schröder 2000). In the U.S. the Flaherty Film Seminar, first organised by Robert Flaherty's widow Frances on their farm in Vermont in 1955, already offered a supportive environment to independent cinema before festivals were founded there. The new themed festivals in the 1970s harked back to these events, in spirit as well as in the formats they applied. One particular film festival that had transposed its ideology into distinct programming practices in the early 1960s can be argued to have provided a blueprint for pending reformations. Founded in 1965 in Pesaro, Italy — a small town on the Adriatic coast about 150 km south of Bologna — the Pesaro Film Festival is worth taking a closer look at.

The Pesaro programming model is characterised by two properties. Firstly, the festival adhered to a different selection logic, which I refer to as *cultural intervention*. Instead of accepting submissions, the festival would actively select films and, with their selection choices, make a cultural statement about what films they considered to be of value. Ideologically, the festival displayed a clearly leftist and activist agenda and a special concern for supporting class struggle worldwide. The programme focussed on experimental and politically explicit films, screening feature films alongside documentaries. Secondly, Pesaro introduced a new format, which I define ideologically as a *politics of participation*. The festival did more than screen films: it provided ample room for discussions, published lengthy documents about its programmes and involved a wide range of people — professionals, academics, cinéphiles and political activists — in its event. It offered, in other words, a rich discursive context in which cinema could flourish as an intellectual and cultural passion.

The development of festival programming practices in the 1970s derives from these earlier initiatives. One can delineate at least four main characteristics of the Pesaro model followed by the new festival sections in Cannes (Quinzaine des Réalisateurs / Director's Fortnight) and Berlin (Forum des Jungen Films / Young Film Forum) as well as the new generation of themed film festivals that made its entry on the festival circuit. The first significant change from the previous period was that the supply of films from which festivals could select was opened up. While before only a limited number of nations was invited to participate in the competitions, thereby reflecting geopolitical power relations, in Pesaro films from all corners of the world were screened, explicitly aiming to offer alternatives to First Cinema (Hollywood) and Second Cinema (European art cinema). It was the first event to offer an international platform for the new cinemas from Latin America, films censored by their governments and neglected by the official programmes in Cannes, Venice and Berlin. The 'discovery' of new Latin American cinemas in Pesaro can be regarded as the first of a series of new waves, the new national cinemas discovered by festivals in the 1970s.[5]

Secondly, the shift to festivals as independent institutions that act as cultural gatekeepers was accompanied by a new set of selection criteria. Following the logics of cultural intervention, festivals adopted a programming philosophy in which value was placed on (cinematographic) innovation, originality, and topicality.[6] Previously, festival competitions had been more conservative, selected by bodies that were mainly concerned with the question of how the submitted films would represent their nations, thereby shying away from things that might cause anxiety in international relations or public offence. With the turn to expert selection, festival programming was put in the service not only of the advancement of cinema as art but also of cinema as a political tool. Festivals set out to 'discover' noteworthy individuals and trends, appropriating the notions of 'auteur' and 'new wave' as their strategic discourse.

A third characteristic of the new practices of the 1970s is that they contributed to the emergence of two main labels to describe cinema: besides considering cinema as a national achievement (national cinema), emphasis was placed above all on film as the artistic expression (art cinema) of an individual artist (auteur cinema). Festivals, in other words, provided the frameworks and language with which people would make sense of certain cinemas. We should however emphasise that these frameworks were created to achieve a clear objective at the time: to distinguish between cinema as entertainment and cinema as art, as well as between cinema-goers seeking escapist pleasures or thrills and cinéphile audiences. The turn to the director-as-creative-genius underlined an association with the fine arts, while downplaying the industrial and collaborative effort necessary for films to get produced. For festivals, these frameworks allowed for a sharper differentiation from commercial cinema circuits and paved the way for governmental and municipal subsidies in Europe and funds and sponsorships in the U.S. The art/auteur frame has proven to be very persistent, not least because the labels are media-friendly. Where Hollywood relies on actors to sell films, festivals are in the business of showcasing directors; spotting new talents and staging mediatised premières of established auteurs.

The fourth and final influence of the Pesaro model is its politics of participation, which continues to be one of the foundational principles behind many programming practices today. Its ideology can be understood as an extension of Henri Langlois' idea that a film is only alive when screened, to the belief that festival programming is more than exhibiting films to a public; it is about offering the public a variety of ways to engage with films. This includes providing synopses and background information in catalogues, programming statements to themed sections, tributes and retrospectives, Q&As after screenings, talk shows and discussions, daily papers with interviews, reviews and picks-of-the-day and much more. It was the Edinburgh International Film Festival that administered this practice most influentially in the 1970s, nurturing the topical feminist and psychoanalytic approaches to film at that time.

I'd like to argue that this politics of participation has been able to flourish at festivals like Pesaro and Edinburgh thanks to the parameters of the festival exhibition space. It is the specific context of festivals as short, intense events that allows for an ideal symbiosis between programmers' outreach and performative reception. The fact that festivals are events is decisive when trying to understand their particular programming practices. Unfortunately I do not have sufficient space to develop this argument in detail (see de Valck 2008 for an elaborated version), but I would like to mention one crucial element here: because festivals take place outside regular exhibition circles, whether these be commercial theatres, art houses or galleries, they assume an atmosphere of being 'out-of-the-ordinary' (also see Harbord 2009). Thus set apart from everyday life, film festivals are able to programme films or draw attention to matters that are unconventional, unfamiliar, break taboos or thwart expectations. The festival setting, in other words, allows for programming practices that challenge the audiences to sample, experiment and be open to new experiences. In the following period we see how the search for new trends and discoveries becomes a standardised programming practice that also has its weaknesses.

Institutionalisation, Standardisation and Self-Referentiality

The third phase begins in the 1980s and runs until today. In this period film festivals are a widespread, global phenomenon, embedded in what we have come to know as the international film festival circuit, beautifully characterised by Julian Stringer as 'a socially produced space [...] a unique cultural arena that acts as a contact zone for the working through of unevenly differentiated power relations — not so much a parliament of national film industries as a series of diverse, sometimes competing, sometimes cooperating public spheres' (2001: 138). Key to understanding this phase is the process of institutionalisation that film festivals went through. Film festivals were, as Stringer pointed out, forced to deal with each other on the terms of what he calls the global space economy, competing with each other for films, guests, discoveries and attention, but also cooperating on the shared mission to screen great films and support a more diverse cinema culture. A side effect of this institutionalisation was that festivals' programming models became self-referential, responding to what people had come to expect of festivals and keeping the system, which legitimised their social function, up and running.

One could, for example, argue that the second series of new waves in the 1980s was also 'produced' by Western festivals looking for specific (political) discoveries. Take China's Fifth Generation: the discovery of a group of young film directors who decided to make films outside the government-controlled academies and travelled to rural areas to show the other face of China, fitted perfectly with the Western preference for anti-authoritarian and 'authentic' stories. After the 1985 première of *Huang tu di* (*Yellow Earth*, Chen Kaige, China, 1985) at the Hong Kong International Film Festival, Western festivals were keen to jump on the bandwagon and continue to promote this type of Chinese filmmaking. Moreover, in the 1980s filmmakers had realised festivals could provide an alternative career track and began to make films especially for the festival circuit. Successful films and festival hits were copied in style and/or theme. Others, like Lars von Trier, played on festivals' preferences for new waves by rigging their productions with manifestos. The self-referentiality of festivals in this phase is most apparent in the emergence of the phenomenon of 'festival films': films that successfully travel the circuit, but fail to 'make it' outside.

Besides the self-referentiality of festivals' programming practices, two developments stand out. Firstly, film festivals attracted new audiences in the 1990s. As cultural organisations, festivals professionalised; they moved into shiny new multiplexes, underwent trendy restyling and improved their logistics. Moreover, in the 1990s the experience economy was in full swing and new types of visitors discovered film festivals; traditional cinéphiles were joined by a variety of urban professionals, students and leisure-seekers. Festival programmers responded to these developments with broader programmes that also catered to the needs of less cine-literate audiences.

Secondly, film festivals turned to pre-programming activities. They extended their industry services to initiatives that actively intervened in the production of cinema. CineMart, organised by the International Film Festival Rotterdam in 1983, was the first 'matchmaking' market. It presented pre-selected filmmakers and projects to potential financiers. Also in Rotterdam, the Hubert Bals Fund financially supported projects from 'cinema-developing countries' from 1988 onwards. Both initiatives functioned as quality labels that increased chances of success in the larger festival network; filmmakers found additional funding more easily and their films won prestigious prizes at festivals and/or better circulation. Other festivals frequently copied both formats.

That programming in this period extended into the handling of audiences and interactions with industry is emblematic of the transformation that film festivals were experiencing. If the previous phase revolved around programmers, the following one was all about the festival director. Festival directors could no longer be only cinéphiles and passionate programmers, they needed to position their festival in the increasingly complex festival circuit, global film market, national cultural agenda and local cinéphile tastes. In order to pull this off they began working with teams of programmers and also cooperating extensively with film industries, local entrepreneurs and policymakers. Some will see this shift as kneeling down to commercial influences. Others will rather stress that the contemporary situation is a democratisation of old programming practices; festivals nowadays are less dependent on the (often idiosyncratic) taste of one man (and programmers then were mostly men) and instead more open to the expert input of several programmers and scouts working for the festival. In addition, the institutionalisation of festivals since the 1980s constituted a welcome professionalisation of a cultural sector that had often been troubled by poor logistics and administration.

Contemporary Programming Practices

For a full understanding of programming at contemporary film festivals it is important that we recognise the formative influence of the practices developed in the 1970s. However, we also need to specify how subsequent developments affected or modified these practices and how they complicate a framework for understanding programming that harks back to the Pesaro model and other earlier initiatives. What stands out with regard to the first two previously specified characteristics — the increase in the number of films on offer from which festivals can make their selection and the concentration on criteria like innovation, originality and topicality — is that these have firmly held ground and, what's more, contributed to a cycle of continuous further specialisation in festival programming. When festivals became *independent* institutions of selection in the 1970s, room was made for refining the division between the various bigger and smaller festivals (de Valck 2007: 214) and, in addition, the way was paved for a new generation of specialised or themed film festivals that really started to blossom in the late 1980s and 1990s. Specialised or themed festivals have a different function on the circuit than the major A-list international events. They do not première the 'best' productions of that year or screen new features of the top range of art cinema directors. Instead they've chosen a niche area that is neglected, underrepresented or ghettoised at major events. Among these specialised festivals are gay and lesbian festivals, children's festivals, documentary festivals, fantasy festivals, short film festivals and also festivals that dedicate themselves to showing cinema from a certain country or region: African festivals, Arab festivals, Japanese festivals, Israeli festivals, Latin American festivals and so on. While the general selection criteria also apply to these specialised festivals (and are relevant to distinguishing them from commercial initiatives), it is problematic to reduce their programming practices to these markers. Some simply want to show all the new productions in their field (or as many as possible), aiming to contribute to a more diversified cinema culture — for example, African-themed festivals responding to a lack of African-made films at major festivals — or hoping for a more comprehensive representation of a region — such as Japanese festivals that counter the prevailing appetite for yakuza films and cult horror with films of modern or working-class life. Others have more explicit political agendas, like Israeli festivals that programme films made by Jews alongside those of Arab, Christian or Bedouin minorities. Scholars should acknowledge that the objectives of specialised film festivals tend to differ, and oftentimes are related to omissions or gaps in festival programming practices elsewhere.[7]

Above I argued that festival programming practices have contributed to three main labels for framing and understanding festival films (national cinema, auteur cinema and art cinema), and provided a critical vocabulary to discuss these cinemas (terms like auteur and new wave). However, in the present-day globalised arts scene, new rules and logics have been added to these classical tropes. Firstly, although the 'national' remains important, it does not extend to all programming practices. In fact, film festivals seem to be playing a big role in the creation and sustainment of an international, cosmopolitan art cinema scene. Once new talents are spotted, they enter a world of international funds, markets, training programmes and producers (Celluloid Dreams, Fortissimo Films, Wild Bunch, Miramax etc.) and the films directed by these filmmakers will over the years become less nationally distinctive as a result. Think of Pedro Almodóvar or Kar-wai Wong as examples. They are no longer mere representatives of Spanish and Hong Kong cinema, but rather heroes of an international art cinema community. Secondly, programming practices have moved beyond the trope of the 'auteur' as well, though less clearly than the move away from national labels. There are several examples of this, such as the growing attention to scriptwriting at training initiatives or funds connected to festivals, or alternatively to organised retrospectives that use a producer, production company or film academy as unifying principle, and also the increasing attention to the role of archives, with whose help different thematically clustered programmes are put together. Similarly, 'art cinema' has become an insufficient term to describe the type of cinema one finds at festivals. On the one hand, festivals have paid increasing attention to various popular cinemas: Korean murder mysteries, Japanese Pink cinema, European horror hits. On the other hand, the relations between cinema and other art forms are being explored: urban screen programmes, media installations, internet experiments and mobile phone cinema. The previously strict distinction between high and low culture, art and popular cinema has become blurred in festival programming of recent years. While specialised festivals have gone further down the path of niche programming, international festivals (particularly major ones) increasingly programme quality films with crossover appeal to a broad audience (this could be called the Miramax effect).

The fourth characteristic of new festival programming practices in the 1970s concerned the festival's engagement with audiences. Iconic figures like Hubert Bals adhered to a programming philosophy that spun from the conviction that great films deserve to be seen. Bals summarised his task as a programmer as 'finding audiences for films', making cinema itself the top priority. When applied in practice, this philosophy meant that if Bals was convinced of the quality and relevance of a film, he'd do his utmost to make sure the film 'was alive' by finding ways to screen it to a public.[8] To this day, one of the main achievements of the festival circuit is the opportunity for screenings of films that might not otherwise have found a global audience. The specific qualities and attractions of the festival as event are instrumental in this.

Since the 'festivalisation' and 'eventisation' trends of the 1990s, however, the ideal of 'finding audiences for films' has come under some pressure. Many festivals cater to broader audiences and most are obliged to present proof of their social relevance in the form of (growing) attendance numbers and (positive) audience surveys.

Maintaining a balance between independent programming ideals and professional management standards is a precarious business for cultural organisations. When the scale tips the wrong way, festivals may find themselves opting for films that will please their audiences instead of challenging, persuading and helping them to sample new fare. If that happens, festivals will have abnegated their legacy and become simply another component of an exhibition logic they were meant to breach.

I hope that my overview of the historical development of programming practices at festivals will contribute to an increased awareness of the effects of different programming strategies and encourage the critical apprehension of what's at stake in festival programming.

Finding Audiences for Films

I have argued for an understanding of festival programming primarily as a cultural practice. I have shown how the art of programming has developed in several historical periods and pointed at defining characteristics, their roots and modifications and the ways in which they complicate existing dominant frames. While I emphasise the need to consider the workings of the festival circuit as a whole when approaching the topic of programming, and attest to the network's flexibility in adapting to transformations, I also set limits to this adaptability. Festivals can deviate too far from what I consider one of their foundational philosophies — finding audiences for films — and cease to be a contributor to the just cause of cinematic cultural diversity.

Currently festivals are faced with developments that will force them to rethink this mission. Digitisation is leading to new channels of distribution and exhibition for niche content. An urgent matter for festival directors today is how to respond to the digital age. Do festivals need to expand into the virtual realm, opening YouTube channels, hosting on-line festivals, and offering year-round video-on-demand (VOD) access via cable or Web-based portals? Do they need to update their industry services and follow the example of collaborative production schemes such as the music website SellaBand? Do they need to redefine the festival as event, or will the magic of watching films amidst a crowd of fellow film lovers hold its appeal for the internet generation?

These are interesting questions, for which time will provide some answers. My concluding thoughts here are preliminary and meant as a stimulus to further reflection on what we think programming should entail.[9] With the shift towards more participatory creative cultures, it can be expected that audiences will demand a greater say in festival programming practices. This could imply that festivals need to incorporate social media to create an environment with ample feedback loops. It will also likely constitute a definitive break with the age of programmers and the reliance on the (idiosyncratic) tastes of a handful of leading figures. Instead festival programmers will need to account for their selection choices — making them more transparent and specifying criteria and objectives — be self-critical about the pitfalls of a highly institutionalised system like the festival circuit, and, above all, continue to put cinema as an art form and potential political tool ahead of other interests. In the spirit of Langlois and Bals, let's hope that the expanded opportunities for audience interaction will bring about the proliferation of communities in which audiences are not simply found but also committed to cinéphile practices.

Works Cited

de Valck, Marijke (2007) *Film Festivals: From European Geopolitics to Global Cinephilia*. Amsterdam: Amsterdam University Press.

___ (2008) "'Screening" the Future of Film Festivals: A Long Tale of Convergence and Digitization', *Film International*, 6, 4, 15-23.

___ (2010) 'De rol van filmfestivals in het YouTube-tijdperk' ['The Role of Film Festivals in the YouTube Age'], *Boekman*, 83, 54-66.

de Valck, Marijke and Skadi Loist (2010) 'Thematic Annotated Bibliography of Film Festival Research – Update: 2009', in Dina Iordanova with Ruby Cheung (eds) *Film Festival Yearbook 2: Film Festivals and Imagined Communities*. St Andrews: St Andrews Film Studies, 220-58. On-line. Available HTTP: http://www.filmfestivalresearch.org or directly at www1.uni-hamburg.de/Medien/berichte/arbeiten/0091_08.html (22 January 2010).

English, James (2005) *The Economy of Prestige: Prizes, Awards and the Circulation of Cultural Value*. Cambridge: Harvard University Press.

Harbord, Janet (2009) 'Film Festivals-Time-Event', in Dina Iordanova with Ragan Rhyne (eds) *Film Festival Yearbook 1: The Festival Circuit*. St Andrews: St Andrews Film Studies with College Gate Press, 40-6.

Heijs, Jan and Frans Westra (1996) *Que Le Tigre Danse, Huub Bals een biografie | May the Tiger Dance: A Biography of Huub Bals*. Amsterdam: Otto Cramwinckel.

Schröder, Nicholaus (ed.) (2000) *Zwischen Barrikade und Elfenbeinturm: Zur*

Geschichte des unabhängigen Kinos. 30 Jahre Internationales Forum des Jungen Films | Between Barricade and Ivory Tower: On the History of Independent Cinema. 30 Years of the International Forum of New Cinema. Freunde der Deutschen Kinemathek. Berlin: Henschel.

Stringer, Julian (2001) 'Global Cities and International Film Festival Economy', in Mark Shiel and Tony Fitzmaurice (eds) *Cinema and the City: Film and Urban Societies in a Global Context.* Oxford: Blackwell, 134-44.

Wijnberg, Nachoem W. and Gerda Gemser (2000) 'Adding Value to Innovation: Impressionism and the Transformation of the Selection System in Visual Arts', *Organization Science*, 11, 3, 323-9.

Notes

[1] Film International developed several activities: it organised the IFFR, but also acted as a distributor for art house films.

[2] For more background on Hubert Bals' notes, see Heijs and Westra 1996: 150-1.

[3] For an overview of writing on film festival programming, see de Valck and Loist 2010: section 6.

[4] For examples of festivals as displays of geopolitical power, see de Valck 2007: 55-57.

[5] The first series of new waves was launched through festival programming in the 1960s and 1970s: Czechoslovakia, Poland, Hungary, Yugoslavia, West Germany, Brazil, Cuba, Argentina, Japan and Russia. The tendency of festivals to look for other national cinemas rather than those already internationally known through the competition programs on A-list festivals led, on the one hand, to a diversified cinema culture. Problematic, on the other hand, was that the old geopolitical power relations, explicitly present in the first festival phase and criticised by the next generation, had not disappeared; the influential nodes in the festival network that were able to present major 'discoveries' — Miramax etc — turned out to be almost exclusively located in the Western hemisphere. Ergo, Western cultural tastes and Western political convictions set the international programming agenda.

[6] For a similar argument about how different selection procedures lead to different selection criteria, see Wijnberg and Gemser 2000: 323-9.

[7] One of the drivers behind the proliferation of specialised film festivals is the universal tension between aesthetic and political selection criteria. Festivals that programme films with a political agenda in

mind will easily give occasion for the foundation of a festival focussing instead on the aesthetic value of films in the niche concerned. For a similar argument with respect to prizes, see English 2005: 60.

8   When Bals was still working for the commercial cinema company Wolff in Utrecht, he developed his talent to 'find audiences for films' he liked: for example, to promote the screening of *Les Parapluies de Cherbourg* (*The Umbrellas of Cherbourg*, Jacques Demy, France/West Germany, 1964) he organised young girls to walk around Utrecht with umbrellas, and for the première of *Alexis Zorbas* (*Zorba the Greek*, Mihalis Kakogiannis, U.S./UK/Greece, 1964) sirtaki dancing lessons were offered in the basement of the theatre (Heijs and Westra 1996: 28).

9   For a more elaborated argument on the effects of digitisation on festivals as cultural gatekeepers, see de Valck 2010.

Chapter 2

Memories of a Film Festival Addict

Gerald Peary

'I think it would be a great idea for you to start sending me to Cannes', pleads an alternative-newspaper film critic in Joan Micklin Silver's 1977 independent feature, *Between the Lines* (U.S.). His editors look unconvinced. That poor critic will be stuck at the office, typing at his desk. Well, lucky for me, my journalist superiors usually have said 'Go!' when I've wanted to flee to a film festival; and that's happened many, many times in my more than 30 years writing about movies, the last 14 of those for *The Boston Phoenix*. There have been delicious occasions on which my newspapers have paid the expenses. More often, it's this way: 'You supply an article from whatever fest, wherever in the world, and we'll print it. But getting to the fest, and staying over at the fest? You're on your own'.

I have managed. I've been a festival guest, dispensed wisdom (?) on festival panels, often served on festival juries, anything to get me places. Lately, I've been invited to festivals in a new role, as the filmmaker of a feature documentary. Ultimately, I've seen the world: Europe, Asia, Latin America. Israel, Egypt, Turkey. Also, hundreds of fascinating movies from myriad countries, and I've been around important actors and filmmakers in an intimate way that would have been impossible if I'd stayed put.

It began innocently in 1976. Visiting friends in Montreal, I was told that a film festival was going on (the World Film Festival). Would I be interested in checking out a movie there? Sure. What I saw was a raw French-Canadian independent work and, though my French is awful and there were no subtitles, there was something so incredibly compelling and romantic about being caught in an enthusiastic Quebecois festival crowd. I was smitten. Two years later, I had my first job as a film critic for the long-defunct Boston weekly, *The Real Paper*. I covered the New York Film Festival. I interviewed Eric Rohmer, Claude Chabrol. I went to a liquor store with Gerard Depardieu. I sparred during a Q&A with Rainer Werner Fassbinder. And then I travelled to Cuba for the first Havana Film Festival. My path was set.

What a fun life! Film festivals have been such a vital, essential — I confess, *insatiable* — part of my existence; I'm really fortunate that it has never stopped. Oh, the endless memories! Here is an edit of what I recall: snippets and snapshots from three delirious decades as a film festival addict.

The Havana Film Festival, January 1979

I'd done the tourist thing in San Juan and St Thomas, but this was a real, break-the-boycott voyage and adventure. Our shy, somewhat intimidated American delegation was led onward by Barbara Kopple, showing off her up-the-union documentary, *Harlan County, U.S.A.* (U.S., 1976). The Cubans loved her, and who wasn't in awe of her charisma and swagger? We saw the famous Havana sea wall. I drank my first mojito, Papa Hemingway's cocktail-of-choice when residing there. I ate my first horsemeat, followed by dreadful diarrhoea under a tree. Ring Lardner Jr., the blacklisted screenwriter, guided me on how to scuba dive. Where was Fidel? We never sighted him, but I had conversations with Cuba's greatest filmmaker, Tomás Gutiérrez Alea, director of *Memorias del subdesarrollo* (*Memories of Underdevelopment*, Cuba, 1968). Despite his ambivalences about the Revolution, he'd never left Cuba, unlike much of the middle class. (In fact, he never emigrated, dying there in 1996.)

As a democratic, 1960s leftist, I had my own problems with Castroism. We'd all heard that gay people were jailed here, and that there were political prisoners. Alas, I mostly kept quiet about my objections, especially among the gung-ho Americans. And then there was the day we saw Stalinist-style Cuban documentaries hailing their brave soldiers putting down the Eritrean revolt in then Marxist-Leninist Ethiopia. Which side was I on?

One afternoon, a fervently friendly Cuban stopped me and a friend in our hotel lobby and invited us to his house. Mixing with foreigners was a crime, subject to arrest, but he was desperate to talk with outsiders. We snuck past the neighbourhood police and into his squalid apartment, where his thrilled children forced on us humble gifts. No, I had to admit to the man's eager eldest son, I didn't know George Harrison.

What has become known as the International Festival of the New Latin American Cinema reached its 33rd year in 2011. Now, filmmakers from Mexico, Central and South America compete for prizes in such categories as First Work, Fiction, Documentary, and Unpublished Script. The Havana fest is arguably the most important in Latin America. Canadians are enthusiastic participants. Meanwhile, the embargo stretches on, for better or for worse, which means there is little presence of U.S. filmmakers, though American films do show: i.e. 22 features and 22 experimental shorts in 2007. That year, Brian De Palma's *Redacted* (2007, U.S.) opened the festival, sans De Palma. It was a high-end example of the kind of American film the Cubans most prefer to show, a movie deeply critical of the U.S. presence in Iraq.

The New York Film Festival, October 1980

Before the advent of the Sundance Film Festival and the ascension of the Toronto International Film Festival in the mid-1980s, the New York Film Festival was the only place in North America to be each fall. The festival director was Richard Roud, a champion of modernist European masters. Bernardo Bertolucci. Werner Herzog and Rainer Werner Fassbinder. Eric Rohmer, Claude Chabrol, and Agnès Varda. This was the year that Jean-Luc Godard and François Truffaut both attended with important films, though they no longer conversed.

Living in self-exile in Switzerland, Godard came to the Big Apple with his first semi-'story' feature in many years, *Sauve qui peut (la vie)* (*Every Man for Himself/Slow Motion*, France/Austria/West Germany/Switzerland, 1980), a slimmed-down, lucid, rethinking of his classic 1960s works. Even Godard professed to like this movie. 'I feel now that I've landed in this beautiful country of narrative for the first time, remembering the full strength of Mack Sennett's arrival in California', Godard said at a press conference after the NYFF screening. 'Of course, I don't pretend to be as good'.

Who ever knows what Godard really believes? He acted unconcerned that the New Wave innovations of his *À bout de souffle* (*Breathless*, France, 1960) — jump-cutting, stop-action etc. — had been abducted by commerce. 'It's a fact that all Eisenstein discoveries are on TV today. Shampoo ads come from *Potemkin*. What can we do? I'm not against advertisement. I was hired to do a two-minute commercial for a men's aftershave lotion. I gave them two hours [of material]'. Godard remained a Brechtian scammer, but was he still, as he'd been in the early 1970s, a Maoist-minded revolutionary? 'I'm a capitalist', he declared. 'I'm a producer. I love money. I love to spend it'.

Godard couldn't leave the stage without getting in a dig at his favourite adversary, his once-pal Truffaut. 'When I tell him, "François, in my opinion, you're not a very good director, but you're a good screenwriter," he gets shocked'. Would Truffaut fight back? The press conference after his *Le dernier métro* (*The Last Metro*, France, 1980) offered Truffaut a chance to respond. 'I'm perfectly aware that Jean-Luc thinks all of my films are bad', he said. 'I say that all of his films are good'.

You could feel the bitterness despite Truffaut's attempt at diplomacy. Godard's cocky animosity brought him much pain. (Truffaut died four years later of a brain tumour. He and Godard never made up.)

As for the New York Film Festival, it goes nobly on, in 2011 still maintaining the highest intellectual standards for movies that are screened, but with a far more global outreach than in Richard Roud's Eurocentric days. Great films are just as likely to be picked from Latin America, Iran, Korea, Taiwan or mainland China. And important slots are reserved for demanding experimental cinema. These days, there are challenges from the consciously hip, and far more conventional, Tribeca Film Festival; and NYFF is no longer where international journalists head to see the unveiling of the art house fall season. That's Toronto. Under Richard Peña, the New York festival is now branded as a 'local' festival, but when 'local' means New York City, there's no problem with unveiling the most rewarding, adventurous cinema, year after year.

The Jerusalem Film Festival, July 1988

The week before, Palestinians in the Old City had stoned archaeologists digging close to their holy shrines, and the Israeli police countered with tear gas and arrests. After several days, the confrontations had ebbed, so it was decided that an historic outdoor lunch could proceed, in the Ben Hinnom Valley below the Jerusalem Cinematheque. Covering this festival for the *Los Angeles Times*, I was the privileged journalist who was allowed at the folding card table. There, Israeli Foreign Minister Shimon Peres, in jacket and tie, sat down for a catered non-kosher meal and a formal conversation with Aleksandr Askoldov, a Russian-Jewish filmmaker who had just arrived from Moscow.

The five-year-old Jerusalem Film Festival at the Cinematheque had gotten a quick reputation as a 'peacenik' event, with a mandate to show films from Arab directors and also from the Eastern Bloc. This was the natural landing spot for the first delegation of Soviet filmmakers allowed by their government to enter Israel. These included Askoldov, maker of the ambitious epic film, *Komissar* (*Commissar*, 1967), and Alexander Chervinsky, also Jewish, the screenwriter of *Tema* (*Theme*, 1979). Both films were made at a time when controversial Jewish subject matter was forbidden in the Soviet Union, and both were to be shown in Jerusalem. Shelved permanently in the Leonid Brezhnev era, they had been resuscitated in 1987 by Mikhail Gorbachev, to be readied for worldwide release.

A lone policeman, with a rifle, stood vigilant on a wall above as

Peres and Askoldov conversed over their outdoor lunch, and I took notes. Peres spoke solemnly through a Russian translator, quoting Leo Tolstoy and other lofty Russians.

'I'm going to ask you a naïve question', Askoldov interjected boldly. 'Are you thinking of candidates for the first Israeli ambassador to my country?' Peres, who promised to attend a Jerusalem screening of *Commissar*, assured him that such discussions were occurring. 'I'd like to raise a toast to this possibility', Askoldov said, and we all clinked glasses.

At this moment, I broke my journalistic objectivity, hoping to intrude on history. I whispered a suggestion in Peres' ear, and he repeated what I said to Askoldov: 'You can invite Mr Gorbachev to Israel'. (I have no idea if this suggestion had any ultimate impact, but Gorbachev did visit Israel in 1992, after the dissolution of the Soviet Union.)

Later, I spoke to screenwriter Chervinsky, about how he and Askoldov had embarked to Israel. 'Andrei Smirnov, the acting secretary of the Union of Soviet Filmmakers, struggled for it. He insisted at the Foreign Ministry that the policy of our union is to enlarge the showings of Soviet filmmakers everywhere. In Israel, lots of people speak Russian. Also, it's a film market. There's money!'

Because Chervinsky's screenplay for *Theme* included a subplot about an unhappy Russian Jew emigrating to Israel, the 1979 film was never released at home. 'In Brezhnev's time', he said, 'a character in a film could be Jewish, but only in a very specific way. He could be in the war, very bold and brave, and die while everyone lives. Or he could be a friendly, funny Jew. I don't have to tell you — it's the same as black persons in American movies'.

I was fortunate enough to return to the Jerusalem Film Festival many years later, in 2009, when I was invited to show my documentary *For the Love of Movies: The Story of American Film Criticism* (U.S., 2010). Little had changed. The festival still remained on the Israeli secular left and showed films, whenever it could, which argued for Palestinian rights. There was more worry about financing with the Likud Party in control and more concern about security with the Orthodox ultra-right on the march everywhere in Jerusalem. A frustration of the festival: when international guests cancel appearances in protest of Israeli government policies such as building Jewish settlements on Arab land; the guests don't realize that the Jerusalem film festival probably agrees with them.

The Berlin International Film Festival, February 1990

I stood on the Berlin Wall! Hoisted up nine feet, I squeezed among hundreds on one section of the Wall, all cheering as the Russians bulldozed another. The festivities stretched from the Brandenburg Gate to Checkpoint Charlie, a mile away.

This was the year that the grim February city of Berlin became, both East and West, a gigantic, euphoric playpen. Virtually every filmmaker, journalist, buyer and seller skipped away often from the 40th Berlin International Film Festival. The lazy people — most of us — simply bought pieces of Wall rock from the myriad entrepreneurs behind makeshift tables. But for a single West German mark, you could rent a pick. For two marks, a pair of goggles to guard against the flying debris. Then, hammer away! An American film critic from Washington got scratched, bloodied hands. 'It's not easy knocking down a concrete wall', he complained. 'Have you ever tried to rip up your sidewalk?'

Meanwhile, the West Berlin-based festival acknowledged the opening of the border with daily showings of forbidden East German films. There were prime pickings especially from 1965 to 1968, when the huffy, intractable, communist government banned virtually every movie produced there — keeping the 1960s from blossoming in the German Democratic Republic. One of those verboten works was *Jahrgang '45* (*Born in '45*, East Germany, 1965), shown finally in the year 1990 with Jürgen Böttcher, the filmmaker, present.

Did he just walk over from East Berlin?

In 1966, the officials had complained: Why did three of Böttcher's characters have to stand against a *black* wall? What does that say of East Germany? And why did the hero stare out the window at a building *not yet completed*? What did that symbolize? In one scene, a tourist bus from West Berlin passed through the frame. Böttcher said: 'I was told that the presence of a Western bus insulted the powers above. We should be happy we don't ride on Western buses!'

Was I surprised that the Wall had come down? I'd had a premonition a year earlier, February 1989. Often before, I'd made the depressing trek, one day of each festival, into East Berlin. I'd visited the awful giant department store, walked into grocery markets where cabbage was the favoured vegetable. And I'd tried to get into Bertolt Brecht's house, a national museum that was always closed. In 1989, I stood inside, by the single bed in which Brecht died. His home was open at last, so Berlin, the Open City, must be next.

I've rarely attended Berlin in recent years. It certainly remains a formidable event, on a par with Venice and just behind Cannes as the most important European film festival. And it's settled easily into East

Berlin for its major screenings. But everyone agrees that, with a united Germany, the festival has lost its political urgency.

The Provincetown International Film Festival, July 2001

What a faux pas, all because I missed a screening of the documentary *Southern Comfort* (Kate Davis, U.S., 2001) at the gay-and-lesbian-friendly third Provincetown International Film Festival. How then could I know, when I met the genial *Southern Comfort* star at a festival party, that Lola Cola was not a transvestite but a transsexual? I referred to Lola as 'him', only to be corrected by Lola's female lover: 'Lola is a she!'

Oops! And I hope I wasn't too much of a pill when I requested a fan for my hotel room to drown out, via white noise, the all-night disco in the basement leather bar. Alone among the guests, I needed my sleep. I did have a cool metrosexual moment: a heart-to-heart with a drag person from Minnesota whose nightclub act, he/she (?) noted, encompassed Celine Dion and Reba McIntyre. Also, I smiled back when cruised by a bearded nun outside a sing-along screening of *The Sound of Music* (Robert Wise, U.S., 1965).

Was there a better spot on earth for 'Doe, a deer' than uninhibited P-town? Raunchy things were yelled out, and boos and hisses rained down on Christopher Plummer's so-straight Baron von Trapp. Who in the gender-twisting audience could abide such a fascistic patriarch? Yet he was forgiven when (a closeted artsy side?) he joined in song with his psychologically battered children.

To find out what was really hopping at the Provincetown film festival, I checked in at the rental apartment of filmmaker John Waters, who has been coming to P-town for 37 Massachusetts summers. A fervent supporter of the festival, he'd agreed to introduce a favourite movie. No Andrei Tarkovsky this time. He chose *Baxter* (Jérôme Boivin, 1989), a French flick about a bull terrier who bites those who are sentimental about dogs.

Mostly, Waters was giddy about the upcoming evening with 1960s songster Connie Francis appearing at Town Hall with a new 35mm print of her super-hit 1960 movie, *Where the Boys Are* (Henry Levin, U.S.). Waters ran through Francis' 'Who's Sorry Now?' tragic tabloid life: a controlling father, a rape, failed marriages, a brother murdered by the Mafia. As we talked, Waters played volume four of her *Greatest Hits*. But his 2001 obsession was George W. Bush's bad-ass daughter, Jenna Bush. Waters: 'She wore a toe ring to court! She was totally defiant!'

Frankly, there was trepidation about Francis' appearance. She'd never heard of Provincetown! Also, she was not in the best of health, having spent five weeks with a broken foot. Would she justify the $25 ticket price? Not to worry. After tanned muscle boys pranced through the audience in bathing suits, Connie hobbled in. CHEERS! She was definitely moved by the reception. 'What a joy it is to be here tonight. Welcome to the groovy Provincetown Festival!' she said. Then the film rolled, the mostly boring, inanely written *Where the Boys Are*, only vaguely improved by a 35mm restoration, made exclusively for the festival at a cost of $15,000.

Back on stage, Francis confessed how little she'd wanted to make the movie. 'I'm a singer, not an actress', she'd told producer Joe Pasternak, who took her to locations in Fort Lauderdale. 'He told me there was a boy in every tree. I didn't see them. I'd rather go to the Jersey shore'. Her father insisted she keep filming. 'I didn't attend the première. I didn't like the way I looked, sang, acted. But *Where the Boys Are* was my *Gone With the Wind*. The rest of my movies — *Follow the Boys* etc. — were downhill all the way'.

'I really have nerve being at a film festival!'

I've attended Provincetown for virtually every year of its existence. It remains a key venue for gay and lesbian cinema, and John Waters continues as the in-house chief attraction. Each year, he screens a little movie — strange and campy — which he adores. Each year, he does a spirited Q&A with a maverick film presence such as Jim Jarmusch. A festival at the level of Provincetown will never exert a major impact, because there are no potential film distributors or television buyers in the house. But it will always do well, far better than most smaller fests. What potential guest cannot be lured for a few late spring days to gorgeous Cape Cod?

The Toronto International Film Festival, September 2001

Here's where I was on 9/11. That morning, I walked out in the middle of a boring screening (it was a film from India) to come upon people at a film festival doing what they never do: eyeing TVs wherever they could find them. Horrific images from NYC. Who could stomach watching movies when, on the fourth day of the Toronto festival, the world appeared to be ending? The many Americans in Canada — press, publicists, directors, movie stars, and so on — stumbled about in collective shock, moving numbly from watching CNN on monitors to struggling to get through to New York on cell phones to, eventually, formulating patchwork arrangements to traverse the Ontario-U.S. border and arrive home —

without encountering a second wave of terrorists. A typical plan: six California show-biz people pooling money for a minibus and a three-day drive to Los Angeles.

On the other hand, there was a solipsistic Hungarian filmmaker who called worried from Budapest: would his screenings at the Museum of Modern Art in New York be affected?

The TIFF closed down for about 40 hours, and then, cautiously, started up. Slowly, those who had disowned the cinema on Tuesday began, on Thursday and Friday, to watch movies again. Me too. Exiled in Toronto, we could do nothing about crashed planes or the downed World Trade Center. Inside theatres, those who so wished could escape a bit in the dark.

Wouldn't you know it? There was a film, Denis Couchard's *L'ange de goudron* (*Tar Angel*, Canada, 2001), so close to real events. It's about an Algerian immigrant family in Montreal in the weeks before citizenship. The grateful father, Ahmed, practises the national anthem, 'O Canada'. To his chagrin, he finds out via TV news that his 19-year-old son, Hafid, is part of an underground organisation that has broken into government offices and deleted computer files. The film climaxes at a rural airport with a confrontation between Canadian police and young Muslims, labelled by the government as terrorists. (To my knowledge, *Tar Angel* never played in the U.S.; Quebec's Couchard is sympathetic to the causes of the Arab youth. The only violence comes from the cops, who beat to death an unarmed Hafid.)

The movie at Toronto which seemed best to address the doom and despair was *Thirteen Conversations about One Thing* (U.S., 2001), by Jill Sprecher. This fine film — ambitious, wryly philosophical — offered a running argument between cockeyed optimism and extreme pessimism, as dramatized in interconnected New York stories, often sad ones. Does everything have to turn to merde? Is the World Trade Center bombing the story of life itself? 'I was mugged in New York and formed a very negative attitude toward other people', Sprecher, an ex-New York University filmmaking student, explained at the screening. The story with actor Clea DuVall, Sprecher said, was the movie's most autobiographical, including — so importantly — the poignant feel-better conclusion. Hopeless Clea, riding on a Manhattan subway, is suddenly waved at, encouragingly, by a stranger on the platform. How stirring! 'We started writing from the end scene', Sprecher said. 'That actually happened to me'.

And then there was *Buffalo Soldiers* (Gregor Jordan, UK/Germany, 2001), about our GIs — Joaquin Phoenix, Ed Harris — stationed in

Germany in 1989 and getting by peddling contraband goods and heroin. Here, post-*M*A*S*H* (Robert Altman, U.S., 1970), post-*Three Kings* (David O. Russell, U.S./Australia, 1999), were slick cynicism and jaded souls. The film's ending had already been staged for real: an apocalyptic explosion, Americans falling off a burning building.

The Toronto International Film Festival is the most important in North America. Each September, hundreds of first-rank journalists and film critics arrive for nine days of previewing the art house movies which will open in North America in the next few months. Along with the movies come the directors and the actors, a tantalizing, accessible dream line-up for a press who live by interviewing movie people. And let's not forget Torontonians in attendance, of all ages, professions, backgrounds. There is probably no festival in the world so connected to the pulse of the city in which it takes place. If Toronto is considered among the most cosmopolitan and sophisticated of world cities, the global status of TIFF is a major factor.

But the Toronto festival has its detractors, those who feel it has gotten smug and cocky, that it's far too beholden to film distributors, that the lovely smaller films which are programmed are overlooked because, these days, they are always playing against several 'hot', trendy movies. Some who have been to Toronto for decades are worried that the festival is becoming 'a second Sundance', though what that means isn't very well defined. More mainstream? More Hollywood-friendly? More youth-obsessed? More American? Whatever, Toronto is so powerful, and so successful, that the criticisms, at least for now, can be pushed off for another day.

The Midnight Sun Film Festival, June 2002

It's certainly surreal, the sun blazing at midnight in Lapland, home of a zillion freezing lakes, where, buzzed on 120-proof Finnish vodka, I jumped in one of them. And who's that bearded, naked man in a towel on the sauna porch? It's Francis Ford Coppola, another high-and-happy camper. Earlier, clothed, he led the gathered in off-key singing of 'Avanti Popolo' and then soloed on 'God Bless America'. Welcome to a VIP party at that June's Midnight Sun Film Festival, where Coppola was a special guest! If blonde Finnish dance partners weren't enough, the *Godfather* cineaste was won over here by a Coppola retrospective, which reclaimed such neglected works as *Tucker* (U.S., 1988) and *Gardens of Stone* (U.S., 1987).

Sixteen years earlier, three Helsinki-based filmmakers (Timo Malmi and Aki and Mika Kaurismaki) envisioned a utopian European festival, as they'd been at enough bad ones to realize what they didn't want. 'The filmmakers use limousines, stay at five-star hotels, and the people attending never talk to them', Mika Kaurismaki explained to me. 'A festival in Helsinki would be too normal. We wanted something strange'. The search ended a 12-hour drive north of Helsinki, to the tiny Lapland municipality of Sodankyla, where the mayor of the out-of-it town (known for alcoholism, suicides, unemployment, and coal-dark winters) was eager for business.

Malmi and the Kaurismakis saw possibilities in this three-street, one movie-house spot. It was geographically exotic, 100 kilometres above the Arctic Circle. And yet each June, transcendence: it was tee-shirt warm, and the sun stayed out 24 hours a day. The Midnight Sun Film Festival was born in 1987. Come one, come all, to the Lappish polar region, where reindeer roam free. The first guests, French filmmaker Bertrand Tavernier (*Round Midnight*, U.S./France, 1986) and American 'B' cult director, Sam Fuller (*Shock Corridor*, U.S., 1963, *The Naked Kiss*, U.S., 1964), got, as promised, 35mm screenings of their films shown round the clock.

What serendipity. Tavernier and Fuller might be the most garrulous filmmakers ever, both famous for talking everyone else into exhaustion. Midnight Sun attendees had all the conversation with celebrities they could desire. 'Sam never slept', said Kaurismaki. 'On the street, if you saw the cigar smoke, you knew Fuller was there, talking about movies'. Filmmaker guests have included Michael Powell, Krzysztof Kieslowski, and Terry Gilliam; I was honoured to be the third American film critic invited there. Still, there was only one Fuller and, after his 1997 death, a Sodankyla street was named after him: 'Samuel Fullerin Katu / Samuel Fuller's Street'.

Standing at that anointed street corner, I imagined cruel February in frozen, lonely Lapland: just the sign of Sam and reindeer. Surreal.

I've never been back. In 2002 I was the recipient of a special invitation to Finland offered to one international journalist. A different journalist each year. In 2010, my documentary, *For the Love of Movies: The Story of American Film Criticism*, was selected for this ever-idiosyncratic, still-vibrant festival. However, the festival's budget wouldn't allow me a second trip to the Midnight Sun, even if I'd crossed over from film critic to filmmaker.

The Cannes Film Festival, May 2003

'Life is short, Cannes is long', quipped an exhausted American critic friend in the midst of the seemingly endless 61st Cannes Film Festival. What bedazzles and seems so glamorous on TV — the azure French Riviera, the red carpet at the Palais, awesome, toothsome international movie stars — makes for the most sleep-deprived, 12-day workaholic week of the year for the 4,000 journalists in attendance. They scramble from screening to cell phone to interview to press conference to computer to e-mail from 8:30am to deep into the night. Yes, there are lush parties down by the sea, each après-midi and evening, but these are mostly gulp-a-wine and gobble-an-hors-d'oeuvres teases for on-the-job reporters.

The Riviera beach? No critic worth his/her salt has gone swimming in years. Sex under the palm trees? Maybe for starlets and collegiate interns, not for the deadline-obsessed fourth estate.

Is that awful enough, dear readers? Also, lots of the heralded world-debut films at Cannes are putrid.

In 2003, the Cannes jury deserved commendation for rejecting all prizes for the mean-spirited film predicted by most there as the Palme d'Or winner: *Dogville* (Spain/Australia/Denmark/Sweden/Norway/Finland/UK/France/Germany/Netherlands), the female-bashing, people-loathing, America-despising tome from Lars von Trier. Legions of misguided worshippers in Cannes, both on-automatic leftists and auteurist-worshipping Europeans, were angered when *Dogville* header Nicole Kidman took no Best Actress, Denmark's von Trier no Best Director, and *Dogville* no Best Picture. For me: hallelujah!

Dogville, based on von Trier's cursory reading of John Steinbeck, Mark Twain, and Thornton Wilder, is situated in a mythic hamlet in the Rocky Mountains of the 1930s. Nicole Kidman plays Grace, a moll on the run from gangsters, who is saved by the Dogville inhabitants. As months go by, these do-gooder quiet Americans turn fuckin' ugly: Grace is put in shackles, and becomes *Our Town*'s sexual slave.

Does this sound familiar to those weighed down by earlier examples of von Trier's perversely sexist point of view in *Breaking the Waves* (Spain/Denmark/Sweden/France/Netherlands/Norway/Iceland, 1996) and *Dancer in the Dark* (Spain/Argentina/Denmark/Germany/Netherlands/Italy/U.S./UK/France/Sweden/Finland/Iceland/Norway, 2000)? At the press conference for *Dogville*, I challenged the Danish cineaste: 'In three recent films, you have had your female stars, Emily Watson, Björk, and now Nicole Kidman, tortured, raped, imprisoned, chained, murdered, or some variant of the above. Why always are your victims women, women, women?'

'That's a superficial way to look at the story', von Trier answered. 'That's not the way I look at the story. I don't think it's important if the victims are men or women. I'm sorry you don't like it. There are other people who do like it'. And a few minutes later: 'I am a victim, the little female within me. When you turn the power toward others, toward yourself, I don't think it matters whether it's a man or woman'.

But Lars, if it doesn't matter, why not a couple of guys instead of gals strung up and anally attacked? That'll be the day! And then there was Vincent Gallo's self-starring cross-country ego-trip, *The Brown Bunny* (U.S./Japan/France).

Cocky and smugly assured before his screening, Gallo shrivelled down to petite because of the scornful laughter during the public screening, followed by the torrent of negative reviews in the English-language press. Nobody could fathom that Gallo could squander that much screen time on himself doing practically nothing: shaving, combing his hair, pumping gas, sleeping, driving, driving, driving. And finally, there was the scene for which every dirty-minded person was waiting (count me in): Chloë Sevigny doing a Monica Lewinsky on his erect member. The blow job was authentic on her part, yet rumours started quickly that what we saw sticking out of Gallo's zipper was a large piece of rubber. Apparently, such an object was missing from the set of Claire Denis' *Trouble Every Day* (France/Germany/Japan, 2001), in which Gallo starred.

'I apologize to the financiers of the film, but I assure you it was never my intention to make a pretentious film, a self-indulgent film, a useless film, an unengaging film', Gallo said in Cannes the sombre day after. He added that the fact that some French critics liked *The Brown Bunny* 'is almost like salt in the wound'.

The Bangkok International Film Festival, January 2005

Would it be obscene to hold the Bangkok International Film Festival just weeks after the Thai coast had been done in, and so many drowned, by the tsunami? A decision was made: the 11-day show would roll on, bankrolled mostly by the Tourism Authority of Thailand. However, the opening-night celebration was cancelled, and proceeds from the festival were announced as going to 'tsunami aid'. As for the much-anticipated appearance of the Thai royal family at the closing night: Princess Uboltrana couldn't attend. She was in mourning for her son, who'd been vacationing that fatal day by the ocean.

The lavish festival moved ahead, with a thoughtful tribute to cinematographer Roderigo Prieto (*Amores Perros*, Mexico, 2000; *Frida*, U.S./Canada/Mexico, 2002; *21 Grams*, U.S., 2003). A career award was bestowed on Hollywood schlock maestro, Joel Schumacher (*The Lost Boys*, U.S., 1987; *Batman Forever*, U.S./UK, 1995; *Phone Booth*, U.S., 2002 etc.), who unveiled his dubious-achievement musical, *The Phantom of the Opera* (UK/U.S., 2004), as a gala première without fear of chortling: the Thai citizenry are famously kind and polite.

David Hockney, pegged to discuss his art-theory videos, was a no-show because he couldn't get a visa to Thailand for his boyfriend. 'I told him, David, don't worry, you can find plenty of boyfriends in Bangkok', a festival organiser confided. Maybe he was put off by the travel time to Thailand? It couldn't have been worse than mine: with woeful connections, 36 hours from Boston's Logan, including a nightmare 3am switching of planes in Fairbanks, Alaska, where reindeer sausage was on the early-bird breakfast menu.

But what's to gripe? I was president of the five-person International Critics Jury; and probably nowhere on earth was a jury treated with such supreme respect. We stayed at a five-star hotel, swam in the pool between screenings, toured ancient Buddhist sites, ate whatever we wished in tasty, spicy Bangkok restaurants. Our jury duty was to select the best Southeast Asian film among 15 candidates. We watched three a day, not in a plebeian movie house but in a plush little theatre at the edge of a multiplex supplied with lean-back armchairs, blankets and pillows. On other days, rich Thais and foreigners paid four times the normal movie price (about $10 instead of $2.50) to see movies so decadently.

In a lobby area, where our jury went between films for tea and finger sandwiches, the walls sported silver-tinted ersatz paintings of American studio golden-age stars: Audrey Hepburn, Elizabeth Taylor. Only one indigenous actor was represented, adjoining Cary Grant. 'He's Mitr Chaibancha, our James Dean', explained my Thai juror, a historian of Southeast Asian cinema. 'He was making a movie, *Red Eagle* [*Insee tong*], in 1970, and fell from a helicopter. He was doing his own stunts, as the rumour then was that he was getting less popular'.

And what did we watch? The first film we'd ever encountered from under-siege Burma (Myanmar), a naïve, inept work about some Burmese in Japan who learn that their homeland (no mention of the military occupancy) is the place to be. Three horrid Philippine melodramas. An intriguing Vietnamese neo-realist film about water-buffalo herders. A

Thai tearjerker with a husband dying of a brain tumour. Our winner? *Mei li de xi yi ji* (*The Beautiful Washing Machine*, Malaysia, 2004) from Malaysia's James Lee, a deadpan sex comedy somewhere between Luis Buñuel and Ming-Liang Tsai.

I was not surprised to find out that the Bangkok International Film Festival, which was, in honesty, a rather wasteful, extravagant event, has fallen prey to political changes. A 29 October 2010 posting on Wise Kwai's *Thai Film Journal* reads, 'After the deadly and fiery end of the red-shirt political protests in April and May, plans for the Bangkok International Film Festival became uncertain [...]. The Festival has now been cancelled altogether, according to a three-paragraph sidebar in today's *Bangkok Post*. I've heard that the festival organizers simply could not get together a budget to hold the festival. There has been no official announcement or word whether the scandal-ridden festival will ever be held again' (Kwai 2010).

The Bergman Film Week, June 2010

In liberal Sweden, five-week vacations are mandated by law, so the prosperous often take off in the summer for the island of Faro (pronounced 'foreh', with a rolling 'r'), southeast of Stockholm, via a plane, a car and a ferry. In July and August, 5,000 tourists pack the place for hikes, bicycling and jolting leaps into the brisk Baltic Sea. But winters are desolate and fierce, and very few (under 100 residents) remain. The last fishermen have moved on; there's one cattle farmer left. The sole filmmaker who resided year-round on Faro died in August 2007. That was director Ingmar Bergman, 89, the island's most famous citizen.

It was 1960 when Bergman first arrived on Faro, for the filming of his bleak existentialist classic, *Såsom i en spegel* (*Through a Glass Darkly*, Sweden, 1961). The craggy, stormy ambience — and the truly extraordinary light — fit perfectly with his vision. Back then, no tourists were allowed on Faro, site of a top-secret Swedish military base. But Bergman loved it immediately. In an epiphany, he told his cinematographer, Sven Nykvist, that he would soon buy a house on the island, and make more movies there. Someday, he would move permanently to Faro. And he wished to die there.

The promises of half a century ago were kept, including the home and the filming of such masterpieces as *Persona* (Sweden, 1966), *Skammen* (*Shame*, Sweden, 1968), *En passion* (*The Passion of Anna*, Sweden, 1969) and *Scener ur ett äktenskap* (*Scenes from a Marriage*, Sweden, 1973). Bergman sold his Stockholm apartment in 1993 and transferred all his belongings to the island. Living alone at the end, he expired in his Faro bed. He's buried in the graveyard of Faro's only church.

2.1. Film critic Gerald Peary (third from left) was among the first group of journalists ever to tour the Faro, Sweden, home of the late director Ingmar Bergman. © Satyen K. Bordoloi

Bergman honoured Faro. How could Faro honour him?

I was one of eight international journalists brought to Faro by the Swedish Institute (figure 2.1). We would participate in Bergman Week, an annual summer film festival open to the world public, with screenings and lectures and special guests. Also, we would see where on the island Bergman shot his famous films. Most enticingly of all, we would be the first press group ever to watch movies in Bergman's private theatre and to tour Bergman's house.

Our initiation to Faro was a conversation with Liv Ullmann, star of four key Bergman features made there, starting with her dazzling film debut in *Persona*. For some years, she was romantically enmeshed with her director and, for months each year, they resided in Bergman's Faro house. She had returned this spring for the first time since his funeral. Said Ullmann: 'I had almost five years here with him, and a daughter, and an incredible creative relationship. It's who I am: Faro, the people I met, the strange seasons, the light in the middle of the night, the barren winters with no colours'.

Linn Ullmann, the Norwegian novelist, and daughter of Liv and

Ingmar, talked to us at the converted barn which, several miles from his home, had been Bergman's private screening room. It was equipped for 16mm and 35mm showings and with a projectionist on call. 'My father

2.2. Director Ingmar Bergman's private library in his home in Faro, Sweden, holds not only videos of accepted classics, but also some surprisingly popular movies. © Satyen K. Bordoloi

would meet us outside on this blue bench', she showed us. 'We'd see two films a day, at three o'clock for the hard-core, an artistic film, often a silent one. At 7:30, there was a film for a bigger audience, sometimes even with children'.

In awe, we ventured inside, where our group would preview brand-new Swedish features provided by the Swedish Film Institute. We looked about, so deeply thrilled: a tapestry on a wall of Bergman's film *Trollflöjten* (*The Magic Flute*, Sweden, 1975), pine-wood walls, and 16 plush chairs in three rows. In the front: the chair where Bergman always sat, supplied with a wool-covered back pillow. We stared at Bergman's seat but stayed obedient to the holy house rule: it's only, evermore, for the Swedish master.

We did more sleuthing in a rushed trip through Bergman's house, pushed through by impatient guides. Some of us lingered in his library to check out his books: lots by playwright August Strindberg, his hero, several bibles, of course, and, surprising to me, many novels by Isaac Bashevis Singer (figure 2.2). Bergman's huge VHS tape collection had the expected classics — Andrei Tarkovsky, Fritz Lang etc. — but also random films revealing, perhaps, an eclectic movie taste. Did this high modernist really watch *The Blues Brothers* (John Landis, U.S., 1980), *Blood from the Mummy's Tomb* (Seth Holt, UK, 1971), *Elvis! Elvis!* (Kay Pollack, Sweden, 1976), and Adam Sandler in *Anger Management* (Peter Segal, U.S., 2003)?

We stood at the double bed with a white cover where Bergman died. And, on another occasion, we were taken to Faro Church, where Bergman, often angrily sceptical of God, apparently worshipped. He's buried in a private spot far from other graves. His grave is shared with his last wife, the non-actress Ingrid Bergman. She had passed on before him, but her body was exhumed and brought here.

Bergman carefully planned out the 2007 funeral with his lady minister. 'He picked the wood for his coffin, and the carpenter', a guide told us. 'People were to be dressed in black, and there should be red roses'. And what about journalists? Our guide laughed. 'The press had to be 100 yards away, in a field where the lambs stand'.

Work Cited

Kwai, Wise (2010) *Thai Film Journal*. On-line. Available HTTP: http://thaifilmjournal.blogspot.com/2010/10/bangkok-international-film-festival.html?utm_source=feedburner&utm_medium=feed&utm_campaign=Feed%3A+WiseKwaisThaiFilmJournal+%28Wise+Kwai%27s+Thai+Film+Journal%29 (5 May 2011).

Chapter 3
Just What Is It That Makes Today's Animation Festivals So Different, So Appealing?

Marcin Giżycki

Over 50 years ago, in 1956, Richard Hamilton created an iconic collage of pop art: *Just what is it that makes today's homes so different, so appealing?* The title was borrowed from an ad which also offered an answer to this question: 'Open planning of course — and a bold use of colour'. Paraphrasing this statement one can say that what makes today's animation festivals so different, so appealing is their open formula and bold programming.

The number of festivals worldwide devoted exclusively or in large part to animated film seems to increase each year.[1] Some of them focus on select aspects of animation: non-narrative or experimental film,[2] auteur film etc. [3] There are several reasons for this proliferation of animation festivals. The most obvious one is that festivals provide artists with the best venues for presenting their work and exchanging ideas. We should not forget about the internet, of course, but as a means for displaying film as a work of art, a darkened room with a big screen is still indispensable. There were times, at least in my native Poland, when short films, animated ones included, had ways of successfully reaching theatrical audiences. They were shown in regular cinemas before feature films. One cinema in Warsaw used to be exclusively dedicated to documentary and animated films. Before the Second World War, owners of cinemas in Poland could count on tax exemptions if they showed short films of artistic value. Later, there were TV shows devoted especially to this kind of cinema, hosted by expert critics.[4] Today, the only way to have your short animation widely distributed in cinemas is to have it included in a touring feature like *The Animation Show* or *Spike and Mike's*. This option is open only to a very limited number of films, typically those with some commercial potential. Festivals may not replace regular cinematic distribution but at least they give filmmakers a chance to display their work in a proper way and to reach small but appreciative audiences. Also, as Kathryn Ramey (2010) points out, a lot of socialising and networking takes place at these gatherings as well. Filmmakers exchange contact information and copies of their work, which might later result in invitations to other events, screenings etc.

On the other hand, many festivals are being organised because local, often predominantly academic, communities are frustrated by not having easy access to art house films, especially experimental and animated ones. An example of this is the Providence Children's Film Festival, launched in February 2009 in Providence, Rhode Island. Festivals of this kind are aimed more at providing their communities with scarce cultural goods and reaching their target audience, rather than setting a platform for professional discussions. Of course these aims are not contradictory, and most festivals try to fulfil them all. There is nothing sadder than a festival without viewers, although I have encountered one or two events of this sort as well.

Another raison d'être for smaller festivals is that big mainstream ones have become victims of their own popularity and are now too competitive and conservative, if not downright commercial, for many independent filmmakers. Festivals like the Hiroshima International Animation Festival, Annecy International Animated Film Festival or Anima Mundi in Brazil, each get around 2000 submissions every year. It is almost impossible for abstract or non-narrative films to make it through the selection process, unless there is a separate category for them, as at the Holland Animation Film Festival or the Melbourne International Animation Festival. Smaller events give more ambitious or more difficult works a better chance for exposure. It was not rare in the 1960s or 1970s for experimental artists of the highest rank, such as Robert Breer, Carmen d'Avino, or Frank and Caroline Mouris,[5] to receive awards at major mainstream festivals like the International Short Film Festival Oberhausen or Annecy. It seems that since then the animation community has fragmented and there is very little communication between those that represent the non-narrative, experimental wing and those representing the more traditional kind of auteur cinema. The former have found other, more avant-garde friendly channels for presenting their accomplishments: galleries, museums, college screenings and smaller film festivals specifically interested in this kind of cinema.

Many well-established animation festivals do not seem to keep up with the rapid technological changes of recent years. Traditional definitions of animated film have been challenged tremendously by the introduction of video and digital recording, motion capture, and computer programs that in many cases make stop-motion shooting obsolete. But even before the digital revolution, there were films rightly categorised as animated despite the fact that they relied extensively on live action. Examples of this are early films by Jan Švankmajer — *Poslední trik pana Schwarcewalldea a pana Edgara* (*The Last Trick*, Czechoslovakia, 1964) and *Rakvickarna* (*Punch and Judy*, Czechoslovakia, 1966) — or the Oscar-winning *Tango* (1980, Poland) by Zbigniew Rybczyński.[6] Moreover, traditional film stock is now used less often and appears destined for obsolescence. In a way we have gone full circle, returning to pre-cinema times when animated 'films' could be made on anything: paper strips, cardboard disks or the margins of books. Giannalberto Bendazzi is probably right when, in the conclusion of his well-informed essay on the definition of animated film, he writes: 'Animation is everything that people have called animation in the different historical periods' (2007: 26). I would go even further and say that today an animated film is one that its creator considers animated. Of course a festival's selection committee does not have to share this opinion.

In light of the above, most dictionary entries explaining animation as a frame-by-frame process have become severely out-dated — as have the entry forms of many festivals. In 2010, the official regulations of some leading festivals, e.g. Annecy and Hiroshima, still called for films made 'frame by frame'.[7] Smaller festivals tend to be thematically more specific but much less dogmatic as far as cinematic techniques are concerned. They look not as much for 'stop motion' films, as for 'made by women', 'surrealist', 'fantasy', '15 seconds long', '60 seconds long', and so on.[8]

Perhaps the most important agent stimulating the development of animation festivals all over the world is the growing necessity among different animators' groups of defining their identities against the mainstream cinema dominated by feature films. Most textbooks on the history of cinema do not pay much attention to animated films. An average moviegoer identifies animation with pure entertainment: TV serials and Disney's super-productions. The film industry treats animation like a poor cousin. An animated film is not considered 'real' or 'noble', terms normally reserved for feature-length live-action films. Widespread attitudes like these have caused an inevitable counteraction. The increasing number of animation festivals is just another proof of the emancipation of animation as an art form.

Despite their growing diversity, animated and experimental film festivals have increasingly tended to become part of a global network of festivals of their type. This process is not unique to animation and reflects a tendency seen in the world of the feature film industry. Festivals serve not only as meeting places for professionals and display windows for their work: they create a circuit, a system; they depend on each other, endorse one another, exchange programmes, jurors and ideas. A festival cannot exist without other similar events at which films and filmmakers are being recognised, judged and promoted; in other words, thanks to the multitude of festivals, artists and films gain a certain 'symbolic capital'.[9] As Marijke de Valck puts it: 'By traveling the circuit, a film can

3.1. In 2008, film scholar Marcin Giżycki co-founded the Animator International Festival of Animated Film in Poznań, Poland. © Animator International Festival of Animated Film

accumulate value via the snowball effect. The more praise, prizes and buzz a film attracts, the more attention it is likely to receive at other festivals' (2007: 35). My personal experience tells me that without going to other festivals, watching films and meeting people there, I would not be able to programme my own festival, the Animator International Animated Film Festival in Poznań, Poland, of which I am the artistic director (figure 3.1).[10]

This network has one surprising rupture, though: there is very little flow of information between North American and European animation festivals, with the exception of the Ottawa International Animation Festival. At least two obvious factors contribute to this situation. The first is that most American festivals charge an entry fee, whereas most European festivals do not. I know some filmmakers in Europe who simply refuse to send films to festivals that require a fee. Another reason seems to be purely technical. Most American festivals use the NTSC television format and they do not accept DVDs or other digital videos encoded in PAL, the European standard. Although there are many computer programs on the market that convert PAL to NTSC, rarely do they offer satisfactory results. Professional labs charge a lot of money for this kind of service. Independent filmmakers can seldom afford the expense.

It also seems that the enormous number of festivals of various kinds which take place in the U.S. leads to the creation of a distinct circuit. There is no question that this country has the largest self-contained community of animators in the world. Or should I rather say two communities? One connected with big studios and the television industry and the other consisting of independent filmmakers. Members of both groups seem to care more about being recognised in their own country than abroad. An animator in the U.S. gains symbolic capital by sending his or her films to American festivals, rather than Asian or European ones. It is not without significance that the majority of 'qualifying festivals and awards' for the Oscars take place in the U.S.[11] For many filmmakers in Europe, the Academy Awards do not have the same importance as they do for their colleagues in the U.S. The former tend to value the Cristal d'Annecy or the Grand Prix at Cinanima in Espinho, Portugal, more than an Oscar, although these particular prizes qualify them for the Academy Awards as well. Of course, it would be a big exaggeration to claim that most American independent filmmakers are Oscar crazy, but there is no doubt that they benefit more from being recognized on the domestic scene than somewhere else, at least as far as grant, fellowship and job opportunities are concerned.

A very different self-contained animation network has arisen in recent years on the internet, and I am not talking here about the well-known Animation World Network (AWN). Although the internet cannot replace the experience of watching a film in a dark screening room, it has already created its own artists, audiences, and aesthetics. Despite sporadic efforts on the part of some festivals to include internet animations in their programmes (Ottawa leads this trend), what can be seen at these venues is just the tip of an iceberg. As Melissa Bouwman correctly points out: 'Now animation is everywhere on the web, from the vast amount of gif animations, to fully interactive web pages loaded with sound and animation' (1997: 6). Internet animations reach millions of viewers. The internet animation community has created its own celebrities, artists virtually unknown to festival-goers who do not follow developments on the internet. Examples include, among others: The Brothers Chaps (Mike and Matthew Chapman), creators of *Homestar Runner* (U.S., 2005), a popular flash-animated series, or Todd Rosenberg (a.k.a. Odd Todd), known for his animated cartoons depicting the life of an unemployed character. There are also festivals and competitions exclusively devoted to internet animated films and similar works, e.g. the Webby Awards, the Flash Forward Film Festival, Minimotion Animation Competition, the NSI Online Short Film Festival, and so on.

Paradoxically, the explosion of web animation has not harmed 'conventional' animation festivals. The opposite seems to be true: apparently it has helped them to flourish in recent years. There is no doubt that the popularity of animated films on the internet has ignited interest in animation among younger users of the internet, for whom projection-based festivals offer a totally new experience with the medium. Not by chance does the vast majority of participants at animated film festivals consist of very young men and women — college and high school students. The internet also serves as a resource of new animators for the regular festival circuit. As a result, animation festivals need not compete with the web; rather, they should look for a symbiotic coexistence. More and more festivals incorporate films made for the internet in their programming. One of the first was the Cracow Film Festival which, in 2002, presented a programme of 'the new motion picture medium' prepared by Jakub de Barbaro. In an article for a Polish design magazine, the curator stated that: 'The majority of films screened had already appeared in www festivals elsewhere, but probably such diverse works had never been shown all together on a cinema screen' (2002: 69). Since then other festivals have followed suit.

The Internet has also become a great vehicle for publicising festivals. Every filmmaker looking for an opportunity to show and distribute his or her new work checks out websites like Withoutabox, filmfestivals.com, Film Festival World, or AWN. The Web has provided a perfect platform for spreading news about competitions, screenings, shows and similar events important to the international animation community. Many festivals have adopted on-line submission systems. On the other hand, festival and museum programmers take advantage of the fact that animators increasingly display their new films on YouTube or their own websites. This facilitates quests for new and promising works and artists. The Internet is a two-way communication tool; artists use it for finding proper festivals, the latter use it for discovering artists.[12] Generally speaking, it is hard to imagine animation festivals without the internet. Their existence relies heavily on it.

Certainly animation festivals have come a long way since their inception nearly 65 years ago.[13] Originally bound up with feature film festivals, they evolved into highly specialised, independent events for select audiences and professional communities. But this is not the end of the road. There are new challenges to confront, such as interactive movies, multi-screen installations and animations for mobile devices. Stereoscopic films are already around. Satellite transmissions are no longer the stuff of science fiction. Movies can be broadcast to a festival from a very remote place. Viewers in different cities or countries can watch exactly the same films at the same time, participating in a single festival which takes place simultaneously in many locations. Filmmakers need not be present at their screenings to discuss their work with viewers in real-time, via Skype or other means.

All this will have an enormous impact on animation festivals in the near future. And in order to survive, to sustain their appeal, festivals will have to accommodate the expectations of upcoming generations of potential viewers. I believe that it can be done without compromising artistic ambitions. What is needed is openness and bold programming.

This is exactly what we are trying to do at Animator in Poznań (figure 3.2). The festival, which started in 2008, is sponsored by the city with some funding from the Ministry of Culture of the Polish Republic and other state agencies. Having several venues at our disposal and a more-or-less secure budget, we have opened our festival not only to conventional films but also to all kinds of spectacle that incorporate animated elements. We try not to stick to one rigid definition of animation, hoping that in this way we will not cut ourselves off from whatever innovations the future will bring to the field. Besides the competition, retrospectives and other programmes typically associated with a film festival, we have presented a wide spectrum of events — from a show of the American Magic Lantern Theater to a lecture on internet art by Olia Lialina — which expand the boundaries of the art of animation. In an effort to find our own niche, we have adopted 'Music and Animation' as our major theme. This has enabled us to host the rock band Pere Ubu, with their staging of Alfred Jarry's *Ubu Roi* (1896), utilising projections by the Quay Brothers, and a number of other excellent

3.2. At the Animator festival, artistic director Marcin Giżycki seeks to program the broadest possible range of animated imagery, including live spectacles. © Animator International Festival of Animated Film

groups — such as the Alloy Orchestra from Boston, the Euphonium Big Band from France, the Francis Wong Trio from Chicago, the Compagnia d'Arte Drummatica from Italy, and Nik Phelp's Sprocket Ensemble from Belgium — all of which have provided live music for different film programmes.

My personal dream is to gradually convert the festival into a broad interdisciplinary and multimedia presentation, maybe a biennale, of any contemporary artistic manifestation that exercises the possibilities of putting inanimate objects into motion — or creating virtual movements — either by means of projection, hidden mechanisms, or pure magic.

Works Cited

Bendazzi, Giannalberto (2007) 'Defining Animation — A Proposal', *Cartoons: The International Journal of Animation*, 2, 26-9.

Bourdieu, Pierre (1979) *Distinction: A Social Critique of the Judgement of Taste*. London: Routledge.

Bouwman, Melissa (1997) 'Animation on the Web', *Frame by Frame, a Quarterly Publication of ASIFA/Central*, Summer, 6-7. On-line. Available HTTP: http://www.asifa.org/newsletter/bowman.php (24 August 2010).

de Barbaro, Jakub (2002) 'The New Motion Picture Medium', *2+3D*, 4, 69.

de Valck, Marijke (2007) *Film Festivals: From European Geopolitics to Global Cinephilia*. Amsterdam: Amsterdam University Press.

Edera, Bruno (1997) 'Animation Festivals: A Brief History', *Animation World Magazine* January, 1. On-line. Available HTTP: http://www.awn.com/mag/issue1.10/articles/edera.eng1.10.html (24 August 2010).

Ramey, Kathryn (2010) 'Economics of the Film Avant-Garde: Networks and Strategies in the Circulation of Films, Ideas, and People', *Jump Cut: A Review of Contemporary Media*, Summer, 52. On-line. Available HTTP: http://www.ejumpcut.org/currentissue/rameyExperimentalFilm/index.html (24 August 2010).

Notes

[1] Poland is actually a good example of the proliferation of festivals. In 2004 there were no international film festivals in this country exclusively devoted to animation. Now there are four of them (in chronological order): Etiuda&Anima in Cracow, Re-Animacja in Lodz, Animator in Poznań, and Animation Now! in Gdansk.

[2] An international experimental film and video festival, 25 FPS, is held in Zagreb, Croatia, and highlights non-narrative works.

[3] OFAFA, the Polish Festival of Auteurs in Animation, takes place in Cracow and features narrative and representational animation from Poland.

[4] One of these TV shows, called *Cinema of Animated Films*, was hosted in the 1960s by my father, the late Jerzy Giżycki.

[5] In 1973 the Mourises won an Oscar for their *Frank Film* (U.S.), which received the Grand Prix at the following year's Annecy festival.

[6] More recent examples of animated films without animation include the splendid work of Paul Andrejco and a clever parody of Dracula movies — *Harker* by Tony Giordano, Jason Murphy and Scott Shoemaker (U.S., 2005). All of these artists, many included in Handmade Puppet Dreams, a touring festival of films programmed by Heather Henson from The Jim Henson Foundation, use puppet theatre techniques rather than stop-motion photography.

[7] See http://www.annecy.org/annecy-2010/take-part/submit-a-film/regulations and http://hiroanim.org/pdf/kiyaku-e.pdf; both accessed August 24, 2010.

8   See, respectively, Tricky Women, Vienna, Austria; the International Surrealist Film Festival, Los Angeles, California; Fantasy World Film Festival, Toronto, Canada, and Fantasy Filmfest, Berlin/Hamburg, Germany; 15 Second Film Festival, Belfast, Northern Ireland; 60seconds, Copenhagen, Denmark, and Filminute, London, UK.

9   The term 'symbolic capital' was coined by Pierre Bourdieu (1979) and adopted by Kathryn Ramey in her interesting essay on networks and strategies in avant-garde film circles (2010).

10   The Animator festival attracts around 20,000 viewers every year, of which 90 per cent are under 25 years of age.

11   See 'Short Films Awards Festivals List' on the website of the Academy of Motion Picture Arts and Sciences, http://www.oscars.org/awards/academyawards/rules/shortsfestivals.html.

12   Curators from the Museum of Modern Art in New York discovered animator Mariusz Wiczyński on the internet; in 2007, MoMA hosted a retrospective of his work.

13   According to Bruno Edera, the first international festival of animated films took place in 1946 as a part of the Cannes International Film Festival. The first international animation festival to be held on a regular basis (and not as part of another festival) is the Annecy festival, which started in 1960 (Edera 1997).

Chapter 4

See Here Now: Festival Red Carpets and the Cost of Film Culture

James Schamus

Film festivals function within and help produce a number of temporalities in relation to film culture. They constitute a place of the 'after' — of restorations, tributes, retrospectives — where pieces of the vast archive of still-extant film texts are reconstituted and reconfigured for the present. Festivals are also places of the 'now' — giving a sense of 'what's happening in film' across cultures and geographical boundaries, affording a sense to their attendees of flows, currents, trends — of contemporary movements that call and respond to each other, of fashions and styles that emerge and fade away. They are also places of the 'before', giving the opportunity to see films in advance of their commercial releases or, for less fortunate films, before their direct consignment to cable, home video, or more ephemeral streaming sites.

The 'here' and the 'elsewhere' for each of these temporalities is different, and these temporalities perform each festival's singularity. In Toronto, among much else, one can catch up with what is happening 'now' in Africa. In Berlin, a newly restored print of *Metropolis* (Fritz Lang, Germany, 1927) or *One, Two, Three* (Billy Wilder, U.S., 1961) reconfigures the festival's relationship to its own geopolitical past and present. Sundance lives with the burden of the fact that 'independent', to the extent it does not mean 'studio', is thus always already 'for sale' — and so, perversely, the festival is forced to exist within and to produce, among other temporalities, that of the auction house or commodity exchange, a mix of the before ('What will sell'?) and the now ('Sold!').

What is called 'film festival culture' aligns with the feeling that, for each festival's particular singularity, the 'here' of each festival is somehow essentially equal to or at least exchangeable with the 'here' of other festivals in general; for bigger festivals, and not just the A-list ones, singularity thus increasingly is seen to rely on a festival's relation to the 'before', to its ability to secure premières, galas, and sneak previews of impending 'prestige' films whose temporal destinies are supposed to be integrated into the

4.1. Zealously guarded by festival staff, the red carpet at Cannes 2009 awaits the appearance of stars and distinguished guests. © Jeffrey Ruoff

commercial-release landscape and from there into the 'awards season', a 'season' which, in North America at least, runs nearly an entire half-year, from September to March. So 'before' becomes the dominant temporal singularity in the eyes of many film festival programmers and directors — before being the creation of a sense of now that is 'news', news of what is to come, so that the festival is a place where what is happening is what is going to happen.

But this 'before' intersects with and produces its own equivalences and exchangeabilities, in particular those we associate with money — money being the exemplar of that which helps turn the singular into the equivalent and the exchangeable. In this brief essay I will explore just one small but exemplary moment of this relation between singular and exchangeable, by asking you to consider a simple piece of news you have probably recently come across — the photo or video clip of a movie star walking the red carpet at a festival gala or première screening of his or her most recent film. Please take a moment to pause and recall that image (figure 4.1). Now also consider that a 30-second commercial aired on a popular U.S. television network show such as *Glee* or *Modern Family* can cost between $350,000 and $1,000,000. Ads played during the Super Bowl have been known to cost upwards of $3,000,000.

So with that in mind, I will now break down the cost of bringing a 'gala' première to an A-list festival such as Cannes, Venice, or Toronto. Such screenings are crucial for the public profile of these festivals, occasions for large donors and local officials to rub shoulders with Hollywood stars, for large red carpets to generate hefty press attention, for big crowds to come out and create a sense of excitement around opening and closing nights. I will narrow my account further by talking about only those costs that I am familiar with in my role as the head of a small, specialised film distributor. I cannot speak to how much the festivals themselves pay on their end (theatre hire, ticketing etc.), though their costs are offset somewhat by ticket and package sales, the revenues from which are not shared, as a rule, with the distributor.

For the large majority of films that screen as part of the general programming at the bigger festivals, costs can be fairly contained. The festival will offer to pay for shipping the print and clearing it through customs, and often will offer round-trip economy or business class airline transportation and a few nights at a hotel for the director and, perhaps, one or two other members of the film team. If one has a film 'making the festival circuit', one can travel the world, meet interesting people, and see movies, while doing the occasional panel or post-screening audience discussion session. I've known filmmakers who have literally spent from half a year to a year seeing the (festival) world this way.

Costs go up considerably if one has independently made a feature film and is bringing it to a festival for its première and possible sale to a distributor or to multiple distributors worldwide. The now-familiar sight at festivals where first-time filmmakers land with large entourages of managers, publicists, cast and crew, represents an often very significant investment, a roll of the dice that the initial screenings will generate a bidding war among distributors rabid enough to pay off the costs of both the film and the expense of bringing the film to market.

Most critical, academic, and even industry attention gets focussed on what happens between the covers, so to speak, of the festival — which films get bought, which films get prizes, which films get the most critical love. The 'galas' are considered mainly as necessary diversions, if not necessary evils — often incongruous appendages adding a dollop of showbiz hype to the otherwise important business of nurturing serious cinema.

By reducing our attention simply to the cost of what it takes to get that photo of the star (and perhaps director) walking the festival red carpet, I hope to help 're-site' the gala screening — and many aspects of the rest of the film festival business — within the context of the industry as a whole, or at least that part of the business devoted primarily to the release of films in an initial theatrical window. How much does that photo cost the studio? What does that cost have to say about our own understanding of film festival culture and business?

I will not provide actual numbers here, but rather a few price ranges. Most of the films my own studio brings to festivals cost substantially less than what I'll lay out here, but some have been in this range (though in the current economic climate, we, like everyone else, are working hard to bring costs down) and big studio festival premières can cost multiples of even the higher-end figures I'll float here. My point is not to give an exact tally, but rather to use the various categories of expense to open a window on what it takes to deliver a single gala screening of a prestige commercial film.

First, of course, people have to get to the festival. (An 'A' festival won't give a studio an opening night or gala, and a studio wouldn't want to pay for one, unless big-name talent is attending.) While many big stars can and will fly commercially to support their prestige films, many simply cannot: would you want to be responsible for what happened if Tom Cruise got on your next flight from Los Angeles to London? And, often, a star will be working on a film at a far-off location. Because a single day of shooting on a big film can cost hundreds of thousands of dollars a day, pulling a star away from the set, in and of itself, can be wildly expensive (studios have been known to offer to defray costs of production hiatuses in order to accommodate publicity needs). So a private jet, simply by being completely flexible, can save an enormous amount of money for a studio.

That said, even simple, flexible first-class tickets can cost well over $15,000 for a transcontinental flight, depending on the carrier and route. But, of course, one never simply flies the star. One or more assistants are crucial for keeping things on track. The star's publicist is also an essential presence, helping manage the crush of press and extraordinary time demands locked into the frenzied festival experience. Given their peripatetic lives, stars often, understandably, wish to travel with their families. Along with partners and children come nannies and personal staff. And because the entire point of the exercise is for the star to appear appropriately star-like at the première and to the attendant press, hair, make-up, and wardrobe artists are often arranged for (and paid, of course — more on that later).

If one is lucky, one has more than a single star to accommodate — and a second entourage to accommodate too, along with the director, producers, and studio executives responsible for the film, as well as finance partners (who often pay their own way), as, usually, do agents and managers. Air travel alone can thus range from $100,000 to $300,000 or more for an international première.

Once everyone arrives, accommodations must be made. Hoteliers in festival towns such as Venice and Cannes naturally take advantage of the festival season, and increase their rates astronomically. Talent must be appropriately accommodated, and not simply for their comfort or status: of primary concern is their security, and only the higher-end hotels can really handle those kinds of demands, so even if a star was willing to stay in more modest digs (as many are) it would be impossible for them to do so. (And besides, even lousy hotel rooms cost a fortune during a festival.) Paparazzi and hysterical fans necessitate genuine vigilance and detailed planning, including sometimes having to book rooms above and below those where our stars are staying. Most major stars have sophisticated personal security teams, who come early to plan and make provision for security and privacy needs — and yes, the studio is expected to share the cost of their travel and attendance, as well as their salaries and incidentals.

On top of it all, hotels often have one-week to two-week minimum booking requirements, so even if the talent are only in town for a couple of nights, the company must buy out the room (and then hope to re-sell the unused nights, if the hotels allow it). A not-too-huge suite at a high-end hotel can easily cost $6,000 a night; simple rooms for executives and support staff often cost more than $1,000 if they are to stay in any proximity to the talent. And whether in the form of per diems or simple minibar expenses, room service and fees for things like access to the gym can also pile up fast. As a result, $200,000 to $400,000 are not unheard-of costs for accommodation.

Once at the festival, talent and filmmaking teams need to have reliable, available, and secure transportation (this in addition to airport transfers). Because schedules and needs can change at a moment's notice, cars and professional drivers (or, in the case of Venice, boats, cars, pilots and drivers) need to be available around the clock. Taxi boats in Venice, for example, can cost thousands of dollars a day — and a big film will need a small fleet of them for the run of its time at the festival, a cost that can easily exceed $100,000.

Large numbers of journalists attend festivals — there are over 3,000 accredited members of the press corps who attend Cannes each year, for example. Press kits, photo sets (now supplied more cheaply on-line), promotional items, gift bags, soundtrack CDs, printed screenplays, and the like are often produced, shipped, cleared through customs, stored, sorted, and handed out. Again, in a modest promotional budget these items may cost little — or sometimes be skipped — but for major studio fare such costs can add up quickly, into the scores or even hundreds of thousands of dollars.

During the festival, intensive press days are organised, where entertainment journalists can arrange for access to the talent for television, on-line, and print interviews and features. In order to facilitate these interviews, rooms and suites — often entire floors — are rented out in the main hotels: holding rooms for talent; make-up rooms; rooms for print and radio 'roundtables', where upwards of 12 journalists at a time can be rotated in to conduct group interviews in shifts of between 10 and 20 minutes or less; video rooms set up so that TV journalists can quickly pop into pre-lit sets for four- or five-minute interviews; welcome suites, and so on. For a big film with major stars, these junket set-ups can cost upwards of half-a-million dollars, when one accounts also for catering, technical support staff and equipment rental.

And, of course, a gala screening wouldn't be a gala screening without a party afterwards. Often, corporate sponsors are found who will cover some of the costs, but an appropriately festive event, at an upscale venue, with mixed drinks, buffet, live music, security, and movie-themed decorations can add up easily to $100,000 to $300,000 — or, in the case of tentpole-style events, multiples of those numbers. In addition, there are private dinners and cocktail parties to be arranged during the course of the festival stay.

A host of other costs must also be accounted for: mounting posters and banners at the theatre; festival badges for executives; booking theatres for additional press screenings, and on and on. These too can easily climb into the tens of thousands.

Let us now recall that red carpet photo and tally the cost of it. Of course, that cost incorporates the ancillary activities and benefits that go with it, in particular the press coverage generated by any junket interviews or press conference appearances by the filmmakers, as well as the (hoped-for) prestige which might accrue to the film as a result of its positioning at the festival. The sum total comes to anywhere from a few hundred thousand dollars to, for big studio movies, millions.

To justify those dollars, they must be understood in terms of their equivalence with the advertising for which they would otherwise have been spent. This is the (partial) price of using the 'before' of a festival to create the 'now' of the 'news' of the film's arrival. The mass circulation of that 'now', the mass production of 'impressions' of the images that that now is both productive of and constituted by, increasingly defines film festival culture's own singularities and exchangeabilities — the equivalence marked by the 30-second TV spots that might otherwise have been purchased in support of a film's commercial release is also an equivalence that more generally invests film festival culture itself.

Part II

Finding Films for Festivals

Chapter 5

Setting the Course:
Directors and Directions at the
New York Film Festival, 1963-2010

Richard Peña

I'm not sure when it first occurred to me that I might want to become a film programmer. Like just about everybody, I grew up watching and enjoying films a lot, although perhaps I seemed to enjoy them more than most people I knew. During a visit to a local library, when I was about 9 or 10, I noticed on a shelf near the end of the art section a very small section (793, in the old Dewey decimal system) about movies. It seemed amazing to me that there were books about movies — movies just were, in some transcendental sense — but there before me lay about a half-dozen books, one of them being Arthur Knight's *The Liveliest Art* (1957). I checked it out, and over the next few days managed to read it all. I was hooked. Knight spoke about how movies began as silents and only added sound later (I sort of knew that, having seen the choppy old prints of Charlie Chaplin and Buster Keaton that would occasionally run on television); of the glory era of the Hollywood studios, now assumed to be in the past (many of the stars' names were at least familiar to me); and of another cinema that came from Europe and other places which was different from Hollywood cinema. That I already knew something about, as I had often accompanied my Castilian grandparents to the Elgin Cinema in Manhattan (now the Joyce Theater) to see Spanish-language films, mainly from Mexico. Even back then I knew they were pretty different from the Hollywood movies I saw with my parents or friends.

My next great epiphany was actually going to the New York Film Festival (NYFF) to see Erich von Stroheim's *The Wedding March* (U.S., 1929). Von Stroheim seemed one of the more colourful characters I had discovered in *The Liveliest Art*: 'the man you love to hate' and all that; moreover, I knew it was difficult to see his movies. The experience of going to the festival that first time was transformative; suddenly I was in a room full of people who also knew about Erich von Stroheim. A man came out and was introduced as the person who had found the print we were about to see: he was Henri Langlois, legendary director of the Cinémathèque Française, although at the time I couldn't figure out his name from the way it was announced. The screening, with wonderful piano accompaniment, was a sheer delight and thereafter, like thousands of film fans, I waited for the Sunday after Labor Day announcement of the NYFF line-up.

Somehow, 23 years later, I found myself on the stage of Alice Tully Hall, introducing films at that very same New York Film Festival, the institution that since my 'tweens had been for many of us the gold standard for determining the direction and shape of American film culture. I'll skip most of the details (high school, college etc.) and jump to my first real job in the field of film programming, first as assistant director, then as director of The Film Center at the School of the Art Institute of Chicago (now the Gene Siskel Film Center). During my first few months there, we accepted a touring package of films from the People's Republic of China, five films sent to the U.S. in an exchange in which we sent them five Hollywood classics, including, I seem to recall, *Singing in the Rain* (Stanley Donen and Gene Kelly, U.S., 1952) and *Bambi* (David Dodd Hand, U.S., 1942). Chinese cinema was — for all but a precious few films — completely unknown back in 1980, usually dismissed with adjectives like 'chop-socky' in the few reviews that mentioned it, although Hong Kong martial arts films had established themselves by that time in at least a few crumbling, inner-city movie palaces. So the series seemed like a great opportunity to see what the Communist Chinese had been up to.

One of the films included was Jin Xie's *Wutai jiemei* (*Two Stage Sisters*, 1965), a film that had been thoroughly condemned as a 'poisonous weed' at the start of the Cultural Revolution, thus making it sound all the more intriguing. At the end of the screening, I could hardly get up from my seat. My amazement extended beyond the fact that the film had completely stunned me, as any artistic masterwork should. The real shock was that this great, great film was completely unknown; I searched in vain for reference either to it or to its director. That such an extraordinary work — and the magnificent level of production that had made it possible — should exist completely outside the purview of even dedicated filmgoers powerfully illustrated how little about film history we actually knew. *Two Stage Sisters* was simply too good to exist entirely on its own — it would have had to come out of some kind of artistic tradition and be the product of strong artistic vision. So, over the next decade at least, learning about Chinese cinema became an interest and a passion, both of which I could indulge somewhat through my work at The Film Center. Indeed, one could argue that Chinese cinema very much dominated the entire field in the 1980s, with retrospectives of older films, dedicated issues produced by leading film magazines, and of course the remarkable new films and filmmakers that began to emerge from Taiwan, Hong Kong and the People's Republic of China (the Fifth Generation). I had always envied those critics and scholars who had been around for the Western discovery of Japanese cinema in the 1950s, and now I had the chance to experience some of the same with Chinese cinema. It was as if a giant treasure chest had suddenly been flung open for all of us, and we couldn't unpack its offerings fast enough.

In fact, my experience with Chinese cinema reminded me in a way of my earlier experience with Brazilian and other Latin American cinemas. Back in the late 1960s I became aware, thanks to some magnificent shows presented at the Museum of Modern Art, of a Brazilian film movement that was called Cinema Novo (New Cinema). The films, by such artists as Nelson Pereira dos Santos, Glauber Rocha, Joaquim Pedro de Andrade, Carlos Diegues and others, were not only terrific in and of themselves, but they seemed to address in exciting, refreshing ways the connection between politics and cinematic expression that dominated so much criticism and conversation during those highly charged years. It wasn't an accident that a still from Rocha's *O Dragão da Maldade contra o Santo Guerreiro* (*Antonio Das Mortes*, France/Brazil/West Germany, 1969) adorned the cover of the January 1969 issue of *Cahiers du cinéma* that featured the seminal Jean-Louis Comolli and Jean Narboni essay 'Cinéma/ Idéologie/Critique'.

Taking a year off from college in 1974-5, I travelled to Brazil, hoping to learn as much as I could about Cinema Novo and the country that had produced it. My admiration for the movement and those who created it certainly increased while I was there, but I also discovered that there was much more to Brazilian cinema. Cinema Novo's defenders — and some of its creators — had implied that Brazilian cinema more or less began with them, with a few rare exceptions; instead, I discovered that Brazil had a rich and complex film history, of which Cinema Novo was but a chapter, albeit a glorious one. Moreover, there were younger filmmakers, the so-called marginals or underground, who had emerged afterwards and whose work was a response/critique of Cinema Novo. Yet again, little of this was known or spoken of outside Brazil. The problem of film history, it was becoming clear to me, was not just to write it, but to see it.

These, one could say, were some of the formative experiences that I brought with me to Lincoln Center in June 1988, when I took up my posts as programme director of the Film Society and chairman of the selection committee of the New York Film Festival. This latter title might need a bit of unpacking: since 1969, the NYFF line-up has been selected by a committee composed of both Film Society staff members and outside critics. In the first six years, the festival was chosen by its two directors, Richard Roud and Amos Vogel. A complicated and ever-changing formula had been worked out between them, whereby there were a certain number of films on which both had to agree, and then each got a certain number of 'solo picks'. After Amos left in 1968, and the Film Society of Lincoln Center was established as the producer of the NYFF (prior to that it had been produced by Lincoln Center itself), the new board of directors suggested that some kind of selection committee be formed, made up of local critics, to make the festival a more 'New York' event. Our selection process has remained the same ever since, and the roster of those who have served on the selection committee over the years is something of which I'm very proud: Susan Sontag, Andrew Sarris, David Thomson, J. Hoberman, David Ansen, Molly Haskell, and many more of the best writers and thinkers on film in America. For my part, I've found it really gratifying to work with my committees — the energy, ideas and commitment they bring to the process have been crucial.

The New York Film Festival was founded, as mentioned, in 1963, a date crucial for understanding its character and on-going development. The festival began at a key moment in two critical tendencies that would change the way films were thought and written about: auteurism and modernism. First articulated in France in the late 1940s and early 1950s (although present as a critical approach both earlier and elsewhere), auteurism essentially proposed that cinema, at its best, was as capable of artistic expression as a poem, a painting or a symphony. Despite the fact that the vast majority of films were made collectively, it was individual expression that elevated a film to the condition of art, and the individual whose thoughts, ideas and visions were most often expressed in this manner was the director. This idea is now so commonplace that it's hard to imagine that anyone ever doubted it or opposed it (see Pauline Kael's 'Circles and Squares' for the opposition's case), but in 1963 it simply wasn't so obvious. (Nor was starting a film festival at a major cultural institution, so three cheers to Lincoln Center's first president, William Schuman.) Andrew Sarris' still-essential essay 'Notes on the Auteur Theory in 1962' had just been published, laying the groundwork for a massive reconsideration of American cinema but, for a number of years at least, sections of the American moviegoing public had been aware of filmmakers such as Ingmar Bergman, Federico Fellini, Akira Kurosawa, and a handful of others whose work was marketed as containing ideas or touching on themes not normally found (it was believed) in Hollywood. Moreover, it was believed that these directors had far more control over their films, as they often doubled as their own screenwriters. This became a somewhat backdoor argument for the validation of cinema: if the people who made such films seemed to fulfil the conditions of being artists (personal vision, identifiable aesthetic style), then what they were creating must be art. Within a few years, it became practically impossible to speak of a film, rightly or wrongly, as anything but the creation of its director.

I think it would be fair to describe the New York Film Festival, with its now 49-year history, as an exemplary auteurist institution. Because the festival introduced and/or defended their work in the U.S., a number of directors are strongly identified with it, including Jean-Luc Godard, Rainer Werner Fassbinder, Krzysztof Kieslowski, Hsiao-hsien Hou, Pedro Almodóvar, and Todd Solondz. We aim to show what we feel is the best on offer in any given year. Frankly, there aren't that many artists who reach the top of their game at any given moment; thus our loyalty (within limits) to a select number of them. Moreover, our focus on these and other directors allows us to offer a sense of where we think cinema has come from, where it is going, and who is taking us there. That said, it must be emphasised that no one, in my 24 years here (nor, I believe, in the 25 that preceded me), has a free pass at the New York Film Festival. Every film we show is seen and considered, and while I certainly might sit up in my seat a little straighter if I'm seeing a new film by Arnaud Desplechin or Joon-ho Bong, we have to select on the merits of a given film, not on a director's career or status. During my tenure we've passed on films by Godard (the festival's all-time champ, with 27 appearances), although I know several people who think we should be ashamed of that fact.

The second sign under which the festival was born, modernism, needs perhaps some background. Modernism itself refers to a periodisation of the arts, a stage both beyond and in some sense in opposition to an earlier stage we could call the 'classical'. If the classical period is characterised by a number of styles, conventions and practices for creating and interpreting art, well understood (and practised) by both artists and audiences, modernism seeks to break that relationship by avoiding, subverting or emphasising those very styles, conventions and practices. Modernism evokes a kind of self-consciousness: we're aware not only that we're experiencing art, but we're aware of the ways in which a modernist work is different from the way we've been used to experiencing art.

The modernist impulse was perhaps always with cinema — some might argue that the medium itself is 'modernist' in the way it calls into question basic notions about art (cf. André Bazin) — or that modernism has been part of cinema at least since the 1920s, since the time of the Soviet constructivists (Sergei Eisenstein, Dziga Vertov) or the various cinematic offshoots of surrealism, futurism, and the like. But it was really the twin challenges from American film noir and Italian Neo-Realism in the mid-1940s that set the stage for the new cinematic forms that would emerge in the 1960s (one could possibly add a third, American experimental cinema, yet its influence was arguably much less important). The mid-1940s in America saw an exponential growth of interest in foreign films, initially the Italian Neo-Realists, and subsequently a whole range of films and filmmakers. These films traded in their difference from Hollywood films — at the very least they were often much franker about sex and, to an extent, politics — and the increasing number of independently owned and operated movie theatres (the result of the Supreme Court's 1948 divestiture decree) gave these foreign films a place to be seen.

Yet by the early 1960s, those American audiences who had come to enjoy such new stars as Sophia Loren or Toshirō Mifune found themselves confronted with some foreign films that were rather baffling. Films such as *La dolce vita* (Federico Fellini, Italy/France, 1960), *Hiroshima mon amour* (Alain Resnais, France/Japan, 1959), or *L'avventura* (Michelangelo Antonioni, Italy/France, 1960) signalled a decisive departure from regular movies. These were films that imagined themselves as being in dialogue with new movements in painting, literature, dance and music — works that saw themselves pushing the boundaries of their respective media. Understandably, not everyone thought this new development was for the good (see Pauline Kael's 'Are Movies Going to Pieces?'), but the presence and challenge of these new films could not be denied.

This is where the New York Film Festival came in. Founded just after the first wave of great modernist films, the NYFF would quickly establish a reputation for presenting and defending this rising tide: Jean-Luc Godard, Jean-Marie Straub and Danièle Huillet, Jacques Rivette, Nagisa Oshima, Michelangelo Antonioni, Miklós Jancsó, Luis Buñuel. These names would comprise the contemporary pantheon erected by the NYFF, a pantheon that argued art over commerce, achievement over popularity. Not surprisingly, the NYFF would be accused of elitism, of obscurantism, of picking films merely because they were audience-unfriendly — charges that continue to be repeated each year, in fact — yet I would argue that since its founding, the NYFF's track record for introducing artists and films that would come to define the way we think about cinema is second to none.

When I took over the reins of the festival in 1988 — its 26th year — these twin legacies of its founding were still very much present. If the above-mentioned pantheon was in large part no longer working (or not working all that much), there was a large number of younger filmmakers extremely willing to take up their positions. If the modernist movement then seemed part of history — and in 1988 there was much talk about something called 'post-modernism' — there also were new film movements, some of them emerging from parts of the world scarcely considered by American moviegoers when the NYFF was founded, that in their own ways expanded and challenged the limits of cinema.

Looking back at my 24 years thus far, I think I have had to contend with two fundamental challenges at the NYFF. The first could be called the structure of the festival itself or, to put it bluntly, its size. Since 1963, the NYFF has remained a relatively small selection of films: somewhere between 25 and 28 each year. Even before I arrived at my desk, a number of people in the field contacted me and asked me to consider increasing that number to 35 or 40 or whatever, in order to 'add more diversity', 'include some popular films', or for various other reasons. Along with those suggestions usually came another: that we should begin giving awards, either selected by a jury of experts, or by the audience, or by international film critics. These suggestions have been repeated often over the years.

I've never really understood the desire to make the festival much bigger. Obviously, our chosen limits are arbitrary: would it make that much difference if our Main Slate contained 35 films? Yet the smaller number of films makes our selection seem, at its best, more like a statement, a vision of world cinema, rather than just a panorama or a catalogue. The smaller number of films means that many people can see a large part of our offering, and thus get some sense of our take on what's out there. What's not in the festival can be discussed as well as what's in it: the NYFF is clearly an event that has to make choices, and be judged on the wisdom of those choices. As the number of films selected is relatively small, we would like to think that the 'competition' is simply getting into the NYFF; no need for other juries or referenda, which have the danger of poisoning the atmosphere for filmmakers, who have often told me that they appreciate the non-competitive atmosphere. For me, the festival is both elitist and democratic: each film is shown in Alice Tully Hall, and given very much the same treatment (press conferences, audience Q&As etc.).

Much of the festival structure described above was already in place when I got to Lincoln Center; it was Richard Roud and Amos Vogel who decided to keep the festival small, and not to offer prizes. But I have embraced these policies and done my best to continue them. Some differences, however, have arisen, along with some significant changes to the Film Society itself. The December 1991 opening of the Walter Reade Theater, our first year-round facility, immediately prompted the question about what to do with it during the festival. My response was to try to use the Walter Reade to expand some of the festival's existing components. From its beginnings, the NYFF has included one or two (or more) older films — NYFF Retrospectives as we called them — films that either were unknown to our audiences or had not been readily available for a long time. Having the Walter Reade created the opportunity to present a retrospective series by a director, actor, or film movement, instead of just one or two films. Thus, in 1992, we were able to offer an in-person tribute to the legendary Mexican cinematographer Gabriel Figueroa, with 10 of his films. Now known as NYFF Masterworks, this series has featured the work of Sacha Guitry, Grigori Kozintsev, Leonardo Favio, Shabana Azmi, Italian divas of the silent screen, the Japanese studio Shochiku, and the Janus/Criterion collection.

The opening of the Walter Reade Theater also afforded an opportunity to revisit the world of avant-garde, experimental cinema. The early years of the festival enjoyed a significant presence of such films, largely due to the influence of Amos Vogel, who had done so much to promote them at Cinema 16. After Amos left the festival, the number of avant-garde offerings declined quite a bit. When I began working at the NYFF, I was determined to address that absence in some way, so I created a programme called Avant-Garde Visions, which screened in Alice Tully Hall as part of the festival. That programme eventually morphed into a kind of mini-festival of its own, Views from the Avant-Garde, now curated by my colleagues Mark McElhatten and Gavin Smith and presented at the Walter Reade during the NYFF's middle weekend.

Of course, it was already somewhat retrograde to speak of avant-garde 'cinema' in 1988 (the year I began at the NYFF), as more and more work was then being created by artists working in video. Although we were the New York *Film* Festival, we could ignore this work only at our own peril so, in 1992, we began the New York Video Festival, which screened in the Walter Reade Theater during the NYFF. That programme continued as part of the fall NYFF for four years, then migrated to July as part of the Lincoln Center Festival. It continued there for a few more years until we decided that the lines between celluloid, video and now digital production had indeed blurred so completely that it would make most sense to address them in a single programme — which was Views from the Avant-Garde.

The 2011 opening of the Elinor Bunin Munroe Film Center, across West 65th Street from the Walter Reade, presented us again with the challenge of making the best use of the Film Society's expanding resources. This new facility contains two film theatres, a large amphitheatre for lectures or digital screenings, an area for installations, plus a café and other offerings. As a result, the 2011 New York Film Festival had access to four screens, and we hope to continue expanding our current programme — offering more restorations of older films, more conversations with artists — while possibly adding performances that include some engagement with projected media. While keeping the number of films screened in Alice Tully Hall relatively constant, we can use these new screens to enrich our programme in many ways.

The other 'situation' that I perceived as a fundamental challenge to the NYFF was the existence of other film festivals. Riding the bus down Columbus Avenue, I passed a bus stop bearing a poster with the words 'FILM FESTIVAL' prominently draped across the top. I wondered how we had found the money for such a campaign, until I saw that the ad was announcing a series of outdoor screenings at the Central Park Nature Conservancy. I'm old enough to come from a time when the New York Film Festival was simply 'the Festival'; now it's one of about 63 film festivals offered annually in New York City, according to research done by one of my Columbia University students a few years ago. It's hard to estimate the impact of all these programmes on the NYFF; happily, we still have almost complete access to the films and filmmakers we want to include each year, and attendance has remained strong. Yet it seems to me that this proliferation of festivals has diluted the brand: what was a special event held once a year is now something that happens two or even three times every weekend. The proliferation of DVDs has led to the (often mistaken) belief that even the rarest things we might include will eventually be found on Netflix. Beyond the local festivals, there have also been changes on the international level: 'mega-festivals', such as the

Toronto International Film Festival or the World Film Festival in Montreal, featuring 300-plus films, offer a far broader, almost encyclopaedic scale, making an NYFF-style selection process suspiciously undemocratic in an era that distrusts canons of any kind.

There's probably little, in the end, that we can do about that. If anything, the NYFF has tried in recent years to emphasise that it's our size and perceived exclusivity that does, in fact, define us. For those who call us elitist, all we can say is 'guilty as charged'. Since the advent of digital production equipment, we have been inundated with films of every conceivable variety. In my first year at the New York Film Festival we received fewer than 800 entries; in 2010 we received more than three times that many, from every corner of the globe. Ideally, a programme such as the NYFF can offer some guidance through that extraordinary thicket of digital dreams, while continuing to herald those works that, by various means, explore new ways to tell stories or create images for our screens.

Over the past 24 years, it's been a great ride for me, personally, at the New York Film Festival. It hasn't always been easy, and I wish I could say there was nothing I would have done or handled differently but, as I look ahead to my last year on the job, I'm delighted to say that the art of cinema seems as strong as ever. Yes, there are probably more bad films than ever before, simply because there are more films in general. But the delights of seeing great masters such as Manoel de Oliveira (*O Estranho Caso de Angélica*/*The Strange Case of Angelica*, Portugal/Spain/France/Brazil, 2010) continue to challenge himself and us — at 101 no less; or young filmmakers such as Abdellatif Kechiche, already admired for earlier works such as *L'esquive* (*Games of Love and Chance*, France, 2003) or *La graine et le mulet* (*The Secret of the Grain*, France, 2007) move to an entirely different level with his film *Vénus noire* (*Black Venus*, France/Italy/Belgium, 2010); or a first-time director such as Jorge Grau breathe new life and great intelligence into his contemporary cannibal film *Somos lo que hay* (*We Are What We Are*, Mexico, 2010), remain as infectious as ever. And I'm even happier that the New York Film Festival, 49 years after its founding, remains committed to spreading the passion.

Works Cited

Comolli, Jean-Louis and Jean Narboni (1969) 'Cinéma/Idéologie/Critique', *Cahiers du cinéma*, October, 216, 11-15.

Kael, Pauline (1963) 'Circles and Squares', *Film Quarterly*, 16, 3, 12-26.

___ (1964) 'Are Movies Going to Pieces?', *The Atlantic Monthly*, 214, 6, 61-81.

Knight, Arthur (1957) *The Liveliest Art*. New York: MacMillan.

Chapter 6
Festival, City, State:
Cultural Citizenship at the
Thessaloniki International Film Festival

Toby Lee

In November 2009, the Thessaloniki International Film Festival celebrated its 50th anniversary, a milestone edition for a festival that is considered to be one of the most important cultural events in Greece. However, this celebratory year also turned out to be one of deep crisis for the festival, which found itself facing the effects of the larger economic crisis in Greece, public criticism for what many considered to be overblown budgets, and an uncertain political environment, with widespread civil unrest, emergency elections in October 2009, and a resulting change in government. Amid these crises, the festival also found itself facing a boycott by a group of over 200 Greek filmmakers, including some of the country's most celebrated directors, who withheld their films from the state-supported festival as a protest against the government. More than any other crisis, the filmmakers' boycott called into question the identity of the festival, its function and its place on the larger cultural map of Greece. In particular, the Greek filmmakers' actions pointed to the tricky relationship between the Thessaloniki festival and notions of Greek national cinema.

Liz Czach addresses this relationship in an article on film festival programming and the role it plays in the construction of national cinemas (2004). Looking specifically at the Toronto International Film Festival and its Perspective Canada series, Czach describes how film festivals contribute to the shaping of a national film canon — and ultimately, she argues, of 'the concept of nation itself' (2004: 85) — through the programming of national cinema series and spotlights. She characterises programmers as powerful decision-makers, in this case defining not only Canadian cinema, but also what it means to be Canadian. However, she ends her article by suggesting that the relationship between festivals and national cinemas is decreasing in importance:

> Its future in an era dominated by so-called postnationalism
> seems uncertain. When coproductions and co-ventures as
> funding models are gaining popularity, the ability to easily
> define and delineate a national cinema becomes increasingly
> more difficult. (2004: 86-87)

The Greek filmmakers' boycott of the 2009 Thessaloniki festival serves as
an interesting counterpoint to what Czach describes. By abstaining from
the festival altogether, the filmmakers effectively made it impossible for
the festival to programme its annual showcase of Greek films, raising
questions about the role of the festival in defining and representing
a national cinema. In this case, we see the category of the national
coming under question; however, rather than becoming irrelevant, it
takes a central position in a larger debate over the relationship between
cultural production, institutions and the state in Greece today. In this
chapter, I examine the Greek filmmakers' boycott and the surrounding
public discourse, to see how the festival and, by extension, the city of
Thessaloniki function as a space of social negotiation. Specifically, I ask
how the protesting filmmakers, as well as different social actors reacting
to the boycott, use the festival to articulate notions of local, national and
European cultural citizenship.[1]

Locating the Thessaloniki International Film Festival

The Thessaloniki festival was started in 1960 as a small showcase for new
Greek cinema and, over the past 50 years, has grown into one of the largest
and most established international film festivals in the Balkans (figure
6.1). It now functions year-round as an institution, organising a number
of separate festivals, screening and educational programmes; sponsoring
industry events; and publishing books and monographs. Among the
various festivals and screening series it organises, the most important is
the international film festival which, for 10 days every November, brings
films, filmmakers, producers, distributors, journalists, and cinema-goers
from around the country, and the world, to Thessaloniki.

Like most international film festivals, Thessaloniki is characterised
by various spatial or geographical orientations — local, national,
regional, international — often functioning on more than one of these
levels, or on all of them, at any given time. Started through the initiative
of a local arts association, Techni, the festival has always been closely

6.1. The 50th anniversary of the Thessaloniki film festival was disrupted by protests from Greek filmmakers. © Thessaloniki International Film Festival

identified with the city. Although Athens has overwhelmingly surpassed Thessaloniki as the centre of Greek cultural, economic and political life, the country's largest — and, for many years, its only — film festival has remained in Thessaloniki. From the beginning, however, the festival was also identified as international, modelled after the large film festivals of Western Europe that blossomed in the post-war period. Indeed, the festival's main founder, film critic Pavlos Zannas, stated that his purpose in starting the festival was two-fold. On the one hand, he wanted to promote Greek cinema and to develop a knowledgeable local public that could engage critically with films. On the other hand, he wanted to attract the attention of the international film industry, and from early on Zannas worked to make the initial 'Week of Greek Cinema' into a festival with international presence (Xanthopoulos 1999: 7-9). The identity of the festival as a local institution is further complicated by the fact that, for the past two decades, its main offices have been located in Athens, where all major programming and organisational decisions are made; a common complaint among festival-goers in Thessaloniki is that the festival has become an Athenian event, organised in Athens by Athenians who are disconnected from the public in Thessaloniki.

On another level, the festival functions as a national institution. The country's most important film festival, it is the one most identified with Greece internationally; since its inception, it has served as the most visible showcase of new Greek cinema. Funded in large part by the Ministry of Culture, the festival is closely associated with the state and, for over 10 years, the festival housed the State Film Awards. On yet another level, the festival is an active presence in the Balkans, promoting and funding film production and distribution in the region. Finally, it is an inherently transnational institution, caught up in the networks of global circulation constituted by international film festivals. These networks of festivals and film industries sustain the festival's activities; the festival not only participates in these networks, but in fact relies on them for its continued existence. In that it trafficks in the latest products, forms, and rhetoric of the international film festival network, the Thessaloniki festival demarcates a translocal cultural space characterised by mobility and ideas of cosmopolitanism, in this sense resembling Marc Augé's 'non-places of supermodernity' (1995: 77-79).

In moving between the local, the national, the regional and the global, the festival reflects Thessaloniki itself, a city that has shifted between the poles of provinciality and cosmopolitanism, between place and non-place. As Mark Mazower illustrates in his book on Thessaloniki's cosmopolitan history (2005), it is a city whose very locality, or sense of place, was built on the waves of movement — of people, goods, capital, armies, ideas — that have passed through it. Historically one of the most important commercial centres in the Balkans, Thessaloniki served for many centuries as a crossroads of diverse social currents, resulting in a complex cultural layering still evident today, in the dense patchwork of archaeological sites from various historical periods dug out from the cityscape — a materialisation of the cultural stratification that characterised life in Thessaloniki for many centuries. However, despite this cosmopolitan history, Thessaloniki has suffered the narratives of ethnic, linguistic, and religious homogeneity that have dominated Greek national identity in the twentieth century; neither has it been able to fend off a growing provincialisation in the shadow of Athens. And in the twenty-first century, cosmopolitanism returns, now in the form of an ever-growing number of immigrants from around the world, as well as cultural and economic initiatives aimed at refashioning Thessaloniki as a worldly, European, and international city.

The Thessaloniki International Film Festival reflects the city's shifting dynamic between the local and the transnational, between place and non-place — a process that we can see unfolding in the filmmakers' boycott of the festival and the ensuing public debates.

Oi Kinimatografistes stin Omichli — Filmmakers of Greece

In March 2009, a small group of directors, producers and screenwriters came together to protest the annual State Film Awards. These awards are administered by the Ministry of Culture and Tourism in conjunction with the Greek Film Center, decided by a committee comprising state officials and members of professional film guilds, and, since 1998, given out at a special ceremony at the Thessaloniki festival. Objecting to what they saw as corruption, nepotism and a lack of transparency in the distribution of the awards and prize money, the filmmakers vowed not to participate in the 2009 State Awards unless new regulations were put in place. They called on the government to do away with the State Film Awards system and to allow for the creation of a national film academy based in Athens, modelled on the American Academy of Motion Picture Arts and Sciences, that would administer its own awards.

As time passed, the group grew to a membership of over 200, including the most established directors in Greece, such as Theo Angelopoulos and Pantelis Voulgaris, as well as the most promising of a new generation of Greek filmmakers, such as Giorgos Lanthimos, Panos Koutras, Constantine Giannaris, and Filippos Tsitos. By the summer of 2009, they had established a loose organisation, calling themselves Oi Kinimatografistes stin Omichli (Filmmakers in the Mist) and, in English, Filmmakers of Greece (FOG). As the group grew, so did their demands (figure 6.2). No longer limiting their criticisms to the State Film Awards, the FOG demanded an overhaul of the existing film legislation and state funding structures, increased government support for domestic film distribution, a re-evaluation and scaling back of the Thessaloniki festival, and improvements in film education. Most importantly, they vowed not only to boycott the State Awards, but to withhold their films entirely from the 2009 Thessaloniki festival until their demands were met and new film legislation passed and implemented. To publicise their protest, they created a website, published a manifesto, held press conferences, and circulated video of their press conferences and other public debates on-line.

For the festival, such a boycott was potentially disastrous. With

over 200 of the most active Greek film professionals boycotting, the festival faced the possibility of a 50th anniversary celebration without Greek films, a prospect especially troubling in a year distinguished by Greek filmmakers' success at major international festivals abroad.[2] A series of negotiations took place between the festival and the FOG; as the festival administration endeavoured to placate the filmmakers and convince them that they were 'on the same side', the filmmakers accused the festival of being too moderate in its concessions, demanding instead a wholesale reorganisation of the 50th edition so that it more resembled a protest than a celebration. In the end, the two sides were unable to come to an agreement. With the government in the throes of an economic and political crisis, and with the change of government occurring one month before the November festival, the demands of the FOG could not be met in time. The 2009 Thessaloniki International Film Festival took place with only a handful of Greek films and with most major Greek filmmakers abstaining.

6.2. A group of Greek directors founded Filmmakers of Greece (FOG) to call for reforms of the Greek film industry and its flagship festival in Thessaloniki. © Filmmakers of Greece

Navigating Between the Local, the National and Beyond

Initially, the actions of the protesting filmmakers resulted in heated public debate, involving politicians, cultural commentators, all the major film institutions and organisations in Greece, unions, professional guilds and associations, and filmmakers who themselves were dissenting from the FOG group. Throughout this time, the protesting filmmakers were careful to point out repeatedly that they had no objections to the Thessaloniki festival itself; rather, they insisted that their protest was against the state and that the festival simply happened to be the best public platform for their protest, because of its high media profile and close connection to the state. The underlying significance of this point of view was made clear to me in a conversation with director Vardis Marinakis, one of the filmmakers who started the protest. Referring to the events of December 2008 — when the shooting of an unarmed teenager by the Athens police sparked massive protests around the country — Marinakis described being inspired by the general civil unrest that followed. Galvanised by what he saw as public expressions of frustration at a corrupt government and ineffective state, he and his fellow filmmakers decided to boycott the State Awards in this spirit of protest. Taking up the rhetoric of rights, responsibility, and government transparency, such descriptions clearly cast the FOG as citizens addressing the state; rather than advancing an aesthetic agenda, the protesting filmmakers often described themselves as a movement of citizens (*kinima politon*). No longer just a group of local professionals looking to better their lot, the protesters are thus elevated onto a national stage and, as a citizens' movement, their protest takes on national significance.

This identification with the national is particularly evident in the form of the protest itself. As the filmmakers insisted, they chose the festival as the site of their protest because it was the one public arena in which their actions would be most visible and effective. What is important to note here is that their protest was effective precisely because of their national identification as Greek filmmakers. As a small group of professionals working in a subsidised industry, they had neither the political nor economic clout to effect change; however, what they did have was their visibility as Greek filmmakers, an important asset during a year in which the state-sponsored festival was eager to present its 50th anniversary edition as a celebration of Greek cinema, new and old. By refusing to participate in the festival, the filmmakers were activating their national identification, putting it to use in negotiating their relationship to the state. In so doing, they also elevated the festival and, by extension, the city of Thessaloniki, to the status of a national space; by refusing to take their films to Thessaloniki, the filmmakers effectively cast the festival and, for the duration of the festival, the city itself, as a space of the state, in contrast to the usual identification of Thessaloniki as a provincial second-city in relation to the nationally dominant political and economic capital of Athens.

Interestingly, public reaction in Thessaloniki to the protesting filmmakers and the boycott focussed on the local rather than the national. A dominant opinion in local press and in conversations with festival-goers was that the FOG's actions were undermining Thessaloniki and its institutions: the boycott was seen as an attempt to sabotage one of the city's most important cultural institutions on the occasion of its jubilee, and the plans for a film academy in Athens were seen as an attempt to take from Thessaloniki its traditional (and mostly symbolic) status as the film capital of Greece. In particular, critics of FOG pointed to the filmmakers' insistence that the Thessaloniki festival and its Greek programme no longer serve as the clearinghouse for new Greek films and that the State Film Awards be dismantled entirely and replaced with national film academy awards given out in a ceremony in Athens. While some of the Thessaloniki public did sympathise with the FOG as citizens negotiating with the state, the predominant view of the boycott was that it was the work of a group of Athenian filmmakers who were uninterested in Thessaloniki, its public, and its filmmaking community and whose actions were a threat to the city; in private, some members of the FOG expressed frustration with the Thessaloniki filmmakers and public, whom they considered to be provincial and narrow-minded. These tensions came to a head during FOG screenings in Thessaloniki when, on the fourth day, an open discussion entitled 'Thessaloniki and Greek Cinema' culminated in a shouting match between representatives of FOG and members of the Thessaloniki branch of the Greek Directors' Guild.

In presenting their case to the public, members of the FOG identified themselves as citizens and cast the stakes of their protest as national, while the Thessaloniki public responded by insisting on the local: on their own local identity as a public, on the specific identity of the protesting filmmakers as Athenians, and on the festival itself as a local institution. However, upon closer inspection, we can see that these categories of local and national are mutually implicated. For example, filmmakers and the cinema public in Thessaloniki saw the FOG and their boycott as a threat to their locality precisely because they felt that something very important was being taken away from them — namely, national status. When faced with the possibility of losing the State Film Awards and the official Greek programme, they responded furiously; not content with the prestige and glamour of the international festival, they made it clear that there was a certain investment in being identified as a nationally significant place. As the site of the Greek film festival and the State Film Awards, the city of Thessaloniki was a place with national dimensions, with national presence, for at least 10 days of the year — it was a place that was defined, understood and experienced as a national one (figure 6.3). The possibility of that being taken away was seen as a definitive threat.

6.3. The Thessaloniki festival commissioned graffiti for its 50th anniversary celebrations in Thessaloniki, Greece, November 2009. © Toby Lee

Similarly, the FOG's insistence on the national was itself not unproblematic. Because the group started unofficially, growing primarily through word of mouth between friends, the vast majority of its membership does indeed consist of filmmakers based in Athens, and little effort was made to reach out to filmmakers outside of this group or in other parts of the country. Thus, FOG cannot truly be said to be representative of the national filmmaking community. In addition, their goal of bringing the national film awards to the capital city of Athens, a seemingly logical move, hides a less obvious but equally powerful insistence on the local: another kind of 'provincialism' which lies at the heart of Greece's perpetual problem of centralisation. In this case, it is the particular locality of Athens, always defined as national and central, that we see at play. Finally, all of the filmmakers' actions unfolded within the larger framework of international film production and the film festival network. The group's claims had more traction because of some of its members' successes abroad. Most interestingly, the protesting filmmakers — many of whom had studied and/or worked abroad — justified their demands by pointing to the vast disparity between the conditions of film production in Greece and the resources and state support available to filmmakers in other European countries. In this sense, the protesters attempted to engage the state as European citizens, demanding rights and privileges comparable to those enjoyed by filmmakers elsewhere in Europe.

6.4. Posters advertise a week of FOG screenings in Athens, Greece, November 2009. © Toby Lee

In this analysis of the FOG boycott, it is clear that the Thessaloniki festival functions as a social space in which the protesting filmmakers could articulate what it means to be citizens on their own terms, leveraging their national identity, but also activating local and transnational identities, to renegotiate their relationship to the state. In turn, different social actors respond with their own articulations of local and national identity, and the city of Thessaloniki itself takes on different identifications.

Post-national?

Thomas Elsaesser has described international film festivals as 'post-national' phenomena; in other words 'another way of transcending the national for European films' (2005: 83) as they address foreign publics, circulate in foreign markets and become transnational cultural products. While film festivals may have had their beginnings in the organisational logic of nations, he states, the nation now exists in film festivals only as a 'second-order concept' (2005: 82) — a discursive construct, a strategic rhetoric, or a self-conscious category. In her article on film festival programming, Czach suggests that even this is no longer the case, as the relevance of the very category of national cinema is now being called into question (2004).

To a certain extent, the FOG's boycott does demonstrate how the category of the national, along with the local and the international, is being self-consciously put to use in the context of the film festival (figure 6.4). However, it is important to remember that the ultimate goal of the protest was to effect real change in national film policy; while the filmmakers were using the rhetoric of citizens' rights, they were doing so in order to actually engage the state, to address and make demands of their government, and to change the conditions under which they, as citizens of the Greek state, produce and exhibit films. In this sense, the nation is not simply a 'second-order concept' — to be a Greek filmmaker, working in Greece, means to be subject to a very real complex of conditions, laws, policies and regulations. For the protesters, it is precisely this complex and their relationship to it that is at stake in their boycott, and it is in this way that we see the nation still very present in the Thessaloniki festival.

The FOG boycott and the resulting public debates are particularly interesting in light of the economic and sociopolitical crisis that has unfolded in Greece since 2009 — a period of somewhat paroxysmal transition for one of Europe's most dogmatic social-welfare states. In Greece, notions of culture — national and ancient — have long been used in attempts to position Greece in relation to Europe, often at its centre and origins, with the Greek state usually considered to be the steward, guardian and financial sponsor of those cultural claims. As the state is now being forced to revisit the terms of its social contract with its citizens, the relationship between the state and cultural production is also being restructured. Public culture is one of the areas of social life in which people are now struggling with the effects of this restructuring and attempting to redefine what it means to be a citizen of the Greek state — utilising and revising local, national and transnational identities in the process. In the space of the Thessaloniki International Film Festival, these different identities are flexible and strategic, in a country that is once again struggling to find its footing on the margins of Europe.

Afterword

Recently, there have been a number of important developments in Greek film culture. The FOG established a national film academy, which held its first annual awards ceremony in May 2010. In October 2010, Greek Minister of Culture and Tourism Pavlos Geroulanos announced that the long-awaited new film legislation had been proposed in parliament; shortly thereafter, a majority of the FOG's members publicly announced their approval of the proposed legislation. In December 2010, Greek films were well represented at the 51st Thessaloniki festival, which showed, among other national productions, the much-celebrated *Attenberg* (Athina Rachel Tsangari, Greece, 2010). In the same month, the proposed film legislation was passed.

Works Cited

Augé, Marc (1995) *Non-Places: Introduction to an Anthropology of Supermodernity*, trans. J. Howe. London: Verso.

Czach, Liz (2004) 'Film Festivals, Programming, and the Building of a National Cinema', *The Moving Image*, 4, 1, 76-88.

Elsaesser, Thomas (2005) *European Cinema: Face to Face with Hollywood*. Amsterdam: Amsterdam University Press.

Mazower, Mark (2005) *Salonica, City of Ghosts: Christians, Muslims and Jews, 1430-1950*. New York: Alfred A. Knopf.

Xanthopoulos, Lefteris (ed.) (1999) *Pavlos Zannas*. Athens: Thessaloniki International Film Festival.

Notes

[1] This essay is part of a larger ethnographic and historical study of the Thessaloniki festival and its relationship to its host city, its public and the state, which looks at how people in Greece today understand and experience place through their engagements with public culture and its institutions. Research for this project was made possible by a grant from the Fulbright Foundation.

[2] The most notable are *Kynodontas* (*Dogtooth*, Giorgos Lanthimos, Greece, 2009), *Strella*, (*A Woman's Way*, Panos Koutras, Greece, 2009) and *Akadimia Platonos* (*Plato's Academy*, Filippos Tsitos, Germany/ Greece, 2009). *Dogtooth* premièred at the 2009 Cannes International Film Festival, where it was awarded the Un Certain Regard prize; it also received an Oscar nomination for Best Foreign Language Film. *A Woman's Way* premièred at the 2009 Berlin International Film Festival, while *Plato's Academy* had its première at the 2009 Locarno Film Festival, where it won an award for Best Actor.

Chapter 7
Film Festivals in Turkey: Promoting National Cinema While Nourishing Film Culture

Gönül Dönmez-Colin

Many international film festivals, while opening a window to the world, serve as a platform for national cinemas to dialogue with foreign buyers, journalists and programmers. In a country like Turkey where cinematheque culture does not exist and the number of cities without movie theatres is embarrassingly high, film festivals also assume the role of a cinematheque, nourishing film culture and extending the festival fervour to the rest of the year. Festivals perform this role despite many challenges. Lack of sufficient funds, lack of exhibition halls, overt or covert forms of censorship, political manoeuvring, rivalries among producers, distributors and other festivals, as well as religion- or tradition-based animosities are often detrimental to the smooth operation of a film festival.

In proportion to the increase in the number of film festivals around the world, film festivals have also started to appear in Turkey, even in the most remote corners of the country. Film studies courses offered in the universities of numerous provincial towns of Anatolia, in addition to those in the prestigious universities of cosmopolitan Istanbul, along with the healthy state of the Turkish film industry in the 2000s, are both causes and effects of this festival boom.

Turkey's most prestigious film event, the International Istanbul Film Festival (IIFF), was founded in 1982 as a small, week-long programme by a handful of film lovers in response to the closure of the Turkish Cinematheque after the 12 September 1980 military intervention. The following year, the event was named International Istanbul Film Days and screened 36 foreign and 4 national films, with Youssef Chahine and Krzysztof Kieslowski as the esteemed guests. In 1985, national and international competitions were introduced. The first recipient of the international award, the Golden Tulip — given to a film that is somehow connected to art and the artist, or adapted from a literary work — was Michael Radford for *1984* (UK, 1984). In the national competition, the first winner was Atıf Yılmaz for *Bir yudum sevgi* (*A Sip of Love*, Turkey, 1984). The event progressed into a full-fledged festival in 1988 with two goals: to introduce quality films of the world to Istanbul audiences (an attempt to build a film culture that was desperately lacking), and to showcase quality Turkish films, creating a platform for national 'art' cinema to dialogue with both national and international audiences. 'The second goal should have been the responsibility of the Ministry of Culture as in some other countries such as in Greece with the Greek Film Centre,' Hülya Uçansu, the former head of the IIFF asserts, 'but the Ministry was not seriously interested in Turkish cinema except for censoring it' (Dönmez-Colin 2010a). In fact, during the 1988 edition, the censorship of five films from the programme of 114 prompted the jury president, Elia Kazan, to lead a protest march with the support of Turkish professionals and the media, pressuring the ministry to issue a decree that, from then on, all film festivals in Turkey would be exempt from censorship.

Uçansu served the festival for 25 years, first as a collaborator, then from 1991 to 2006 as its director. As she explained in an interview,

> In that epoch [the 1990s], Turkey was still a closed country. Filmmakers were not familiar with film festivals and the festival circuit except for Cannes, Berlin and Venice. Publicity channels did not exist. Advertisement strategies were unknown. The festival served as a bridge. Foreign critics and festival representatives began to come to Istanbul to see Turkish films. (Dönmez-Colin 2010b)

During the turbulent 1970s, a period of dictatorship, street clashes and curfews, families stayed home to avoid a stray bullet and entertained themselves with the newly arrived television, although it had only one channel: the state-controlled Turkish Radio and Television. Even if they ventured into theatres, there was not much to see. Foreign films would take years to arrive and the national product was reduced to soft porn or action yarns due to heavy political censorship.[1] An audience was hungry for quality cinema, especially the younger generation, curious to discover the world. In 2007, on the 25th anniversary of IIFF, many esteemed filmmakers of New Turkish Cinema commented on the importance of the festival in their careers. Nuri Bilge Ceylan (*Uzak/Distant*, Turkey, 2002; *İklimler/Climates*, Turkey/France, 2006; *Üç maymun/Three*

Monkeys, Turkey/France/Italy, 2008), who started as a photographer, said that he would wait for the festival like waiting for the spring: 'If it weren't for the Istanbul Film Festival that really injected the passion, perhaps we would never have started in cinema' (Anon. 2006: 3). Yeşim Ustaoğlu (*Güneşe yolculuk/Journey to the Sun*, Turkey/Netherlands/Germany, 1999; *Pandora'nın kutusu/Pandora's Box*, Turkey/France/Germany/Belgium, 2008), an architect by training, pointed out that her generation was 'nourished by the Istanbul Film Festival, where we had the opportunity to follow [Robert] Bresson, [Michelangelo] Antonioni, [Andrei] Tarkovsky and [Theo] Angelopoulos' (Anon. 2006: 6). For Derviş Zaim (*Tabutta rövaşata/Summersault in a Coffin*, Turkey, 1996; *Nokta/Dot*, Turkey, 2008), one of the greatest discoveries was Tarkovsky. 'I still remember the first screening of *Nostalghia* [Italy/Soviet Union, 1983] in 1984, which was packed. The International Istanbul Film Festival has raised a generation of filmmakers' (Anon. 2006: 6).

Unlike some other festivals in the country, which have suffered from a lack of infrastructure or monetary backing from the government, the Istanbul festival became established in a short time under the umbrella of İstanbul Kültür Sanat Vakfı (IKSV), the culture and arts foundation, which had already been organising festivals in other art forms. A non-profit, non-governmental organisation founded in 1973 by 17 businessmen and art enthusiasts under the leadership of Dr. Nejat Eczacıbaşı, IKSV's initial goal was to introduce Istanbul to the best examples of art from around the world, while promoting the national, cultural and artistic assets of Turkey through an international platform of communication. The project has grown over the years; in addition to its festivals in Istanbul, IKSV has organised several film events in major European cities and, since 2007, Turkey's pavilion at the Venice Biennale.

One major obstacle to the smooth operation of the IIFF has been the lack of exhibition space. Multiplexes in shopping centres have been detrimental to local cinemas, which have been closing regularly. The festival conveniently operates around the old Pera, where Turkish cinema was born. Renamed Beyoğlu, the area is a hub of culture and entertainment, with bars, cafes and bookshops running until the late hours of the night. Alkazar Cinema, with its art deco-cum-rococo charm, was the venue for the best European films in the 1920s; it was saved from its decrepit state as a soft-porn movie house and restored to its ancient glory, re-opening to the public in 1994 and subsequently serving the festival. When Alkazar was closed for unknown reasons (it remains closed at this writing), the festival tried to appropriate the Rüya (Dream) cinema

7.1. Protestors demonstrate against the closing of the historic Emek Cinema during the Istanbul film festival, April 2010. © Kanber Altıntaş

across the street which, with its double and triple bills of soft porn, had been the eyesore of Beyoğlu. Although it lacked the architectural appeal of Alkazar, the seedy and colourless Rüya was cleaned and renamed Yeni Rüya, the New Dream. (During the first year, one of its old customers, ignorant of the transformation, was shocked to see women in the ticket line.) But the real venue of the festival was always Emek, one of the oldest operating movie theatres in the world. Unfortunately, it was closed just before the 2010 edition. A cinema that had served the festival since the beginning — welcoming Bernardo Bertolucci, Elia Kazan, Bertrand Tavernier, and Jeanne Moreau to its stage — was going to be sacrificed to a shopping mall. Thanks to a campaign that included impressive demonstrations during the festival and a collection of signatures via the internet, the project has been halted, but no one knows for how long (figure 7.1).

Other elements threatening the future of festivals such as Istanbul include the recent advancements in technology and mass communications. The festival's role as a bridge between Turkish filmmakers and the international film world has become obsolete. The generation that entered the national film industry in the late 1990s and early 2000s includes mainly film-school graduates already in close contact with the world of cinema, and several who work in the transnational milieu of filmmaking. Most of the films screened in the 2010 edition of Istanbul had already made the rounds of several film festivals, in the East and the West, and some had been released nationally. The festival also is not instrumental in the distribution of local films. Film exhibition is in the hands of Warner Bros., United International Pictures and their Turkish partner, which gives precedence to its own films. Important art films are released under difficult conditions, in bad cinema halls and during bad periods. The new generation of filmmakers/producers (Tayfun Pirselimoğlu, Atıl İnaç et al.) assert that the IIFF does not play a role in the recognition and promotion of their films, nationally or internationally (Dönmez-Colin 2010b).

The International Istanbul Film Festival sells around 150,000 tickets annually. For a city of 15 million, this is not a large number. Apart from a population of two or three million that congregates in certain parts of the city — and prefers to remain oblivious of the rest, as filmmaker Pirselimoğlu has pointed out (Dönmez-Colin 2010b) — the public in general is conservative, traditional or poor; they are either indifferent to, do not approve of or cannot afford such an extravagance as a film festival. Many would be intimidated to set foot in such an atmosphere. In an epoch when Turkish women are increasingly supporting the headscarf, their numbers are limited among the festival audience. During the 2010 screening of Reha Erdem's magical *Kosmos* (Turkey/Bulgaria, 2009), I counted one woman. Islamist filmmakers no longer enter their films in the festival, arguing that they would either not be accepted or would be prevented from winning a prize.

Turkey is more than a handful of intellectuals and students gathered around certain centres of the big cities with visions of becoming European. National identity is a serious matter. One could expect the IIFF to form a bridge between the cinemas of the East and the West, but the gaze of the Istanbulites has been conventionally Orientalist. China and Japan are still exotic, and India is still backward. Istanbul's liberal middle-class urban audience does not feel any affinity with the East and the choice of films reflects this Eurocentric sentiment. Homages to European masters are repeated regularly, but great masters from Asia are systematically ignored. Kar-wai Wong was a total unknown until he became a household name with *Fa yeung nin wa* (*In the Mood for Love*, Hong Kong/France, 2000). Most film buffs were not cognisant of the thriving cinema of Thailand until Weerasethakul Apichatpong won the Golden Palm at Cannes 2010. Prominent Iranian directors, recognised by the West, are regularly invited to Istanbul, but an unknown Iranian with a very good film would not have much chance. Films from Palestine or Iraq (mostly co-productions with France) may be screened for their attraction as current news, but films from other Arab countries have difficulties. Indian films are hardly shown. A Shyam Bengal or Adoor Gopalakrishnan masterpiece would not find its way easily to Istanbul. Some years ago, a film by Keralite master Shashi Kharun — *Vanaprastham* (*The Last Dance*, France/India/Germany, 1999) — won the Special Prize of the Jury but the film was a co-production with European countries and had already been shown at Cannes and released in France.

If the IIFF is blotchy eyes, strained backs and late nights in the dark caverns of Beyoğlu's ageing cinema halls, the International Antalya Golden Orange Film Festival is a constant battle with the conscience, the lure of the sea and the sun easily triumphing over ultra-modern multiplexes in ultra-modern shopping malls, popcorn and all. The oldest film festival in Turkey, the Golden Orange, was started in 1956 as part of the Antalya Art Festival, with very little interest in cinema. The Golden Orange Film Competition began in 1964, when the city's mayor took the initiative to invite the Turkish Producers Association — the only authoritative cinema organisation of the period — to enter their films. However, the lack of professional foresight was a strong handicap. The efforts of the municipality to seek the support of famous film personalities and to exploit their presence for political gains resulted in several stars avoiding the festival, which did not surpass an ordinary tourism event.

The early years of the Golden Orange were laden with scandals, from jury irregularities to fame- and fortune-hunting starlets. The lack of audience has always been a drawback, one that has not been resolved over the years. In its 11th year, the festival tried to organise henna parties, fashion shows and poolside extravaganzas, but these activities only entertained the guests from Istanbul. The interest of the Antalya public in the festival did not go beyond the annual parade of stars in decorated convertible cars. Trying to bring art to the festival with street concerts, exhibitions, symposiums, poetry competitions, sculpture and graffiti happenings did not help. Portraits of national and foreign actors were vandalised by the enemies of freedom of expression.

Some producers systematically withdrew their films after entering them. Others tried to block the entry of better films. In 1976, pressure from competing producers prevented *Kara çarşaflı gelin* (*The Bride in Black Chador*, Süreyya Duru, Turkey, 1976) from entering the competition — with an explanation that a 'secret order from above' had censored it.

The film was successfully entered the following year and received the Best Film award. In 1978, the jury refused to evaluate the censored version of *Maden* (*Mine*, Yavuz Özkan, Turkey, 1978), one of the classics of Turkish cinema today. The jury won that dispute, and *Mine* was shown in its uncensored form. In 1979, as the festival committee was preparing the programme, news came from the capital Ankara that three films in competition, including *Yusuf ile Kenan* (*Yusuf and Kenan*, Turkey, 1979) by Ömer Kavur, one of the great masters of Turkish cinema, were forbidden by the censorship board. With a change in government, the censorship regulations had been ameliorated on paper, but not in practice; the new government continued to suppress artists and the arts. The jury, the prefect and the mayor of Antalya appealed to the prime minister, but their pleas did not bear fruit and the 1979 festival was cancelled. In the following year, the deadly coup d'état of 12 September took place; again the festival was cancelled.

In 1981, the festival administration refused to accept for competition two films that are now among the most important classics of Turkish cinema, *Sürü* (*The Herd*, Turkey, 1978) and *Düşman* (*The Enemy*, Turkey, 1979) both directed by Zeki Ökten, with scripts by Yılmaz Güney. *The Herd* was rejected because the Turkish citizenship of its principal actress, Melike Demirağ, had been revoked for her role in the film as the wife of Tarık Akan (of *Yol* fame), who had already been blacklisted; *The Enemy* was refused a screening licence from the inspection committee of the Ministry of Interior (Özgüç 1991: 77-85). Erden Kıral's masterpiece, *Bereketli topraklar üzerinde* (*On Fertile Land*, Turkey, 1980) received the Best Film award, but that award was withdrawn due to pressure from the military government. Kıral was given the Best Director award, which he refused. *On Fertile Land* was subsequently banned (Kıral chose self-exile in Germany) and the remaining copies were stolen. Discovered 28 years later in a warehouse in Switzerland, the film has been restored by Groupama Film Foundation in France and was shown to audiences at the IIFF in 2008.

Over the years, the Golden Orange has served the film industry as a national festival with prestigious awards, becoming semi-international for a period, and finally establishing a parallel International Eurasia Film Festival, which was discontinued after a few successful runs (figure 7.2). The demise of the Eurasia film festival was attributed to the extravagance of its organisers, the Turkish Foundation of Cinema and Audiovisual Culture, who depleted their budget by practically competing with Cannes in their efforts to bring Hollywood stars to this

7.2. The Eurasia film festival, a sidebar of the International Antalya Golden Orange Film Festival, was cancelled after several extravagant editions. © The International Antalya Golden Orange Film Festival

Mediterranean town, but municipal elections played an important role in a shift in management and policies. The former mayor was a member of the ruling Justice and Development Party (AKP); the new mayor — from the opposition Republican People's Party (CHP) — decided to make drastic changes in the 2009 Golden Orange festival, resulting in a rather uninteresting event.

For the 2010 Golden Orange, the mayor appointed another artistic director and enlarged the spectatorship to include prisoners, providing makeshift screens in local prison yards. The prisoners also benefitted from scriptwriting workshops. Focussing on the theme of 'Cinema and

Social Interaction', the festival organised thematic screenings, panel discussions, exhibitions, talks and workshops that concentrated on sociopolitical and economic interaction as well as interaction between cinema and the general public. One of the festival's highlights was the screening of some lost films of the past, including Ernst Marischka's *Enis Aldjelis, Die Blume des Ostens* (*Enis Aldjelis, The Flower of the East*, Austria, 1920), thought to be the first film shot in Istanbul,[2] and *Kara lale bayramı* (*The Black Tulip Festival*, Turkey, 1918), by Muhsin Ertuğrul, the only prominent filmmaker of the early years of Turkish cinema.

Organised by the Antalya Foundation for Culture and Arts with the support of the Antalya Metropolitan Municipality, the Golden Orange festival plans to establish social responsibility and awareness projects, including a 'Responsibility in Art' award to be presented annually to artists who act as leaders in art education. The new administration aims to create a new image for Antalya, famous as a package tour resort, by promoting its possibilities as a film production centre. Whether these are genuine attempts to serve the Antalyan public and the national cinema, or simply election promises, time will tell. One important concern is that the social missions which the municipality has set for the festival may override the selection of quality films.

The 47th edition of the Golden Orange was not immune to political manifestations and manipulations. Emir Kusturica, invited to serve as a member of the jury, was made 'un-welcome' for his alleged sympathies with Serbian nationalists and their war crimes against Bosnians following the violent disintegration of Yugoslavia. Bosnian associations and women's groups demonstrated against his presence, and Turkish Minister of Culture Ertuğrul Günay and filmmaker Semih Kaplanoğlu — who won the 2010 Golden Bear in Berlin for *Bal/Honey* (Turkey/Germany) — boycotted the festival. Kusturica quit the jury and left Antalya. The film industry and the press were divided in their sentiments, while the opposition CHP blamed the ruling AKP for using Kusturica to target the mayor.

Politics have always been detrimental to the fragile position of film festivals in Turkey; another good example is the Festival on Wheels, which began in 1995 with the mission to present outstanding examples of European and Turkish cinema to film enthusiasts living outside the country's cultural centres. In many Turkish cities, seeing a movie on a big screen is still a hopeless dream. In the city of Kars (made famous by Nobel laureate Orhan Pamuk's novel *Snow*, reportedly to be made into a movie by Atom Egoyan), 1,042 films were shown in 1978. In that year, 297,500 tickets were sold to a population of only 60,000. At least five cinemas were in full operation, one of them in a converted church. Over the years, the church burned down and the remaining cinemas were converted to shops. The Festival on Wheels had several successful years in Kars, but a new mayor — whose campaign speech included the promise that he 'would not let a film festival set foot in Kars again' — kept that promise. Festival organisers did not give up easily, moving to Artvin — where it is difficult to find even a half-decent hall to show movies — but Kars has been deprived of its only major cultural event. The Festival on Wheels does more than show movies. Directors, actors, writers, film critics and students — from Turkey and abroad — take part in workshops, Q&A sessions and film shoots. Bridges are built between cultures, even historically unfriendly cultures. The year I was in Kars, film students from Armenia were invited with their teachers. They attended seminars and made documentaries with their Turkish colleagues. It was touching to see them working in the ruins of Ani, an Armenian heritage sight, now inside the borders of Turkey, where only a river marks the border between the two countries. Furthermore, the enthusiasm created by the festival drew established filmmakers to this remote border city to shoot films, such as Erdem's *Kosmos*, screened at the 2010 Berlin film festival; *Kars Stories* (Turkey, 2010), a portmanteau film that has been invited to several European film festivals; and Kutluğ Ataman's mock-documentary *Aya yolculuk* (*Trip to the Moon*, Turkey, 2009), shot nearby. For the hospitable people of Kars, it was a delight to meet some of the stars of Turkish cinema, including actor Tuncel Kurtiz of international fame (who danced with the mayor on stage the closing night), actress Müjde Ar (the woman who, in the 1980s, liberated Turkish actresses of their sexual hang-ups on screen) and actor Tarık Akın, who was location scouting for a film of his own.

Although Festival on Wheels originates in Ankara, its mobile character means that it cannot be appropriately labelled as the festival of the capital. Flying Broom International Women's Film Festival is the most important film event in Ankara. Although some women filmmakers (Yeşim Ustaoğlu, Handan İpekçi) prefer to compete with men on equal terms — arguing that women's film festivals have a stigma attached to their specificity — they do not mind entering their films after having made the rounds of other, more important film festivals. Flying Broom as an organisation was founded in 1996, with the aim to increase communication between women's groups and the general public, to share their experiences with the next generation, and to secure national and international links. The women's film festival, the first of its kind in Turkey, was started in 1998 and screens features, shorts, documentaries and animation by women from Turkey and abroad. Since 2004, the International Federation of Film Critics (FIPRESCI) has been authorised to give a Best Film award in a competition section called 'Different Colours'; the festival promotes itself as the only women's film festival in the world to give this prize. The documentaries in the programme are shown on the campuses of the three major universities in Ankara without charge.

For its 12th edition in 2009, the festival mounted an exhibition titled 'On 12 September', the date of the notorious 1980 coup. Limited to women only, participants could enter handwritten letters, sound recordings, cartoons, graphic designs, photos, drawings, paintings or videos. The exhibition was interactive, with visitors invited to write their own letters, with the goal of remembering — and making others remember. Turkish cinema's landmark films from the 1980s were part of the programme, including *Mine* (Turkey, 1982) and *Ölü bir deniz* (*A Dead Sea*, Turkey, 1989), two important works by the late Atıf Yılmaz that celebrate the liberation of the female body, reflecting the delayed arrival of feminism in Turkey.

The slogan of the 2010 edition was 'She is bad, and you?' — a question designed to provoke a discussion of 'badness' attributed to women in real life and in cinema. A special section called 'The Other History' was organised for the 'denied identities' of people who become victims (Dönmez-Colin 2008: 89). Films included the documentary *Nahide'nin Türküsü* (*The Song of Nahide*, Turkey, 2009) by Berke Baş, whose grandmother had to hide her Armenian identity, and a powerful drama, *Iki tutam saç — Dersim'in kayıp kızları* (*The Disappeared Daughters of Dersim*, Nezahat Gündoğdu, Turkey, 2010), about Kurdish girls given to military families for adoption after the massacre of their birth families in Dersim.

The Flying Broom festival is often reproached by conservative and Islamist circles for screening films against the moral and religious values of the country. One Anatolian newspaper was particularly enraged by the screenings of *Baise-Moi!* (*Rape Me!*, France, 2000) by Virginie Despentes and Coralie Trinh Thi and *Parfait Amour!* (*Perfect Love*, France, 1996) by Catherine Breillat, accusing the organisation of showing pornography in the name of art. These are some of the perils of running a festival in a Muslim country, especially a women's film festival called the Flying Broom with strong-headed 'witches' at the helm!

Not as bold as the Flying Broom, but more in tune with the

traditional atmosphere of Adana — the cotton-growing southern city which gave the film world Yılmaz Güney and several other distinguished filmmakers — the International Adana Golden Boll Film Festival screens feature films along with nationally produced short films and student films. Beginning in 2008, its municipal organisers decided to broaden the scope of the festival to Mediterranean countries, with the aim of showing films by other young filmmakers living along the coast and establishing a dialogue between countries in the region.

The festival was held for the first time in 1969, but was cancelled between 1973 and 1992 for political reasons. In 1997 and 1999, it was cancelled again because of an earthquake and, in June 2010, a few days before the curtain was to rise, the 17th edition was cancelled because of the Israeli attack on a Turkish ship carrying humanitarian aid to Gaza, which resulted in the murder of several Turks. Film lovers, the film industry and foreign guests could not understand why several pop concerts planned for the same dates in Istanbul were not cancelled as well. The theme of the festival was to be 'Palestine: Longing for Peace,' and scheduled events included a panel discussion with several Palestinian filmmakers and critics. The festival's supporters argued that it was the city's most important cultural and artistic event of the year and a valuable resource for filmmakers who wished to connect with an audience; postponing the festival would signify a capitulation to terror, whose aim is to silence. Nonetheless, the festival was postponed, dealing a significant blow to the budget, as most of the guests, which included Theo Angelopoulos, had already been invited, the film reels ordered and the rentals paid. The 2010 festival was eventually held in the autumn, with an attractive programme of Mediterranean shorts and national features, documentaries, short films and homages to film personalities, which included an award to the doyen of Turkish film critics, Atilla Dorsay, a rarity in world cinema. Angelopoulos' photography exhibition was itself worth the trip to Adana.

Most international film festivals include documentary sections, but two festivals in Istanbul focus solely on documentaries. Documentarist — Istanbul Documentary Days is an independent initiative geared towards the new generation of filmmakers and film students as well as film-lovers. The event was originally founded to support creative documentary filmmaking and to bring the best examples of the genre to Istanbul. In its third edition in 2010, more than 120 films from 35 countries, including Sweden, Denmark, Iceland, Argentina, Korea, India and the U.S., were screened at six different venues with a geographical focus on Balkan countries, Poland and Switzerland. The festival does not have a main sponsor; neither does it receive financial support from the Ministry of Culture and Tourism. As part of the Eurasian Art Collective (Avrasya Sanat Kollektifi), it takes place with limited monetary resources, mostly with the support of various consulates in Istanbul and of volunteers.

The International 1001 Documentary Film Festival, started in 1997 by the Association of Documentary Filmmakers in Turkey, aims to encourage quality documentary production. The first National Conference of Documentary Filmmakers in Turkey, convened in 1997, laid the foundation for the present professional association, which is recognised by the Ministry of Culture. The association has a broad range of membership, including freelance filmmakers, private production companies, documentary makers at Turkish Radio and Television, university professors and film students throughout Turkey, with membership predominantly in the Istanbul, Ankara, Eskişehir and İzmir regions.

Short films have had a long history in Turkey. The Golden Orange film festival has been honouring national short films since its inception, although during the nine editions of the festival between 1965 and 1977, one man, Behlül Dal, systematically received the Best Film award. The first short film screening and competition in Istanbul was held in June 1967, organised by the film club of Robert College, an American private secondary school, and called the Hisar Short Film Competition. The most mature short film festival of today, the Istanbul Photography and Cinema Amateurs Club Short Film Days, was started in the 1980s. That organisation was instrumental in changing the general attitude toward short films by showing good examples of the form from the West; soon afterwards, short film competitions were begun within established film festivals or as separate events.

Other specialised film festivals also are in operation, mainly in large cities: !f Istanbul AFM International Independent Film Festival is daring and provocative in its choice of films. The latest titles from acclaimed independent directors, as well as award-winning recent festival favourites from Toronto, Cannes, Sundance, and others are included in the programme. The !f Inspired International Film Competition is designed to reward new directions in cinema. Open to emerging directors from around the world, !f Inspired aims to highlight films which show technical innovation, bold narrative and courageous storytelling. Other festivals that attract specialised audiences include the Istanbul International Meeting of History and Cinema, Istanbul Animation Film

Festival, the International Architecture and Urban Film Festival, the Bursa Silk Road Film Festival and Film Harvest, also run by IKSV. None of these festivals features a market. The efforts of the short-lived Eurasia film festival in Antalya, discussed previously, also failed to establish a productive international market.

While researching this chapter, I came across yet another film festival, held in the summer in a small Mediterranean town, Köyceğiz. The Kaunos Golden Lion Film Festival is in its fifth year. Organised by the Ministry of Culture and Tourism, the municipality, Turkish state television and the International Culture and Dialogue Association, the festival promises air-conditioned screening halls to viewers in the middle of summer's scorching heat, in addition to selections from the latest crop of Turkish cinema.

Is it necessary to have so many film festivals? Does every festival truly have an audience? 'Each festival has its own function', according to former IIFF director Uçansu,

> Istanbul Film Festival has its audience: it exhibits quality products of the world to Istanbulites. Bursa Silk Road has an attractive national competition. Adana has done well mainly due to the tradition of cinema in the city, which goes back to its native son, Yılmaz Güney. Except for Istanbul, most festivals are in a race to grab the national films by offering attractive cash prizes. The loss is Istanbul's because it happens at the end of the festival season (in April) and before Cannes. Distinguished filmmakers do not enter their new films if they want to go to Cannes. *Distant* of Nuri Bilge Ceylan was shown in Istanbul before Cannes, but this is no longer possible. Festivals like Cannes, Venice and Berlin eschew a film already reviewed in *Variety*, etc. And films that are not accepted by major festivals do not enter Istanbul either, waiting for other Turkish festivals with higher cash prizes. Some Turkish films are released long before they participate in the Istanbul Film Festival, hence the media attention is very low. (Dönmez-Colin 2010a)

Running a film festival in Turkey is slightly different from running a film festival in the better-established democracies of the West. For one thing, the political issues can be particularly complicated. Even when government support is negligible, the presence of the state is felt in overt or covert ways. Handan İpekçi's *Büyük adam, küçük aşk* aka *Hejar* (*Big Man*,

Little Love, Turkey/Greece/Hungary, 2001) was forbidden to compete at the IIFF due to a plea from the police, who argued that officers were shown committing cold-blooded murder during a raid scene. İpekçi was tried for 'insulting the police'. That charge was later dropped, as 'no element of crime' was found. Because selection committees often ignore films that touch upon sensitive issues, self-censorship dominates both scripts and productions, and such films are rarely made.

When a festival follows a liberal policy, daring to screen controversial films, some segments of society are invariably offended (even by rumour, without having seen the films themselves). For example, a screening of Ferzan Özpetek's *Hamam* (*The Turkish Bath*, Italy/Turkey/Spain, 1997) might cause the Hamam Owners Organisation to protest that 'such things [homosexuality] do not happen in our hamams', or provoke a jury member in Antalya to cry, 'Who gave this man permission to insult our traditions'?

But festivals do survive (and thrive) in Turkey, despite all odds. Considering the longevity of many such events, perhaps the attraction of the spectacle is what really counts.

Works Cited

Anon. (2006) *Anlar: Uluslararası Istanbul Film Festivali'nin 25 yılı | Moments: 25 Years of International Istanbul Film Festival*. Istanbul: İstanbul Kültür Sanat Vakfı.

Dönmez-Colin, Gönül (2008) *Turkish Cinema: Identity, Distance and Belonging*. Reaktionbooks: London.

___ (2010a) Interview with Hülya Uçansu, 15 April, International Istanbul Film Festival.

___ (2010b) Interview with Tayfun Pirselimoğlu, 9 August, Locarno Film Festival.

Özgüç, Agah (1991) 'Antalya Film Festivali ya da Bir Festivalin Perde Arkası' | 'Antalya Film Festival or Behind the Curtain of a Festival', *Antrakt* (November), 77-85.

Notes

[1]   The 'soft porn' furore of the 1970s surfaced with the availability of video cameras that permitted the shooting of clandestine films with starlets and insignificant budgets in a few hours. The censorship board closed its eyes to such sexploitation as long as cinema stayed away from politics.

2   Long before he became famous for his Sissi series, starring Romy Schneider, director Marischka shot this silent movie about 'intimate Turkish life' in Istanbul, with an all-Austrian cast, including his wife Lily Marischka as Enis. *Enis Aldjelis* was discovered in the EYE Film Institute Netherlands' collection and restored by Filmarchiv Austria in 1991.

Chapter 8

24 Hours @ 24FPS:

A Programme Director's Day

Zoë Elton

Prologue

A mountain. Redwood forests. Ocean trails. A community of artists, entrepreneurs, environmentalists, activists, hikers and bikers, movers and shakers. Minutes from San Francisco. A great location for a film festival: Mill Valley. The festival that takes its name from this small town began at a time — the late 1970s — when northern California and its independently minded, innovative film community was a crucible for new cinema. It was a time of experimentation with film, form and technology, in a community that included those who eschewed Hollywood for the relative freedoms of the San Francisco Bay Area, a vibrant community of documentary makers, and experimental filmmakers and video artists whose work knew no boundaries. Local names of note in early editions of the Mill Valley Film Festival (MVFF) include Francis Ford Coppola, George Lucas, Philip Kaufman, James Broughton and cinematographer David Myers; Mill Valley's hometown critic, Sheila Benson, who segued from the *Pacific Sun* to the *LA Times*, remembers describing it as 'the little festival that could' (Elton 2011). Within its first five years MVFF proved itself not only a festival that could, but one that did, by 1982 counting Jeanne Moreau, John Sayles, Jack Arnold and Lucasfilm's Industrial Light & Magic among its alumni. Also, radically for film festivals at that time, MVFF's Videofest showcased video art, experiments in HDTV and film/tape transfers. It was out of this distinctive culture — innovative and smart, creative and socially aware — that MVFF grew and defined its sensibility, celebrating renowned film artists alongside innovators and newcomers.

Fast forward just over three decades and MVFF is a festival of note, included on *Screen International*'s 'Best of the [U.S.] Fests' list (Anon. 2005), and, per Benson in the *Variety International Film Guide*, 'a notable

8.1. Coming out of the northern California counterculture in 1978, the Mill Valley festival has expanded to embrace Hollywood as well as the best of American independent and world cinema. © John Casado

asterisk on the world calendar of serious, well-managed festivals, ones with continuity, imagination and backbone' (1998). Being part of that continuity, as MVFF's long-time programme director and former Videofest director, I've witnessed its growth and recognition: our programming emphasises significant new films and legendary artists as well as emerging talent, and MVFF is a place where many take their first steps towards the red carpet of the awards season. As much a sensibility as a place, I notice that Mill Valley has become adjectival ('It's a Mill Valley film') and, for some, synonymous with its festival ('My film is in Mill Valley').

A single day at the festival is like a microcosm of the whole, revealing the essence of MVFF's roots even as these elements have grown over the years (figure 8.1).

The months before the festival are like training for an 11-day marathon in which each day is an endurance test. During the festival, I find that any one day is like living in accelerated time, shifting among the joys of introducing new work to audiences, of hosting guests from around the world, of encounters with celebrities, and of coping with the endless details of producing a new show every two hours on six screens in two cities. What follows is a composite portrait of a day in the life of this film festival's programme director.

I: Morning, Early

The alarm ruptures the darkness and heralds day two of MVFF, but my mind woke up ages ago in a cacophony of details and to-do lists. I pull myself out of bed and open the industrial-strength blinds. The intense morning sun hits like a spotlight; I refocus to a view of Mount Tamalpais, whose presence overlooks the whole of this part of Marin County. For the duration of the festival, I'm staying in a hotel midway between Mill Valley and San Rafael, the two towns where the festival takes place: it's a location that's much more strategically placed for these long days than my home in Oakland, 25 miles and a bridge away.

I throw on some clothes and go downstairs to the breakfast room. A TV in the corner jovially blasts the news; no one watches. A woman with immaculately coiffed blonde hair, tight jeans and tank top stands ahead of me, browsing the bagels, the cereals, the toaster waffles. She picks up an apple, puts it on a plastic plate. I get some cereal to take back to my room. As I reach the door, a festival guest shuffles in. It's Seymour Cassel, whose work with director John Cassavetes is legendary. He was at the opening party last night, but I didn't get a chance to meet him; I am too bleary-eyed for introductions now. He joins the woman, says something brief, quiet. He doesn't notice me. I leave.

Back in my room, I make tea, check phone messages. There's one from Alex, our print shipper. The first conundrum of the day: a problem with a print coming in from China. I call Alex. She updates me: there's a national holiday in China that wasn't factored into the shipping schedule on their end. So, between the time difference — they're 15 hours ahead of us — and the holiday, it's unlikely the print will arrive on time. Not impossible, but a challenge. And yes, it's their error, not ours; but the problem's ours. So: Alex wants to phone them, have them expedite the package, then have someone on standby at San Francisco airport to clear it through customs as soon as it arrives. If everything goes smoothly, it could work.

But just in case, we brainstorm alternatives. Is there another 35mm print? Another format — HD, DigiBeta, anything — other than the preview DVD we have? Alex has already tried that: no luck. Tomorrow I'll think about backup plans in case the print doesn't arrive.

Now, the big question is, do we know someone who speaks Chinese? Somewhere filed in my brain is a memory of someone who does. Yes: one of our former staffers did her Master's in Chinese cinema, speaks Mandarin or Cantonese, or maybe both — and lives in Mill Valley. Alex is on it.

Back to breakfast: I've got to eat it, as this may be the only meal of the day. I browse the paper: the headline on the arts page is 'Ang Lee Opens Mill Valley Film Festival', with a picture of Lee and James Schamus at the opening gala. I look at the clock and realise they had an early flight; they'll be at the airport already, on their way out. Opening night already feels like months ago.

Onstage last night, Ang Lee credited Mill Valley with having supported him long before anyone else. He joked about Sundance turning him down. After the show, a friend who used to work at the Denver Film Festival tells me Lee said something similar at Denver once, too. I am momentarily crushed. But I remember we've been showing Lee's films since discovering his first feature in 1992, *Tui shou* (*Pushing Hands*, Taiwan). Lee, delightfully, was a gracious guest, charming the crowd with stories that connect him with their festival. Many audience members crave a connection with immortality, and Lee is definitely on track to immortal status.

U.S. fall festivals share a lot — not just longevity with Ang Lee and James Schamus. There's a season that kicks off on Labour Day weekend with the Telluride Film Festival, followed by the New York Film Festival, Mill Valley, the Chicago International Film Festival, the AFI FEST and Denver: all festivals that are, ultimately, a conduit to major U.S. theatrical markets for independent and world cinema. Festival staffs coordinate the flow of people and prints between events. It's an informal circuit that savvy distributors and sales agents — and filmmakers like Lee and Schamus — know how to utilise.

I scan my day's schedule: film introductions in Mill Valley in the morning; then, to San Rafael for more intros and a meeting; a tribute in the evening; and a music event in Mill Valley after that. Before I leave, I make a couple of phone calls. First, my morning call to Mark Fishkin, our executive director, who founded the festival in 1978 and, subsequently, the California Film Institute (CFI), our parent organisation. I let him know about the China print and the shape of my day. His day includes a panel on distribution. Our paths won't cross until the tribute, late afternoon. Next, I phone the hotel where the subject of tonight's tribute is staying and leave messages in welcome. Then I grab my notes, badge, schedule, and a change of clothes.

As I leave the hotel, I see Seymour Cassel and the woman with immaculately coiffed hair leaving the breakfast room. It still doesn't seem the moment to introduce myself.

II: Morning, Later

Drive to the Sequoia Theatre in Mill Valley. One line of people eases slowly into the theatre, while another on the uphill side of the theatre waits to get in.

The theatre's bottleneck of an entrance is full of people with questions: Where's the sponsor line? Is this the Indian film? My friend is stuck in traffic, can I leave his ticket here?

To navigate the crowded doorway, I make eye contact with the two doorkeepers, septuagenarian volunteers and lifelong friends who have manned the front door at the festival for two decades. As ever, they obligingly make space for me to squeeze through.

The lobby is buzzing with people and popping with corn. The house manager, wearing headset and clipboard, quietly manoeuvres out of house one, softly easing the door closed, avoiding letting in light. We check in. So far, so good: the screening for our outreach programme, CFI Education, is going well, and it's almost time for the Q&A. For the show I'm introducing in house two, we're running on time, the filmmaker is in the house, sponsors are getting seated; all is good.

A familiar face hovers, beaming at me, as the house manager and I talk. It's one of our long-term members: eager to talk, she jumps into a pause in the conversation, gushing about how she loved the Ang Lee film — wonderful opening, plus she got to talk with Seymour Cassel at the party, *and* got her photograph taken with him. She is bright with excitement, with that momentary brush with celebrity. She was ready to be charmed, and Seymour charmed her. Ah, a festival story. Consciously or not, programmers are story brokers — for the stories in the films, obviously, but also for all the other little stories that happen as lives intersect in the maelstrom of festival time.

The house manager takes my arm and guides me towards house two. Inside, I see the filmmaker, Guarav Jani, from India, who's at the festival for the second time. We greet, check in, talk about his introduction and Q&A. Like his first film, this one is about a journey into a remote borderland region of northern India on his 50-year-old, 350cc Royal Enfield motorbike. Guarav makes ultra-low-tech, low-budget movies and is a one-man crew on the journeys of his films: camera, sound, talent, everything. It's the kind of digital work we would have shown in the Videofest, years ago. His openness and unassuming wisdom is charming, both onscreen and in person.

The house manager approaches: it's show time. House lights and sound go down, the festival trailer heralds the beginning of the show. Lights back up, I approach the microphone for my first intro of the day: I welcome everyone, thank the sponsor, give some background to the film, acknowledge the motorcyclists in the audience, Guarav's dedicated biker-geek fans. Guarav stays so he can watch his film with an American audience for the first time. I wait for a few moments to make sure the sound and picture are OK, then leave: in the theatre's other house, the education screening is still happening.

I sneak into the back to see how it's going. A film about women who resisted the Chinese invasion of Tibet in the 1950s just played to an audience of teenagers from around the San Francisco Bay Area and the post-film discussion is in full swing. Two Tibetan women from the film, Ama Adhe and Dolma Tsering, are onstage. Ama's traditional dress is a striking contrast to the jeans, tee shirts and hoodies of the audience.

Ama Adhe, now in her seventies, was incarcerated for 27 years after resisting the invasion. Dolma is a member of the Tibetan government in exile. It's a minor miracle that the filmmaker, Rosemary Rawcliffe, was able to bring them from Dharamsala, India, to the festival. Seeing these two women speaking with a group of American teenagers is like crossing both time and culture in the same bound.

Ama talks, at length, in Tibetan. Dolma listens, translates, then adds: 'You see, we, as Tibetans, are stateless. Our experiences, what you saw in the film, tell us that sometimes truth is not what you see'. She pauses, serious, thoughtful, head cocked to one side. 'Seeing can just be an illusion'. Through the shorthand of her words, she is explaining the depth of their experience, as people who stood up — and continue to stand up — for the truths they believe in.

It's heady stuff, and the young audience is riveted. Not even anyone texting. As John, our education programme director, calls for questions, a young man dressed in goth black, with piercings and tattoos, raises his hand to speak. He's visibly moved, and speaks directly and passionately, right from the heart. He thanks the Tibetans for being there, he tells them he just wants them to know that they're role models for him. There's a gasp of surprise from his classmates, nods of assent: he has spoken for many. John catches my attention with a teary-eyed smile: it's moments like these that make all the late nights worthwhile.

I sneak out. Our print shipper Alex is in the lobby. The update: she's contacted our Chinese translator and has set up a phone call at 4pm our time (which is first thing tomorrow morning in China); fingers crossed. I look at her, take a deep breath, check the time, and hurry to my car. My next show, in San Rafael, is in half an hour.

As I leave Mill Valley, I hit the first of three traffic lights that lead to the freeway; traffic is at a standstill. The lights change; I move two car-lengths forward. Not good. It's Saturday, shopping day, beach day, kids-to-soccer day. Inch by inch, traffic light by traffic light, I make it to the freeway. Now I have 13 minutes to get to San Rafael: time is tight. I call to alert Holly, the theatre manager at the Smith Rafael Film Center, which is both our year-round, non-profit art house cinema and the festival's other home, and pound up the freeway.

At three minutes before show time, I'm a block away. Holly meets me at the loading zone in front of the theatre, tells me that someone else needs the parking spot right after my intro. With the focus of someone running a well-oiled political campaign, she speaks into her headset. 'Holly to House One: Zoë's here, we'll be right there'.

III: Noon and After

Holly walks me into house one, just on time. The filmmaker, from New Zealand, is here, plus her editor, an American whom she met at the Sundance Lab. We review the introduction and Q&A. The house manager calls the booth, cues me, the show begins.

Back out in the lobby, Holly intercepts me to make sure I'm not leaving. I'm not, just moving my car. Which I do, and come back for the next introduction, the Russian film *Stilyagi* (*Hipsters*, Russia, 2010) — the latest by Valeriy Todorovskiy, who first came to MVFF with his film *Lyubov* (*Love*, Russia, 1991). This would have been his first time back since then, but he contacted us a few days ago to say he was sick and couldn't attend. So, no guest. Pressure off, a shift in script.

Except: Atissa, our development director, comes over. She suggests that since the filmmaker won't be here and we have time, this would be a great opportunity to give the Screening the Future pitch. Ah. Pressure back on. Another script shift. You always have to be in the moment.

Screening the Future is a campaign we are launching for the Rafael Film Center's 10th anniversary. I hadn't planned to talk about this now; script-less, I panic a bit. Atissa talks me through the bullet points: it's time to refurbish, we need digital projection systems, energy efficient lighting for the exterior, solar panels, new eco-friendly carpets... We walk and talk, going into the theatre. I pause, wait for the trailer and the lights, trot onstage, and tell the story.

Ten years ago, we renovated this theatre, which had been closed for a decade. We reopened it as a place for independent and international filmmakers to show their films, with or without U.S. distribution. We saw this initiative as an important way to serve filmmakers year-round. To provide a high-quality theatrical venue in this region for films, including festival titles about which people ask: Will there ever be a chance to see this again?

Now, 10 years later, things have changed. When the Rafael originally opened, the festival used three projection formats: 35mm, 16mm, and Beta SP in NTSC, the American format. In 2009, the festival is projecting in eight different formats: 35mm (but not 16mm) along with seven digital formats, from DVCAM to a Cinema Server. Which means a lot of equipment. Big expense. A lot of switching for our projectionists. A lot of variables to consider when scheduling. A lot of focussing and refocussing, colour correcting and sound balancing. The digital revolution may be upon us, but it's still in transition. Hard to believe that one universal format, trusty old 35mm, was the stalwart in projection booths worldwide for 100 years. So, a new campaign is upon us, to raise the funds to re-equip the projection booth.

I leave the stage, pondering whether standardising digital projection worldwide will be a nightmare or a dream. While Hollywood and the big movie theatre chains have begun the shift, independent theatres are pretty much on their own. And for festivals, whose stock in trade is international cinema, who knows where other countries, from Austria to Zimbabwe, will be on the digital learning curve? Instead of a print traffic person and shipping costs, we'll need a traffic geek who can navigate the nuts and bolts — no, the bits and bytes — of downloading and uploading films from countries that are often, at best, internet-impaired. With low-speed connections that may or not be working — I remember spending hours trying to connect at the Pan-African Film

Festival of Ouagadougou. It could be a nightmare. It could be a dream. But without shipping those hefty 35mm prints, it should, at the very least, be green.

Dan, the Rafael manager, is dashing between a format change in one projection booth, a reel change in another, and popcorn replenishment in the lobby. He pauses a moment to acknowledge what I just said onstage. We connect with the clarity of busy people, seeing exactly where this will go in the next year or two. We talk with brief intensity, estimating what projector upgrades we will need, how many cinema servers, how we could share resources with other festivals, how to train filmmakers to transfer their films for cinema servers. The wish list, renewed and reviewed each year. But the house manager interrupts: it's almost time for the Q&A in house one.

In the dark of the theatre, the last minutes of *The Strength of Water* (New Zealand/Germany, 2009) roll, its frames transporting me to New Zealand. I find the director, Armagan Ballantyne, and we watch the final credits. Enthusiastic applause as we make for the stage. Armagan talks about the genesis of the story, how she developed it; and fields questions from the audience about finding the kids who play the leads, about Maori culture, about what a good editor brings to the project. It's an engaged conversation — with 300 people.

As I leave the theatre I walk out of New Zealand and into the festival hospitality lounge next door. It's a hangout for filmmakers, festival guests, publicists, press — and it's buzzing.

A filmmaker from Los Angeles who is premiering her first feature is deep in conversation about the costumes from her film, which she has on display in the lounge for the weekend. She is more proactive than any filmmaker I've ever encountered: she and her partner came to Mill Valley a month before the festival, essentially to scout locations, discovered that CFI Education has a 'film in the schools' programme, and offered to do one with her actors. A techno-geek herself, she also pitched a Girl Geeks panel to us and invited colleagues from Industrial Light & Magic, Pixar and the like.

I scan the room and catch sight of two programmers. Karen is deep in conversation with Seymour Cassel; she will be introducing his film. Janis catches my attention and asks me if I've heard about Todorovskiy. I assume she means the news about his illness, forcing him to cancel his appearance at our festival. But, no: it seems his film has won a prize at the Abu Dhabi Film Festival, and executive director Peter Scarlet has offered to fly him out to receive it. Todorovskiy tried to bow out gracefully with

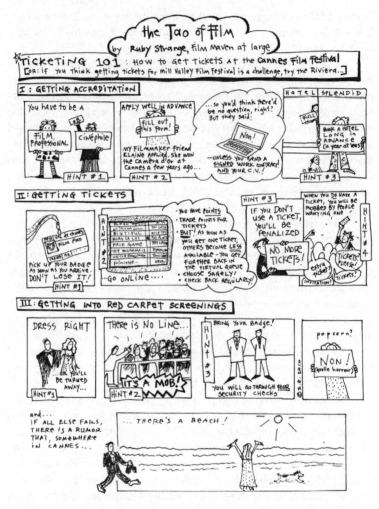

8.2. Drawn by MVFF programmer Zoë Elton under the pseudonym of Ruby Strange, 'the Tao of Film' outlines the byzantine accreditation and ticketing process at the Cannes film festival. © Zoë Elton

us, but the world of festivals is small; word gets around. And who could turn down an all-expenses-paid trip to such an exotic location? Still, I'm disappointed he's not here. I'd first noticed the film in the market at the Cannes International Film Festival earlier in the year, though another screening meant I couldn't see it — not untypical at Cannes. Of all the festivals I regularly attend in the search for films — like the Berlin

8.3. The marquee at the Smith Rafael Film Center, the California Film Institute's beautifully restored theatre, announces the 2009 Mill Valley festival tribute to actress Uma Thurman. © Mitch Ramos

International Film Festival, the Fajr International Film Festival in Iran, the Guadalajara International Film Festival in Mexico and FESPACO — Cannes is the most densely populated in every way, a non-stop ride of screenings, meetings, events, networking, madness and celebrity, with 20 or more screens running simultaneously (figure 8.2). And, for our October festival, its position in May makes it the most important strategically. So, even though I missed *Hipsters* there, Cannes put it on our radar, and Janis ran with it and booked it.

Karen pries herself away from Seymour to check our schedules; my next introduction is the South African film, *White Wedding* (Jann Turner, 2009) and Karen will do its Q&A. But neither of us has met the guest yet, the British actress Jodie Whitaker, who is stopping at the festival en route to a wedding in Las Vegas — ironically, given the wedding/

road trip subject of the film. A call from our hospitality director tells me Whitaker is arriving outside — I go out to meet her; we go straight to the theatre. Jodie tells me she hasn't yet seen the film, which has already had a successful theatrical run in South Africa, as she's been working in England. Now, she gets to introduce its North American première. The house manager cues us: lights, sound, trailer, spotlight, mike. Another beginning, another show.

I go back to the lounge looking for something to eat: it's long past lunchtime. I find some strawberries and a cracker, and munch while walking down the block to our San Rafael office. Our conference room is being used for press interviews with Uma Thurman, which gives me the chance to meet her and, I hope, her publicist, whose blessing I'd like on some final, dangling logistics for the tribute this evening (figure 8.3).

Like many indie films, this one starring Uma Thurman is being released as a service deal, with a distribution team that includes a New York publicity company. But I've been repeatedly asked to deal with a different person, each with a different take on the order of the evening. Add to this picture Uma's personal publicist, who needs to make sure that everything makes sense and that his client is properly taken care of. And then there's the San Francisco publicist who, in daily conversations with me over the last month, has been taking everyone's requests into consideration and juggling and re-juggling the day's schedule. So we want to make sure that things run smoothly — and to make sure our guest has a good time.

As I arrive at the office, Shannon, the local publicist, gets me up to speed. Everything is going well so far: Uma is holding court in the conference room with three writers, all of whom seem entranced. And she tells me that Uma, her director and her publicist drove to Muir Woods National Monument at 7am to go for a hike in the redwood forest — early enough that, by the time they left, the tour buses were only just beginning to arrive. Great: a perfect Mill Valley experience. But Shannon reminds me of our next challenge: the Blue Angels are doing their annual aeronautics display over the Golden Gate Bridge today, so traffic back to the hotel, to change for the evening, may be snarly.

Shannon introduces me to Stephen Huvane, Uma's publicist. We review the order for the programme and, to my relief, sanity reigns and the original show-flow, which had been chewed over, changed and ultimately rejected by the bevy of New York publicists, is reinstated. We review the party at a Mill Valley restaurant following the tribute. The owners have been long-time supporters of the festival, and have flown back from Tuscany in time to be at the event. So, I want to make sure that our guest meets them, and Stephen wants to make sure that she has an easy way to exit. I draw a picture of the layout of the restaurant, and he chooses the area that will let her presence be felt, then allow for the simplest, most direct way out, avoiding the inevitable throngs.

At that point, the door to the conference room flies open, and Uma emerges like a burst of light. She takes a quick break before the next interview. We are introduced, chat briefly, then she's back to work.

I get the updated show-flow to the stage manager, then call our events director with the instructions for guest seating at the restaurant, by which time the last interview is over, and Shannon is poised to lead the party to the hotel and back for the evening. Goodbyes exchanged, we all move on to the next thing.

The evening plan is to have Katherine Dieckmann, the director, introduce the film, *Motherhood* (U.S., 2009). Then Mark, Shannon and I will take her to dinner during the screening and return for the tribute clips programme, interview with Uma, and Q&A with Uma and Katherine.

I pick up my cell and notice a text message. It's Alex: the China print is a go. Relief! I call Mark to check in, review the evening's schedule, and see how his distribution panel went. On the latter: great, except he stepped in to moderate at the last minute. He added that it was a little too premature to mention publicly the launch of CFI Releasing, his distribution initiative, a work-in-progress that would be announced a few months after the festival.

In regards to the evening, he asks who has the MVFF Award, the bronze sculpture we give to our honourees, which he'll be presenting later; although not a competition, the festival gives an award, designed by a Mill Valley artist, to recipients of tributes.

The 'competitive versus invitational' discussion comes up every so often. Since almost every other festival has some kind of competition, including all the small, low-to-no budget festivals that spring up every year — the festival equivalent of garage bands — the pressure has been on. There can be an odd legitimacy in having a competition and giving prizes, and occasionally sales agents won't let their films go to a festival that has no competition — even a festival with a three-decade track record, a theatre and a history of backstage distribution deals. Considering its ambience, its proximity to LA, its reputation as a premier non-competitive festival for distribution-seeking filmmakers, and its relationships with U.S. distributors, MVFF is a natural for acquisitions directors, who scan the festival for possible titles, sometimes incognito.

8.4. Actress Uma Thurman arrives at the Mill Valley festival for her 2009 tribute. © Margot Duane/margotduane.com

It was months after the fact that we discovered that *Genghis Blues* (Roko Belic, U.S., 1999) was picked up by Sony Pictures Classics at MVFF.

And the distributors, sales agents and filmmakers who regularly work with non-competitive festivals like MVFF and Telluride understand — and factor into their marketing plans — the value of aligning themselves with the prestige and visibility of those brands as they launch into the U.S. market. It's a stamp of approval worth more than a 'Winner, Yet Another Film Festival' moniker.

Mark and I sign off: got to go. Just time to change and get back to the Rafael. I have precisely 20 minutes.

IV: Evening

At the Rafael, there's a buzz of anticipation outside. People mill around the entrance: the festival publicists, several volunteers, autograph hunters clutching photos and posters. One of the latter has collared Seymour Cassel, who obliges by exchanging banter as he signs a lobby card from *Minnie and Moscowitz* (John Cassavetes, U.S., 1971). A couple of burly security guards mingle, looking a little out of place in the laid-back, sunny-day casual-coolness of the MVFF crowd.

Hovering close to the entrance is Waldo, an MVFF regular who can always be counted on to be front and centre whenever celebrities are around, and is an expert at talking his way into theatres, parties, wherever the action is, with or (mostly) without a ticket — and always with a smile. He's benign, but über-persistent and knows no boundaries. I begin to cross to the ticket takers to mention his presence and ask them to make sure everyone has a ticket.

But another regular, Hattie, corners me, and virtually without breathing or pausing tells me how much she loved that film earlier, how she *lived* that film, how she thought about Sidney Poitier and that other film — she fixes me with her eyes — you remember? Hattie's train of thought is constantly running, and at this point, it's at express speed and somewhere between stations; it's hard for me to jump on, there's not enough context for me to know where she's coming from or going to, and she doesn't pause long enough for me to ask. So I muster a gracious smile, although I have no idea which film she's talking about. In the last 24 hours there has to have been a couple of dozen. And — uh-oh! — I see Waldo approaching the ticket takers. Hattie pierces me with a look, then smiles and says, 'Oh, but you must be busy — Great festival! See you soon!'

In a flash, she is gone, off into the theatre. And so is Waldo.

Mark arrives, then — almost as soon as we get the call saying Katherine's car will be here momentarily — she too arrives. Some photos outside, then we take her into the theatre. It's packed. Ushers help people from the rush line to the few seats left. The stage manager cues us; I follow Mark onstage. As he begins, I look out and scan the audience: there's Waldo, front and centre. I hear Mark thanking sponsors, alighting on the Rafael's anniversary; I pick up my cue, setting the scene for the evening and inviting Katherine onstage. We talk a little about her work, the genesis of the film, how Uma became involved. No spoilers, just context.

The film begins. I check the start and finish times before leaving the theatre, then Mark, Katherine, Shannon and I go to a restaurant a block away from the theatre. Actually getting to sit down and eat real food during a festival is a relief — a miracle, even. We cue the waiter to the time frame we're on. We order. We chat, we eat. An oasis of relative sanity, until Shannon's phone rings: Uma is five minutes from the theatre (figure 8.4). We pay, we leave, we trot back. With the film in progress, the arrival is low-key, and we all sneak into the back of the theatre. Credits roll, I introduce the clip reel of Uma's work. Two decades of career and a dozen or more films, all in a snappy 10 minutes, opening with the smouldering 'Hello' of her Venus-in-the-shell entrance in *The Adventures of Baron Munchausen* (Terry Gilliam, UK/Germany, 1988), via *Henry & June* (Philip Kaufman, U.S., 1990), her dance with John Travolta in *Pulp Fiction* (Quentin Tarantino, U.S., 1994) — which inspires, of course, spontaneous applause — to her gun-wielding 'I'm the deadliest woman in the world' moment in *Kill Bill: Vol. 2* (Tarantino, U.S., 2004): even at this image-byte speed, the career is astonishing.

Lights up, I welcome Uma to the stage: svelte, long sheath of a black dress with long white pearls knotted flapper style, she immediately connects with her audience, telling a story about her Swedish, former-model mother. She has everyone in the palm of her hand. The interview is rife with stories, insight: her mom, her Buddhist dad; watching Audrey Hepburn films as a little girl; being a teenage actress; Tarantino anecdotes. She's eloquent, insightful, charming, funny, poised. Katherine joins us, and they take questions from the audience, an easy banter. Then Mark presents the MVFF Award. It's heavy — sometimes people want us to ship it for them — so Mark begins to offer to take it from Uma. She throws him a look, grabs it back, laughs. No shipping for Uma; it will go with her.

But as she leaves the stage, Waldo jumps up from his strategic spot, wielding his camera. Uma sees him and goes for it, graciously stooping down and giving him his photo op. She is a pro. And, I guess, so is Waldo, in his way. I make a quick getaway so I can be on meet-and-greet duty when she and her party arrive at the restaurant.

V: Evening, Late

I make it to the restaurant in time. Guests are arriving, tickets are being checked, security guards are observing. Shannon coordinates: Uma's car is parked outside, she will come in soon for her agreed-upon 20 minutes.

The restaurant fills, Uma makes her entrance and we usher her to her spot. The guards hover nearby, to the frustration of several well-wishers. We choreograph a moment of meeting and photos for the night's sponsors, two couples who, for years, have been phenomenally generous to the festival. They each have their graceful moment. That fulfilled, the pressure is off.

The Thurman group sits, chatting and hanging out and looking like they're doing OK. And we're well past the 20 minutes we'd been promised, so it looks like everyone's happy.

Our sponsor opportunities over, I relax for a moment, join a friend who has made it a tradition to come to these tribute events for years. A filmmaker and events person herself, she understands the parties-as-work concept, and cuts me some slack as I move about to take care of business. At festivals, particularly my own, I am a bad friend: I cannot be counted upon in social situations — most people's entertainment is my work. We sit at the bar adjacent to Uma, but my phone rings: the music show playing in conjunction with *Soundtrack for a Revolution* (Bill Guttentag and Dan Sturman, U.S., 2009), a film about the music that gave voice to the American civil-rights movement, is beginning and I am supposed to be there for the introduction. Two big events playing against each other. A challenge I'd counselled against — but, here we are. We regroup: I'm not going to make the beginning of the concert. We check timing of the first set, the intermission: I will make it for the second set.

Then, with a blurry swiftness that reminds me of some kind of otherworldly presence from a Harry Potter movie, the Thurman group rises and, flanked by the two guards, moves out as one body. They're gone. With no goodbye!

I feel an odd emptiness: another part of the production, another of the events-within-an-event is over. These moments come and go so quickly: months of work and negotiation, dozens of emails and phone calls, hours of watching movies and choosing clips, writing programme copy and press releases, booking airline tickets and hotel reservations — not to neglect selling movie tickets — all become distilled into a couple of hours. And then, it's over.

But then there's the next one. I shift gears, check back with my friend, leave to go to the music show, arrive at the intermission. The theatre is set up cabaret-style, people are mingling and getting drinks before the second half. I head backstage: in the cramped dark space, the excited word is that Emma Jean, a gospel soloist from San Francisco's Glide Ensemble, got to sing with the headliners, the Blind Boys of Alabama. They loved her, and a music producer wants to work with her; connections were made. But the second part is being called and, although we've talked many times, I still haven't met the film's co-director, Bill Guttentag. Hastily, I ask someone to point him out; I introduce myself. Seconds later, the band onstage plays a quick *ta-da* and a drum roll, then Bill and I introduce part two.

I sneak off stage, go into the house, and find a chair at the edge of the front row. As soon as I sit, I realise how exhausted I am. But the house band fires up another set of rock-out gospel music that culminates with everyone onstage, handing off solos, from the Blind Boys to Emma Jean to a guest appearance by Taj Mahal. Riotous applause, everyone on their feet. And then, people leave. A bevy of volunteers flows in to gather up glasses, tidy the chairs and tables, sweep the floor. I go to the green room, say thank yous to the Blind Boys and Emma Jean, and go for my moment of hero worship with Taj. I take my leave too, joining the general exodus.

As I walk out, the square at the centre of Mill Valley — it used to be the terminus of a small railway line — is deserted. A huge fir tree oversees the small businesses, all of them high-end, well-appointed — the baby store, the dog boutique, the bookstore-café, the perennially popular Italian restaurant. All is quiet.

I drive back to the hotel. It's late, and it looks like I'm the last person back: all the parking spaces are taken. I circle the building. Finally, on the far side, I find a place. Then I pull together my stuff: clothes, shoes, schedule, badge.

Walking into the central courtyard, I notice something that smells like — what? skunk? fox? Not as pungent. Ah: *cigar*. Bizarre, in health-conscious Marin County — it's almost an anachronism for anyone to smoke any kind of tobacco. Who smokes cigars anymore? I look around, but no one's in sight. Lights still illuminate the pool. I pause before making towards the staircase. Where's the cigar?

Then, finally, I see the source. A lone figure moves along the walkway by the pool, away from me and towards the reception office: an older man, flash of silver mane, loose tan pants and short-sleeved plaid shirt, his loping walk like an aging cowboy. It's Seymour.

I stop and watch him turn the corner to his room. I enjoy the moment of stillness. Maybe, tomorrow, I'll finally meet him.

Works Cited

Anon. (2005) 'The Best of the Fests', *Screen International*, 18-24 February, 15.
Benson, Sheila (1998) 'The Mill Valley Film Festival's First Twenty Years', in *Variety International Film Guide*. New York: A.S. Barnes, 353-62.
Elton, Zoë (2011) Interview with Sheila Benson, 27 April.

Chapter 9

Programming the Old and the New: Bill and Stella Pence on the Telluride Film Festival

Jeffrey Ruoff

Bill and Stella Pence have extensive backgrounds in film exhibition and distribution. In the early 1960s, Bill was a pioneer in the distribution of specialised and foreign films in small U.S. college towns. He became vice-president and part owner of Janus Films during its transition from distributing current foreign films to specialising in international classic films (1965-78) and, with Stella, headed national theatrical sales. Bill created the 'films in repertory' concept of distribution, which included the highly-successful 'Janus Film Festivals' that toured major cities and college towns in the 1960s and 1970s. He was instrumental in the creation of Janus' extensive library of classic motion pictures, which served as the foundation of the Criterion Collection. In 1979, the Pences founded Kino International, still a leader today (under different management) in specialised distribution in all media.

A film collector, Bill Pence built his first theatre in 1965 and, with Stella, owned and operated more than a dozen art and commercial theatres in the Rocky Mountain region until the 1980s. In 1983, he was appointed Director of Film at the Hopkins Center for the Arts at Dartmouth College in Hanover, New Hampshire, and remains at that post today, programming year-round film series. Stella is a trustee of the Flaherty Film Seminar and both are advisors to the Chuck Jones Center for Creativity. They have also consulted with Turner Classic Movies in the creation and programming of its TCM Classic Film Festival, launched in Hollywood in April 2010.

In 1974, Bill and Stella Pence co-founded the Telluride Film Festival with James Card, director of the George Eastman House International Museum of Photography and Film, and Tom Luddy, director of the Pacific Film Archive at the University of California-Berkeley. For 33 years, until

2006, Bill served as the co-director/president and Stella as the managing director of the festival.[1]

Origins

Jeffrey Ruoff: How did the Telluride film festival start?

Bill Pence: Well, that first year, 1974, none of us knew anything. We expected this to be a one-time thing. The idea for the festival came from James Card, the film curator at George Eastman House. He was one of the three most influential founders of the international film preservation and archive movement, with Henri Langlois of the Cinémathèque Française in Paris and Iris Barry of the Museum of Modern Art in New York. Card had a romance with the old West: he imagined himself being in one of those old theatres in the mining towns where Lily Langtry performed, like in *The Westerner* [William Wyler, U.S., 1940] with Walter Brennan. Jim was a fellow film collector, and he came to visit Stella and me in the early 1970s, when we ran a chain of movie theatres in the Rocky Mountains. He brought some film prints which played in our opera house in Aspen, Colorado, and the next night in our opera house in Telluride. The programme included two silent films, *Lonesome* [Pál Fejös, U.S., 1928] and a Japanese film, *A Page of Madness* [*Kurutta ippêji*, Teinosuke Kinugasa, 1926]. In Aspen, the theatre was between 50 and 100 per cent full. In Telluride, the place was jammed; all 232 seats. Of course, there was nothing else to *do* in Telluride.

Stella Pence: We had a captive audience of disaffected hippies, alternative types; people who had moved from the cities to eke out their lives in a hardscrabble community. Most of them painfully well educated. The garbage man probably had three PhDs. Telluride was a town in transition, just right for a film festival. The ski area hadn't been built. Lots of the young people were there.

BP: At the time, I was one of the partners of Janus Films, and Stella and I ran the theatrical division from Colorado. As a result, we knew film exhibitors in art theatres across the country. We presented Janus Film Festivals. Traditionally, they were nine-week festivals: a week of Bergman, a week of Fritz Lang, a week of Kurosawa, a week of Truffaut. So we already knew by phone the best theatre owner in Atlanta, and Bob Laemmle in L.A., and Mel Novikoff in San Francisco. When we decided to do a festival in Telluride, Stella and I would say, 'Gee, we're having a party, this is going to be fun, you know? Francis Coppola, Leni Riefenstahl, and Gloria Swanson are going to be there.' And luckily, a lot of these exhibitors came. I think this planted the seeds that Telluride, from the beginning, was a festival for cinéphiles who cared about and loved the movies.

SP: The exhibitors' outreach into their own communities helped us. There were a lot of people from Denver. Do you remember that first year we ran that bus from Denver?

BP: Yes, exactly. We offered a deal for that first festival: you could get lodging, full pass for Telluride, and your transportation to and from Denver — $50 a person. *And* you got to meet Coppola and Swanson. We were worried it was too high-priced.

SP: One of the things that's interesting to me about Telluride is that we never started it with high ideals. We were not interested in increasing tourism. We certainly had no great desire to spread the word about how fabulous film was. We mostly wanted to have a big party. James Card came and said, 'Wow, this could be really fun.' He brought us Leni Riefenstahl.

BP: Card also brought Tom Luddy, director of the Pacific Film Archive at the University of California-Berkeley. Tom is probably world cinema's best matchmaker. His phone directory of movie people is infamous.

SP: We thought it would be a one-time, cool event. But it just kept going, took on a life of its own.

BP: Card was a roué, a man who had an affair with Louise Brooks. Tom and I loved the balance of the threesome. In the first couple of years, Card was silent film, classic film; Luddy was the future of film, what's happening now; and I was sort of the entrepreneur in the middle, balancing both sides.

JR: What festivals had you attended before starting Telluride?

BP: A now-defunct film festival in Aspen, the San Francisco International Film Festival a number of times, Filmex in Los Angeles a number of times, Venice, Cannes, New York, the Flaherty.

SP: The Cork Film Festival in Ireland. Tom has been to a lot more of the exotic ones.

BP: For us, the key ones were San Francisco, which so influenced our tributes, and Filmex, where we learned how eclectic and exciting a festival can be and how much showmanship is involved. San Francisco was the pioneer of great tributes. Unfortunately, they would take all day. I mean, for example, a Howard Hawks tribute would come after seeing eight full features. *A Girl in Every Port* [U.S., 1928], *Rio Bravo* [U.S., 1959], *Hatari!* [U.S., 1962], and *The Big Sleep* [U.S., 1946], or whatever. You'd have to sit there for hours. But how wonderful it was to be there with John Ford, Howard Hawks, and David Lean. And, if you talk about a sense of family, nobody does that better than Cork, where everybody sees a film together, then goes to the festival club for drinks. I also liked the Flaherty seminar ideal of a family, with civilised discourse, in a remote, quiet place.

JR: And perhaps the excitement of Cannes?

SP: I don't think Cannes is exciting, I think it's terrifying, frenetic beyond belief. On the weekend, you literally can't walk down the Croisette, it's so crowded. And there are police cars everywhere, things are roped off, it's a miserable place to be. Unless you're doing business and you have to be there. Or unless you're in a suite in the Carlton Hotel with more money than God.

BP: In the 30-plus years that we have been going to Cannes, I don't know the total number of celebrity actors and directors we have seen, but not many. Truffaut once gave you a rose, Stella, in an elevator. But we have seen fewer in number over the course of 30 years than an off-the-street, regular guy would experience at Telluride. Because the talent are all kept with their entourages away from people at Cannes. One of the big, magic things about Telluride is that you're bumping into these people all the time.

SP: I think the magical thing about Cannes is the red carpet. By nine in the morning the barriers are in place and people are lining up.

BP: But those aren't the film lovers, those are the French people.

SP: And there's lots of screaming and flashbulbs going off.

Programming

JR: The mix of old and new films is really one of the novel, defining features of Telluride. What was exciting about this mix?

BP: There were very few festivals in this country in the 1970s, and the big ones were pretty much all about new films. We began with Jim Card and Tom Luddy, two archivists. The first year, 1974, a lot of the festival was in Card's hands. And his shtick was the classic cinema, older cinema, German films.

SP: Bill was the sole showman. And all his life he's been in love with older films, so Telluride began with people who were enamoured with classic films, as opposed to being star-struck by new movies. We started from a position of zero strength, and a lot of what we could get were older films that we admired. It changed a lot as the festival grew and became bigger and more complicated, as the town grew and became more expensive, less funky.

BP: Less edgy.

SP: More commercial, more high-end. The festival became more powerful, and we could get more new films to go with the old, good films.

BP: In terms of programming, initially Telluride was much more in the direction of the George Eastman House kind of programming — rare treasures and undiscovered masterpieces, King Vidor, Gloria Swanson, Henry King — than it was contemporary filmmakers. That took a long time to change: the balancing act between new films, for example, which had no priority in the beginning, with the focus on retrospectives, rediscoveries, and restorations. Both have been an important part of Telluride. Today I think the balance is 60/40: 60 per cent new films, 40 per cent revivals.

JR: Telluride really participated in the rediscovery of silent and classic films, didn't it?

BP: When Jim Card left, we went to Bill Everson, another classic cinema guy, for the same reason. Everson was a wonderful man — easy collaborator, delightful to work with. He shared classic films at the festival for over a decade.

SP: Bill Everson had a huge following at Telluride. His films were always shown in the community centre because they were on 16mm, from his own collection. He wore a leather cowboy hat, an Aussie hat and a suit and tie. He was the only person in Telluride who ever wore a suit and tie.

He'd go down the street with his 16mm film reels under his arms. He was much loved in Telluride.

BP: If you were to ask me what the watershed event for Telluride was, I would say the revival of *Napoléon* [*Napoleon*, Abel Gance, France, 1927] in 1979. That screening changed the attitude towards film preservation worldwide, of film archiving and silent film. Francis Coppola had his father write a score that travelled internationally to the world's biggest arenas and palaces, to full houses, starting in 1980 at the Radio City Music Hall in New York. That really marked us.

SP: It used to be easy to fill the house with silent films or lost foreign films, difficult films. It's much harder now. The audience has changed substantially at Telluride and the accessibility of films is everywhere. I mean, you press a button on your computer and you can get virtually anything that you want to see. Consequently, the desire to programme those difficult kinds of things is waning a little bit.

JR: What were you looking for with the tributes in the early years and afterwards? What were the ones that most pleased you?

BP: First of all, the tributes really identify and stamp what Telluride's all about: the art of film, the appreciation of film. When James Card came, and he wanted to give tributes to Swanson, Riefenstahl, and Coppola simultaneously, it just seemed like a perfect way to do it. Riefenstahl's appearance generated a lot of controversy and got us on the map immediately. Now, tributes are everywhere. But when we started Telluride, some of these greats were alive — what would you have given to talk to Jeanne Moreau, Lillian Gish, Hal Roach, Fritz Lang, John Ford or John Wayne?

SP: The tone for that was set the first year. Coppola represented the new and current, Swanson was the classic Hollywood, and Riefenstahl was the one you hadn't heard about.

BP: In terms of tributes, the ones that I think are the most perfect are the ones that are rare. In the early years, I think it would have been Chuck Jones. He would have been pretty much forgotten by most people in 1976 (figure 9.1). Michael Powell. I asked Powell years later what Telluride did for him, and he said, 'There was life before Telluride, but life after was much different. I was looked upon as a film director once again.' It was always wonderful to spring a surprise on the audience. 'Where in the hell did they come up with that?' One of the best tribute ideas came from casting director Fred Roos, who suggested a tribute to the American character actor, to the profession. There they were at Telluride 1981: John Carradine, Elisha Cook, Margaret Hamilton, Woody Strode. It was a tribute to that profession, and so to have those faces all within a three-block area in Telluride was really extraordinary. After that, one of my favourite tributes was Joel McCrea, who'd always been an elusive figure. Never liked to mix

9.1. Mixing old classics and new films, Telluride has stayed true to its cinéphile origins while becoming one of the most influential festivals in the world. © Chuck Jones

with the public. We found him at his ranch, somewhere between Los Angeles and San Francisco. The process of getting him to Telluride was like a dance. I'd say two of the defining tributes were Abel Gance and Andrei Tarkovsky, which I think was probably Telluride at its best.

JR: How did you manage to bring Tarkovsky in 1984?

BP: We were persistent. It took years. Finally, it became possible to bring Tarkovsky after *Nostalghia* [*Nostalgia*, Italy/USSR, 1983]; he had a visa that would permit him to come to the U.S. It was really a very brave thing for him to come. He put his freedom on the line. Then, at a panel for the public, on Main Street — this was not for the press — came the famous debate between Tarkovsky and Richard Widmark. The art vs. commerce debate.

SP: Yes, what was the origin of art? Was art born in sorrow and sin, à la Tarkovsky, or was film for fun, à la Widmark? It was wonderful.

BP: Over the years, tributes became less important to the festival itself. They were very important to Tom and me because they were promises to the pass-holders that, although they didn't know the programme, they were for sure going to have three major tributes.

SP: In the early years, Tom started a tradition in which he would fly to Las Vegas, about a week before the festival started, and pick up a bunch of filmmakers, often Eastern European filmmakers. Tarkovsky was on one of those journeys. Tom would load up in a van and drive everyone through Las Vegas, through Monument Valley, up through the American West to Telluride. As you can imagine, they were dumbstruck.

JR: Unlike most festivals, Telluride doesn't announce its programme in advance. How did this come about?

BP: We announced our programme ahead of time only for the first three years. The thing that precipitated the change was in the third year. Jeanne Moreau was invited as a tribute guest. She accepted. Then, the week of the festival, she had to go into oral surgery and couldn't make it. We felt we had egg on our face. As people came into town for the festival, the headline on the *Telluride Times* newspaper read, 'Moreau cancels'. That was the final straw. I said, 'Tom, we are *never* going to announce our programme again!' It has paid enormous dividends. It remains almost unique to Telluride. Not announcing creates a certain flexibility when hot films are available at the last minute, or people cancel whom we thought we had on board. It's also part of the egalitarianism since no one has any advance information.

SP: As a result, we're very tough on a new film being a North American première. It's a pact with our audience. We don't tell them what's coming, but they can rest assured they won't have seen what's on the slate before.

BP: I think part of the mystique of the Telluride Film Festival is *anything* could happen. We can fill in a spot that's been cancelled, like five days before. It provides the audience with a great sense of anticipation. It enables us to have a spot for an important film that arrives at the last minute. Often some of the hottest films — *Brokeback Mountain* [Ang Lee, U.S., 2005] or *Slumdog Millionaire* [Danny Boyle and Loveleen Tandan, UK, 2008] — aren't even finished until the very, very last moment.

JR: What has been Telluride's relationship with the press?

BP: Difficult, although we have received good press over the years.

SP: For starters, there's no such thing as a press pass. Some festivals in the past even had paid press junkets. At Telluride, the press was required to buy a pass just like everybody else. Although we've always had a respectable amount of press, it's never been a love fest. There are no special arrangements made for the press, there are no press rooms.

BP: They're not guaranteed an interview. We certainly don't do screeners so the press can see things in advance. One result was, when Clint Eastwood came, or Helena Bonham-Carter, they didn't feel they had interview obligations. They could let their hair down and enjoy themselves like other pass-holders.

SP: I think that we didn't want the festival ever to be about hype. And don't forget we thought it was only going to be one year. We've always felt that it was better to under-promise and over-deliver. Also, we never wanted it to be about the press; we didn't want the press to overwhelm the film. We were fearsome about entourages. Telluride was not about your publicist's fourth secretary from the left. We wanted to try to keep it as pure as possible, keep it about the films. We were significantly unpleasant to producers for years. After the audience, the people who were important were first the directors and the actors. Also, we never wanted it to be a festival for rich people. Unfortunately, it has turned out that way because of the economics of the town.

JR: For whom is Telluride programmed and designed?

BP: The audience. The pass-holder. We've always felt that way from the very start. At the top of our mission statement, in fact, it *says* that the pass-holder is king. At festivals I attended before we undertook Telluride, I always noticed the difference in the way that audiences and press and filmmakers were treated. For instance, I remember a screening at the old film festival in Aspen, in the 1960s. Showtime was 8:00pm. The theatre was full, except for the best seats in the house. And it wasn't until 8:25pm that this entourage of festival sponsors, rich people in Aspen, and a couple of the directors, came and sat down in those prime seats, so that 'we the people' could ...

SP: ... admire them as they came in.

BP: That made an impression on us. Also, every time I attend Cannes, which is a festival for the press, I note that everyone else is a second-class citizen. At Telluride, we try to treat everyone equally, to create an egalitarian film festival experience.

JR: How is the Telluride pass system different from that at Venice, or at Cannes?

SP: Oh, completely! I mean, at Cannes, there are multiple hierarchies. There's the press, then there's probably filmmakers, distributors, then there's the dweebs on the street. But even within the press, there are seven or eight categories, and if you have the lowest press pass, you are untouchable. You can't get in. We actually worked our way up through various string-pullings, tantrums and fits, to the second-highest pass, which was pink. And even then, there were times when we did not get in at all. It's very frustrating when you're there on business. But it has to have been a nightmare for the people who paid for a pass to see something, and never got in.

JR: I would imagine that the system at Sundance is similar.

BP: Their priority is for press, and for filmmakers.

SP: I think you diverged from Tom in this. His concern was always the filmmakers: would they be happy, would they be comfortable, would they mind if they stood in line. We always felt that the pass-holder was more important and that guided everything. In the years we were at Telluride, the only filmmakers who received the best passes, which would enable them to get into the theatre first, were tributees. And people who were infirm. So, it was a difference in philosophy.

BP: And it has worked well. While waiting in line, pass-holders at Telluride inevitably run into filmmakers. You'd never, at Cannes, for example, be able to stop at a concession stand with Roger Ebert, or be in line with Jodie Foster, or something like that. And it just happens all the time at Telluride.

SP: But it's interesting that you asked for whom we programmed the festival. I always had the sense that we programmed the festival for ourselves. It was what Bill and Tom loved, with me kibitzing somewhere in the background. But what was important was that we were proud of the films that we played. We programmed for us under the assumption that either you liked it, you came, and kept coming, or that you chose somebody else's taste and went to another festival. The pass-holder has to trust in us. We promise that we're not going to pander to your tastes. We'll feed you the peas, the coinage of the day, because we think you ought to know about this, and we won't let you down. In his opening remarks at Telluride, Bill always said, 'Don't go see the things that you know all about. Don't go to the things that are familiar to you. Go and see the things that you've never heard anything about, and open your eyes to those things.' People absolutely did that. Those are the great discoveries that you wouldn't get at Sundance, or Toronto.

JR: To programme Telluride, how did you learn about films that you might want to show?

BP: The only festival that Stella and I traditionally went to was Cannes. Tom went to many. We relied on 1) what Tom got wind of; 2) Cannes, which is really the gathering place for most films; 3) film distributors calling us; and 4) by our being aware of what films were coming up from important directors, and from studios that we dealt with all the time, like Miramax and Sony Classics; and, finally, 5) an open submission process that brought some pleasant surprises like *The Civil War* [Ken Burns, U.S., 1990]. Tom prepared a list of films that we should be tracking all over the world: Japan, India, and so forth. But most of what had been seen in Europe and not in the U.S. came from Cannes. If we found a film we were interested in, we would contact the film's producer — 'Would you like to show your film at Telluride?'

SP: The only time it was difficult was for an obscure foreign film, if there was a pending distribution deal. Then that was a fine line to walk. They had to be sure that the distribution company would be happy if it played in Telluride. I think for American films, it's a little trickier.

BP: It's how it fits into marketing. Most of the high-profile films that play at Telluride have distributors attached. Sometimes, you'd start as far back as the director, then go to the producer, and then to the distribution company; it depends on how far the film has progressed. That was the way with *Lost in Translation* [Sofia Coppola, U.S./Japan, 2003]. We went to Sofia Coppola first and worked our way up. It helped that we had been film distributors. We have long-term relationships with distributors and also with sales agents, like Wild Bunch, MK2, Fortissimo.

JR: Once you have the films, what is the process of deciding when, and where, to show them at the festival?

BP: With seven theatres, you have to make sure that every new film, for example, plays four times, and you don't want to butt up the only screening of a very specific retrospective, a revival, with another of the same type. You want to give people who love movies the opportunity to see all of the films. I really start thinking about the retrospective choices even before Cannes. It's called slotting. I enjoy the mathematical thing — who would be exiting theatres at a given time. We also wanted to give breathing room. For example, the best possible year was when the theatres would rest for two hours at noon, and people would take time out for lunch, attend the seminar. One theatre now has a noon show, for those people who do not eat lunch and insist on cinema 24 hours a day.

JR: How do you go about putting the right film in the right-sized theatre?

BP: I could pretty much tell what belonged where. There were a couple of instances that took us by surprise; for example, *Roger and Me* [Michael Moore, U.S., 1989]. The world première was in our smallest theatre, 151 seats, and the lines stretched around the block. It ended up with eight unscheduled screenings, a total of 11. Until they open you really don't know what films, what programmes are going to catch on. TBAs, those 'to be announced' shows, are very much a part of the festival. One of the most exciting things to think about at Telluride, if you look at the programme, is that a clear third of it isn't determined until people get there and start going to movies, letting us know by the seats that they're occupying how that final third is going to play out. This means that the participants are really programming that last third.

SP: And it's kind of an unspoken pledge that we'll keep playing a film until everyone who wants to has seen it.

BP: Film exhibition is primarily, in my mind, the comfort of the patron. Are the sight lines good? You would be amazed how many theatres are designed with bad sight lines. I learned from ushering the importance of ventilation. It used to annoy my managers at Telluride that I would constantly be biking from venue to venue and feeling the air. Was it cool enough? Was the air moving fast enough? You can't imagine how quickly an audience tires if they don't have good airflow in the theatre. I've always had a pretty good sense of how bright the picture should be, what the right aspect ratio is, how you integrate a live introduction as smoothly as possible to the on-screen performance.

JR: Could you talk about your relations with other festivals?

BP: Competition with other festivals is significant. With the New York Film Festival, the rule is pretty simple; the opening night film at New York must be a North American première.

SP: Is it not true for the closing night film as well?

BP: Sometimes they try to press that.

SP: We have always had a really amicable relationship with New York. If we hear that they are seriously considering a film for opening night, we don't tear after it. I think it's still pretty edgy with Toronto. Periodically, they'd yell and scream at the distributors, 'You've played it at Telluride, we won't play it.' But most of the distributors say: 'It's going to play in Telluride, and then you can have it.' I think Venice has been an issue.

BP: It's more a question of timing, because we run at the same time as Venice. And they really do want the world première. But in some cases, we beat them to it.

SP: It's been a little bit of a downside for Telluride, because you'll actually see a film listed as premièred at a grand event like Toronto, when it actually played two weeks earlier in Telluride. Or you see 'worldwide première in Venice', when 24 hours earlier it played in Telluride. The bargain with the devil is that if we agree not to talk about premières, if we don't have grand soirées, then Venice says, 'OK, you can play it 24 hours earlier, but we had the world première.' Fine! I think the festival that provides the greatest pressure is Sundance. That pressure comes from distributors who play a film at Sundance and then, later in the year, want it to play at Telluride. We're pretty fearsome about that not happening. There have been a handful of exceptions over the years, sometimes depending on a tribute. We showed *Reservoir Dogs* [Quentin Tarantino, U.S., 1992] for a tribute to Harvey Keitel, following its debut at Sundance. This is rare.

Festivity

JR: Let's talk about the festive aspect, the ways in which Telluride is much more than a series of film screenings.

BP: The really important thing about Telluride is that I don't think there's another festival where it takes over the entire town. The theatres are located in such a position that you can't get away from it. In Cannes, if you wanted to get away from the festival, in a few hundred yards you can. But Telluride is really like a film festival carnival. It's very festive, with flags flying from all the previous festivals.

SP: We have always tried to promote Telluride as a big party. For the Opening Night Feed — a gigantic meal for everybody — we'd lock down all of Main Street. We feed the pass-holders, because a happy, well-fed pass-holder is a happy person standing in line. And then there are three seminars in the park, one each day. That's a big thing because each day everyone comes together in the same place.

JR: What's the role of the gondola, which ferries pass-holders up and down the mountain?

SP: A gondola ride is like a mini-seminar. You know, eight people go up or down together for fifteen minutes. It's one of the best places to discuss the films. You can sit next to strangers. You can go up the gondola next to Clint Eastwood or come down next to Laura Linney.

BP: When we set up the first Telluride festival, I just asked myself, 'How do I like to attend film festivals, not as a guest, but as a participant?' And when I thought about Filmex or San Francisco, I liked an intensive, three- or four-day period of time. After that, it became counterproductive: you were too tired to really enjoy yourself.

SP: We needed a three-day weekend in Telluride because you actually had to *go* to Telluride. It wasn't like in a city where you could work and then attend a festival screening in the evening.

BP: One of the genius ideas of the festival, developed totally by accident, was choosing Labor Day weekend, three days at the beginning of September. We realised it was the first major festival after Cannes. And of course, now, it fits in perfectly with everyone's Academy plans. The fall is when they start coming out with their Academy pictures.

JR: When films are shown, they're presented and there's a conversation, there's something else that happens in addition to the screening. Tell me about that.

BP: Well, it's a way to make it an experience, make it come alive with a three-dimensional aspect. We made it a requirement that the director be present. In some cases, we know that it's not realistic. But from the beginning, we required that somebody be there representing the film, usually the primary artist. And there's another purpose behind the policy. While that director is walking around the street, or riding in a gondola, audience members can talk to him about their film experience, and filmmakers love that. It's something that they don't usually get.

SP: Telluride is not a fan festival, so there are very little, if any, autograph issues. People don't rush up and say, 'Please sign my fingernails.'

JR: For other kinds of screenings, you might have B. Ruby Rich, or Stan Brakhage, or Werner Herzog introduce the films or interview the directors. Why?

SP: That's what we call our intelligence quotient. It's exciting to have interesting people talking to interesting people. You know, each theatre has an 'introducer'.

BP: A ringmaster.

SP: It's fascinating to watch Salman Rushdie interview a filmmaker. He has a specific way of looking at things, and so does the filmmaker. So you're really getting double bang for the buck. Think of the interview that Ebert did with Peter O'Toole.

BP: Oh, my god! That was magical.

SP: And at the end of the interview, they traded Keats quotes.

BP: Roger would start, and O'Toole would finish, then he'd give a line and Ebert would finish.

JR: Telluride sounds like a community, a kind of a family, which is a term Herzog used to describe it. Could you talk about that aspect?

SP: Look at the staff. The rate of return is huge. People come back year after year, and people get to know one another from all parts of the country. And then there is a real corps of people who come to produce the festival, the intelligence quotient of the festival, those people who do the interviews; it's the same people year after year.

BP: In the early years, the corps was Chuck Jones, Werner Herzog, Stan Brakhage, and Ken Burns. It's hard to imagine four more dissimilar people, yet there they were, year after year.

JR: How did you come up with the idea of annual guest programmers?

BP: When Bill Everson left, Tom and I decided to try replacing him with one-time guest directors. This was one of our best inventions. I think we started with the film critic Donald Richie. We've had wonderful guest directors such as filmmakers John Boorman, Errol Morris, Peter Bogdanovich, Edgardo Cozarinsky.

SP: Steven Sondheim, the composer, was very good.

BP: Major player. Usually, Tom or I would say to the guest director, 'Think of a half-dozen programmes that you'd like to present.' One of the biggest risks was somebody I suggested, after I'd moved to Dartmouth: Peter Sellars, a New England legend. I'd never seen his work, but Tom thought that he was a great idea. Sellars turned out to be one of the best directors ever, and he comes back every year now. He's on the street and people get to talk with him.

SP: The critic John Simon was wonderful, smitten with Ingmar Bergman's muse, Harriet Andersson. She was a tribute guest and he was supposed to interview her on stage. He was dumbfounded. He didn't know what to say. He was acerbic to everyone else, in typical John Simon fashion, but I think he loved being a guest director.

BP: From the beginning, we thought the guest director should be a person who could bring other arts to Telluride; a musician, a visual artist. We tried to expand the view of what a film lover could be. We've had authors — Don DeLillo, Guillermo Cabrera Infante. They really put a stamp of quality on the festival.

Periodisation

JR: In retrospect, would you divide Telluride up into separate periods, three or four different eras?

SP: There were the pre-1979 years, sort of halcyon years, when the festival was small, when it was just hanging in there financially.

BP: 1979, in addition to the landmark revival of *Napoleon*, was the year that we were thinking about leaving Telluride. We had had enough of financially supporting the festival with our office help and our services. We didn't get any salaries, and it was taking more and more of our time, so we thought, 'Gee, let's move this baby to Aspen.'

SP: We had already written a National Endowment for the Arts grant to move to Aspen.

BP: And we'd written the press release!

SP: But the ski area and the town of Telluride got the word — 'rumble, rumble, they're going away', and the owner of the ski area came to us and said, 'You can't leave, and I will give you a lot of money if you stay.' So, after 1979, we had more financial backing. We still didn't get paid, but we did pay our key people a pittance. What, going from 1979 forward, was the next big change?

BP: The première of *My Dinner with Andre* [Louis Malle, U.S., 1981].

SP: You think that made a difference in being able to get bigger pictures?

BP: Yes. We recognised the importance of a world première. *My Dinner with Andre* was a big, big hit. It was offered to us by Louis Malle, and we heard afterwards that it made Richard Roud of the New York Film Festival really unhappy.

SP: Andre Gregory and Wally Shawn, who play themselves in the film, came. They were very much part of the New York art world and that helped to expand us out there. That year, 1981, was also the year that Keith Carradine came riding in to the festival on his motorcycle. He was the very first Hollywood dude to build a house in Telluride. The door to the town was opened to the Hollywood population.

JR: In the 1980s, what happened to expand the festival and put it on more solid footing?

BP: After a decade of running the festival, we still weren't getting paid for our work. It was around 1985, I think, when it suddenly occurred to us that it would be good if that changed. The town of Telluride was taking off like crazy, in terms of being a ski area. And everything was getting more expensive.

SP: One of the horrible anomalies about dealing with this event is that, in being a ski area, Telluride has different rates for different times of the year. The Telluride film festival is a high-season week. A room that would have cost $200 now costs $950. And the irony was that they would charge *us* $950 to put our guests in those rooms. Anyway, in the mid-1980s, we hired somebody to fundraise for us on a full-time basis.

BP: We decided to grow the festival. Telluride has sold out every single year since its beginning. We knew we could sell the seats, so we built another 500-seat theatre, converting a gym into what became The Max. This literally doubled, overnight, the number of passes that could be sold. And that had a huge effect. More recently, in 1999, we built the Chuck Jones Theater on the mountain, adding another 500 seats. These theatres were necessary to bring the festival into economic solvency.

SP: And then there was the Galaxy.

BP: The Galaxy, another 500 seats. So we went from a festival with around 800 seats to one with 2,600 seats. All of this growth was wanted and, we felt, needed. It made it possible to pay the airfares of the guests.

JR: How did the Pence family make the transition from Colorado to Hanover, New Hampshire in the mid-1980s?

SP: Well, it was pretty easy, I guess. We were living half in Colorado, half in Santa Fe. We had recently sold our distribution company, so we began to think about the possibility of moving East and about different things in film that we had and hadn't done. Neither of us was interested in production, so the next thing was academia. Shelton Stanfill, who was the director of the Hopkins Center for the Arts at Dartmouth College at that time, was a good friend of ours from Telluride. He told us, 'I think there is an opening for a position in film here, why don't you apply?' So Bill did, and we picked up and moved when he got the job. We continued our work on Telluride from the East Coast.

BP: There was another transformation at Telluride around the time of *Lost in Translation* [Sofia Coppola, U.S./Japan, 2003], which was ...

SP: ... kind of the entry into the blockbuster period. Over the last 10 years or so Telluride has been hot for the next Oscar picture. It's a blessing and a curse. It's the Faustian bargain.

BP: Now, everybody's sweating bullets that they won't be able to top *The*

King's Speech [Tom Hooper, UK, 2010]. Well, they probably won't be able to top *The King's Speech*.

SP: And before that it was *Slumdog Millionaire* [Danny Boyle, UK, 2008] in 2008, before that *Juno* [Jason Reitman, U.S., 2007], *Brokeback Mountain* [Ang Lee, U.S./Canada, 2005] in 2005, *Girl with a Pearl Earring* [Peter Webber, UK/Luxembourg, 2003]. Naturally, the audience has changed. It's very expensive to go to Telluride. The demographic is quite wealthy. Many are there because they want to be the first ones to see *The King's Speech*. So we have fewer and fewer diehard cinéphiles who are making the trek.

BP: Now there is an awareness of Telluride — particularly on the part of producers and distributors — as the launching pad of Academy Award kind of stuff. *The Last King of Scotland* [Kevin Macdonald, UK, 2006] was part of that trend. Since that time, there has always been at least one picture that became important in the Academy Awards cycle.

SP: And now it's expected. People are assuming that Telluride will have its finger on what the next Academy Awards stuff will be.

JR: What do you think the future of a festival like Telluride is in a world where everyone has mobile devices for watching movies and everybody can watch films on Netflix?

BP: Well, I think your introduction to this anthology makes a case for festivals becoming increasingly important.

SP: I am less inclined to go see *Casablanca* [Michael Curtiz, U.S., 1942] on the big screen, when I can go see it on our own 47-inch at home. But I think for the communal experience of watching films, festivals may be the only way that we have left.

BP: There will always be a New York Film Festival.

SP: Always. And I think that for a city like Seattle, where it is important for a film festival to bring stuff that will never come otherwise, it will sustain.

JR: Why, in 2006, did you leave Telluride?

BP: Thirty-three years is a long time. There's very little additional change that we felt we could effect. We were getting the rare films that we wanted, we were getting the Academy Award kind of attention. It sort

153

of seemed like, where could you go from there? Telluride was at the top.

SP: Also, our daughters referred to Telluride as the third sibling. Their lives were constantly affected by the festival, as were ours. They grew up with this phantom sibling in their lives, which is not a bad thing. I don't want to make it sound like an onerous thing, because it was a lot of excitement for them to be a part of it. But it was so all-consuming for us — we ate, drank, and slept the film festival. We worked all day in the office. Then we'd go home and screen two or three movies. I mean, it was absolutely all-consuming, and 33 years of all-consuming is really all-consuming. So it finally just became time to do other things.

Notes

[1]   I met Bill Pence in 2001, when I came to teach at Dartmouth College, and have enjoyed many fruitful interactions with him. More recently, I had the pleasure of meeting Stella. I interviewed Bill and Stella on 13 July and 15 July 2011 in Wilson Hall at Dartmouth. Martha Howard transcribed our discussions with speed and aplomb. I edited the transcript, which was checked for accuracy by the Pences.

Part III

Programming Identity

and Themed Festivals

Chapter 10

A Complicated Queerness: LGBT Film Festivals and Queer Programming Strategies

Skadi Loist

A very obvious factor that distinguishes queer film festivals from other film festivals is the content they offer. While many larger festivals — at least those situated in the global West and pursuing a liberal agenda — now also show films with gay characters, queer film festivals have historically been the venues where queer images could be seen and celebrated. Today, queer film festivals are still the places where community representation is the central factor around which festivals and their programming revolve. Thus, I will analyse the specific programming routines of Lesbian Gay Bisexual Transgender (LGBT)/queer film festivals. I want to show how programming at LGBT film festivals differs from other — non-specialised, non-identitarian — festivals, mainly by working out the ways in which these programming strategies are bound up with the history of LGBT identity politics.

In a first step I will briefly sketch out the historical development of queer film festivals. I also want to highlight the different nuances between LGBT and queer politics, as they draw out the complexities of programming in these identity-based settings. This will also explain how the difference in speaking about routines of programming in LGBT film festivals and queer programming strategies comes about. As a background to the discussion of the specifics of LGBT film festival programming, I will also make a few brief comments about general festival programming.

A Short History of Queer Film Festivals

The history of queer film festivals goes back to the 1970s and was influenced by the social movements that came out of the transformative

1960s. In his dissertation Ger Zielinski (2008) discusses the influence of the political changes after 1968 on the development of lesbian and gay film festivals. The controversy around the proposed dismissal of Henri Langlois as director of the Cinémathèque Française preceded a general strike in France and both these events contributed to the cancellation of the 1968 Cannes International Film Festival. When the festival reopened in 1969, the festival circuit had been transformed from a system of national programming driven by government officials and diplomatic politics to one managed by programmers who were also film connoisseurs. At the same time, new socially oriented film festivals appeared, taking their cues from oppositional social movements.

Several strands of identity-based film festivals — all with a corrective and self-affirming nature — came out of that era and the social movements that revolved around identities and representational politics. The civil rights movement spawned black film festivals, second-wave feminism provided the base for a surge of women's film festivals,[1] and the sexual revolution following the 1969 'Summer of Love' and the spread of contraceptives sparked a brief outbreak of erotic film festivals (Zielinski 2008: 66-111).[2] Gay and lesbian film festivals proliferated in the 1980s in the wake of new social movements — especially the gay liberation movement which is officially recognised as beginning with the Stonewall riots on 28 June 1969 — but they also borrowed from existing feminist and civil rights movements. These social movements and their respective festivals served as a model for gay and lesbian film festivals, along with other activist and exhibition practices such as clip-show lectures and screenings at community centres or cinemas (Zielinski 2008: 101).

The oldest LGBT film festivals date back to the late 1970s. The first — advertised as the 'Gay Film Festival of Super-8 Films' — occurred in San Francisco in 1977. This prototype festival eventually became Frameline: San Francisco International LGBT Film Festival, organised by an LGBT media arts organisation. In 1979, the New York Gay Film Festival was launched; it terminated in 1987 and was succeeded in 1989 by NewFest: The New York LGBT Film Festival. The gay and lesbian movement strengthened, and film festivals spread across North America and Western Europe in the mid-to-late 1980s.

At the same time — and coinciding with the AIDS crisis — gay and lesbian activism came under attack from right-wing elements in the U.S. The movement was also challenged by feminist and anti-racist activist camps, as well as by queer theory and politics. Lesbian feminists criticised

10.1. The Lesbisch Schwule Filmtage Hamburg | International Queer Film Festival celebrated its 20th anniversary in 2009. © Lesbisch Schwule Filmtage Hamburg | Querbild e.V. | Design Bax Bartmann | Photography: www.timokerber.com

the gender bias of the movement. Several festivals reacted with name changes: gay film festivals expanded their names to 'gay and lesbian' film festivals to mark their inclusive politics. Other events highlighted the (not always obvious or customary) collaboration of lesbians and gays by forefronting lesbian visibility, as did for instance the Lesbisch Schwule Filmtage Hamburg | International Queer Film Festival in 1990 (figure 10.1). Gay and lesbian activists also faced criticism for the neglect of racial issues by queers of colour, which was reflected in programming strategies which will be discussed later.

The gay liberation politics of the 1970s, aiming at inclusion of homosexuals into mainstream culture and marked by positive imagery politics, were criticised and opposed by a new generation of sexual deviants. Unlike the gay liberationists of the 1970s, whose credo was to stress equal rights and the similarity of homosexuals to heterosexuals, the new activists radicalised their politics under a proudly reappropriated moniker — the formerly derogatory term 'queer' — and defended their difference. Queer theory became one of the fiercest opponents to traditional identity politics as well as heteronormative (and homonormative) structures. The term queer promised an all-inclusive, non-normative, non-identitarian activism and theory: gender and racial hierarchies were to be fought and new alliances should be sought. This spirit also carried over to film production and the successful New Queer Cinema (Rich 1992).[3] These on-going, non-linear developments and complications of gay and lesbian politics, as well as queer theory and activism, pose 'quite a linguistic challenge', as Ger Zielinski has noted; indeed, 'several distinct phases in their historical development require some attention and reveal the cultural politics of their times. Not only have their names changed, but also the meaning of the words comprising the names' (2009: 982).

Following these parallel and overlapping discourses, many existing festivals continued to expand their names to LGBT, adding a B for bisexual and a T for transgender, in order to follow their imperative of inclusivity and diverse representation of their constituency. With the new respectability and marketability of gay and lesbian content in the media, the 1990s saw another expansion of these festivals. New festivals not only sprang up in North America, but also in Eastern Europe and Asia. Many of the new programmers followed the contemporary discussion in theory and activism and started specifically named 'queer film festivals'.

It is interesting to note that the newer festivals around the globe are mostly called queer film festivals. This has to do with the circulation of the concept of queer with globalisation. However, the term does not always convey the same meaning after a cultural transfer, but rather is informed by local politics. Sometimes the term queer brings a new concept of lifestyle and sexuality to a place, where it is locally transformed in meaning and merged with the existing culture. Other times the term queer offers a certain kind of security from persecution or violence because it is either unknown or does not convey the same abject connotations as the equivalent words for 'gay' and 'lesbian' in the local language might. As in all processes related to globalisation, the transfer of the term queer brings with it a whole set of issues involving cultural import and displacement of meanings.

General Film Festival Programming

Programming is one of the most important activities of film festivals and has been since their post-1968 change in organisational structure. Although there are significant differences between film festivals in terms of size, budget, profile, position in the festival circuit and thematic orientation, there are a few general programming criteria that are true for most (if not all) festivals.

Film festivals usually showcase new, aesthetically innovative content. As the festival circuit has grown and film markets have shifted, however, these basic requirements for film selection have become more complicated. Apart from interest in a film, the main question for programmers is whether the film is available. Availability depends on the specific festival and its position within the circuit and festival calendar. Festivals usually aim for international or national premières because timeliness secures interest and media coverage in this era of the 'attention economy'. Films often launch at festivals before their wider release, to make use of the press reviews and the buzz; this benefits both producers and festivals. In the past few years, however, the time span between a world première and a national release in theatres or on DVD has been shrinking, leaving shorter windows for festivals to show a film and thus limiting their selection. Another limitation, especially for smaller festivals below the A-level, is the cost of screening fees. If a festival is interested in a particular film, it might be able to negotiate a waiver of the screening fee in exchange for an invitation to the director — again benefitting both the festival and the film, as a director's attendance adds to the event character of the festival and creates an extra incentive for press coverage.

All these mechanisms of programming, which reach far beyond taste and aesthetics, also apply to queer film festivals. However, on the level of content and aesthetics, queer film festivals function very differently.

LGBT Film Festivals and Programming

The early gay and lesbian film festivals were started by filmmakers and gay activists as platforms for alternative representation. They created counterpublic spheres where non-stereotypical, non-negative images could be seen, images that the mainstream did not provide. Beyond the function of counter-representation, the festivals had a formative influence on the community, as people came together to see themselves on screen and support their own art and artists. The history of LGBT film festivals as a specific platform for positive and political images has had an impact on the programming of these festivals, and that impact continues today. Queer filmmaking and curating for LGBT film festivals is bound to representational and identity politics and loaded with rules and expectations. Thus, it differs significantly from the usual programming business at international film festivals, where the main imperative usually involves selecting new films and presenting the best of the crop (Klippel 2008).

In the following section I will trace common programming mechanisms of LGBT film festivals and place them within their historic context. Here I should mention that I mainly refer to short film curating, because here the strategies become more apparent, and not only because of the condensed forms. Due to a shortage of resources, minority film production has created more output in the short format, which is often bundled together to compensate for the lack of feature-length material.

The first type of LGBT programming aims to comply with the demand to show positive images of community members. This imperative goes back to the history of the counterculture and what Zielinski calls the 'corrective motif' of the early gay and lesbian film festivals (2008: 129). These festivals set out to correct the (mis)representations produced by the dominant culture and circulated by mass media at the time (2008: 68). Many festivals wrote this concept explicitly into their mission statements and vowed to present films that fit the formula 'films by, for and about' gays and lesbians or the LGBT community.

As feminist discussion spilled over into gay discourses, lesbians demanded a level of representation equal to that of gay men. This helps explain the 1980s wave of renaming 'gay' film festivals as 'gay and lesbian' ones. Along with that official recognition of this constituency came the demand for equal presentation on screen; for example, in the same number of time slots or the same number of programmes. This was harder to achieve, since gender hierarchies have great impact on film production; women — and especially lesbians and transgendered persons — are an under-resourced group. In a 1986 incident that went down in Frameline's history as the 'lesbian riot', audience members reacted violently when a lesbian short film programme they were watching included Midi Onodera's three-part *Ten Cents a Dance: Parallax* (Canada, 1985) which, in addition to lesbian themes, also features heterosexual and gay male sex scenes. Many lesbian audience members had been frustrated with unequal presentation for years and were not willing to take it any longer (Stryker 1996: 366-7). Frameline took this

10.2. The Verzaubert Queer Film Festival travels to major cities in Germany. © Verzaubert Queer Film Festival | Rosebud Entertainment Veranstaltungs + Medien GmbH

incident very seriously. The board of directors ordered parity in gay and lesbian content and specifically created the post of 'women's guest curator' to find enough appropriate material (Loist 2008: 169).

The creation of a lesbian programming position within this organisation is symptomatic of the larger trend of involving audience members in selection committees that Zielinski identifies as beginning in the late 1980s and continuing into the 1990s. Such committees help pre-screen and review a vast number of submissions, then offer comments and a collective vote for consideration to the head programmer. Selection committees typically represent a diverse range of community members and serve as sounding boards for a variety of tastes and identity issues. This part of the selection process, with its commitment to community representation, marks a stark difference with general film festivals, which 'place their confidence in the connoisseurship of their respective programmers to select films and group them into enticing, relevant programs' (Zielinski 2009: 982).

As the twentieth century came to a close, discussions about identity and representational politics shifted. Other groups demanded representation in turn; in the past decade, the B for bisexual and the T for transgender were added to many festival names. Along with the new names, festivals added programme slots that cater to these groups (Loist 2008). In parallel with the demand for diversifying representation along gender/sexuality lines, criticism by black feminists and, later, by queers of colour prompted awareness of racial and ethnic diversity within the community. As a result, festivals also made efforts to include these subgroups, creating what Richard Fung calls 'dedicated' programmes (1999). Thus, festivals that responded to community criticism simultaneously expanded their audiences. Since the 1990s, programmes like 'Jewish queer shorts', 'Latino shorts', 'Asian-American shorts', and 'Queers of Colour shorts' have appeared in the programming of larger LGBT festivals.

This pattern of diversification could be summarised as a programming strategy of addition, which is only possible at the larger festivals. While this strategy is motivated by good intentions, trying to please groups through the promise of visibility, it is quite problematic. With the creation of separate programmes featuring trans* or bisexual films, or Asian-American or Jewish shorts, these themes started to drop out of the more notorious 'mainstream' programmes of gay male or lesbian short films which almost every larger LGBT film festival features. San Francisco's Frameline festival, for example, has the long-running 'Fun in Boys' Shorts' and 'Fun in Girls' Shorts' programmes, while Germany's Verzaubert Queer Film Festival (which recently converted to a biennial Verzaubert/Leibe Filme Festival) features its traditional 'Gay Propaganda Night' and 'The Elle World' (figure 10.2). Writing about such programming in the 1995 Frameline festival, Marc Siegel noted that these slots had a tendency for white, clean, sanitised programmes with short, happy, 'fluffy' films (1997). These programmes conveniently left out issues of trans* or racial politics, which then became mere minority issues in terms of programming structures, assumed not to be of interest to the overall queer community. Thus, these programmes could be said to cater to a mainstream, homonormative, sponsorship-friendly group — an imagined white, affluent homosexual (male) middle-class. This issue was stressed in the work of Ragan Rhyne (2007), who pointed out that LGBT film festivals are intricately intertwined with neoliberal economies.

Queer Programming Strategies

In contrast to the traditional programming strategies that have grown out of the long history of gay and lesbian activism, I want to highlight a few examples of what I would call 'queer programming strategies'. In accordance with the political imperative put forward by the concept queer, one would want to create a truly inclusive and diverse counterpublic. That is, one where guys would not only go to 'boys' programmes' and queer women of colour would not (only) be hailed to go to a 'queer women of colour' programme. It would mean a public sphere where these and other groups meet between programmes and are not separated because certain programmes only show in certain venues.[4]

For the purpose of clarity, I would like to point out that the programming strategies used by many LGBT film festivals have developed over time in accordance with the then-current discussions in the gay, lesbian and queer movements. And, for any individual festival, the use of certain programming strategies often has grown out of that particular festival's historic relationships with its audience and community. Thus, the fact that a festival carries the term LGBT or queer in its official title does not necessarily characterise its programming strategies. As we will see in the following examples, queer programming strategies can also be employed by so-called gay and lesbian film festivals. Similarly, traditional programming modes can be found in festivals that call themselves queer.

One strategy for avoiding separatist programming along gender/sexual identity or racial/ethnic backgrounds is the obvious move to mixed programmes. New York's festival of lesbian and gay experimental film and video, for instance, has a long tradition of including work that ranges across gender and racial categories (Rastegar 2009). This strategy is even reflected in the festival's name; it became MIX NYC in 1993 and is currently called MIX: New York Queer Experimental Film Festival. The programming staff and their invited guest curators focus the festival's thematic programmes on current issues — such as unemployment, capitalism, gentrification, AIDS etc. — rather than on gender or ethnicity (Zielinski and Jusick 2010).

For a study of queer film festivals, Jamie June asked festival programmers what they regarded as queer cinema. The motivation for this question is not a trivial perception: while filmmakers create a very diverse pool of works, it is the selections made by queer film festivals which define what audiences identify as queer cinema (June 2004). The results of her study showed that the majority of festivals still hold on to the traditional rule of films 'by, for and about', while sometimes adding 'of interest to', the LGBT community. A smaller fraction of festivals actively pursues inclusion of work that is not easily identified as LGBT. In order to engage with an audience that might question this practice, events such as question and answer sessions with curators and/or filmmakers are offered to contextualise such work.

I want to present two examples of curated programmes of short films which followed this route, aiming to create non-essentialist programmes by challenging the imperative of direct representation and ultimately asking, 'What is queer cinema?' Both programmes screened at the Lesbisch Schwule Filmtage Hamburg | International Queer Film Festival in 2008. The first was a programme of Canadian experimental shorts called 'A Complicated Queerness' (from which I borrowed my title); the second, a programme featuring teenage heroines called 'Girl's Room'.

'A Complicated Queerness' moves beyond one-dimensional target groups and the imperative of film 'by, for and about' (with a stress on the *about*). Lauren Howes, head of the Canadian Filmmakers Distribution Centre, Canada's foremost non-commercial distributor and resource for independently produced film, curated this programme of 13 short films. Howes set out to question established assumptions of LGBT programming by asking: 'Is there a queer aesthetic beyond the overtly queer statement?' She goes on to describe the programme in the festival catalogue as follows:

> This selection of films by queer artists presents us with a range of complex images and ideas. A post-queer doctrine of work that is both complex and ambiguous. These filmmakers use visual mosaic, hand-processed film, found footage, and carefully crafted works of art on film to invoke feelings of memory and loss, heartache and struggle, often with the influential power of song. This program weaves both the very personal with political points of view in subtle and powerful ways, and celebrates the work of these queer artists through their complicated queerness. (Querbild e.V. 2008: 17)[5]

Although the films selected were made by queer artists, they did not depict explicitly queer material; there were no representations of overtly sexually determined stories, no films with a coming out, a same-sex kiss or a graphic depiction of a sex-change operation. Apart from going beyond the mode of direct queer representation (around which revolves an intricate discourse itself), this curatorial strategy has the advantage of supporting queer filmmakers at a point in their careers when they have turned away from overt statements about identity or sexuality. One hopes that other festivals also will develop their curatorial practices in order to continue supporting such filmmakers.

'Girl's Room', curated by Melissa Pritchard for the 2008 edition of the Hamburg festival and subsequently shown at the 2009 identities Queer Film Festival in Vienna, appropriated the specific reception context that exists at queer film festivals (figure 10.3). Due to their history, most LGBT film festivals have created a counterpublic sphere, a safe space where patterns of mainstream reception are disrupted and suspended. In this space, where certain set identitarian and social assumptions are negated, films can be seen differently: even potentially homophobic and racist films can be reinterpreted (Searle 1996: 51-2). The specific reception context — and the expectations that come with it — can encourage a 'queer reading' or reveal a film in a different light.

'Girl's Room' compiled six films featuring teenage girls. The programme description in the festival catalogue gives an idea of the individual films:

> Shy encounters, confusing feelings and the search for self: In *Pitstop* the silent Margaret is left behind by her family at an intermediate stop at a gas station in the middle of nowhere. And in the time before the family wagon realizes she's missing, Margaret has the chance to get to know the gas station owner. Seven-year-old Sidsel learns that the very first love can hurt when jealousy awakens. *Blodsøstre/Blood Sisters* shows that rejection can have serious consequences. What surprising adventures can be had in the scary and none-too-welcoming *Girl's Room*. Composition of some water music, and almost the chance to try a kiss … *Sexy Thing* has two stories to tell us: one of violence and escape, and also how dreamy tenderness found between sea stars and glittering fish can help. One thing most of us have experienced is the fear of the first kiss. *Saliva* has a few ideas about how to overcome the fear: a bit of practice in the mirror? Test-run with a boy, or better kisses through pink plastic with the best girlfriend? And you can drown it in longing? The heroine in *No Bikini* knows only the fear of the three-meter board, but otherwise tumbles like a fish in the waters of the summer

swim camp. Even without a bikini top she feels not for the smallest moment naked. (Querbild e.V. 2008: 30; ellipsis in original)[6]

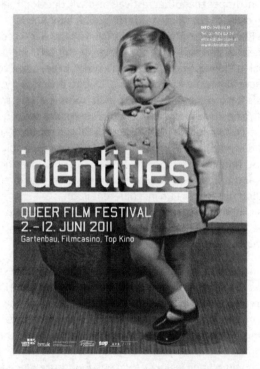

10.3. Inspired by critic B. Ruby Rich's writing on New Queer Cinema, identities, Vienna's Queer Film Festival, was founded in 1994. © identities 2011 | DV8 Film

In these short films, the protagonists share a pivotal moment in their coming of age, their awakening to adult identities and sexuality. These films are not specifically lesbian — whether because the girls are too young or because there are no explicit depictions of lesbian (sexual) desire. Instead, the films offer moments of same-sex contact that are special, ambivalent, and touching (not sexually or bodily, but emotionally). Seeing these films individually or within another festival might make for a totally different reading. But the compilation of these films, set in a queer festival context, surely resonates with queer audiences — as a filmic (and perhaps abstract) memory of fleeting moments that might have meant something special for the youthful individual and her identity.

Conclusion

I have tried to point out the epistemological problems related to tendencies within LGBT festival programming. The mere addition of representational segments on a superficial level, without integrating criticism of identity politics, perpetuates structures of inequality and discrimination based on gender/sexuality and race/ethnicity while pretending to offer visibility, which is often confused with political power (Schaffer 2004). Programmers and festival organisers often legitimise this decision by invoking established reception behaviours based on presumed one-dimensional identification patterns — i.e. gay men or women are said to watch only films by, for and about gay men or women, respectively. The same goes for racialised and ethnicised audiences. By this practice, curators neglect their responsibility to truly 'strengthen the diverse lesbian, gay, bisexual and transgender community and further its visibility by supporting and promoting a broad array of cultural representations and artistic expression in film, video and other media arts' as, for instance, Frameline's mission statement suggests.[7] Instead, programmers mask their own curatorial apathy and compliance by selling their audiences to sponsors in readily packaged, homogenised segments.

Queer programming strategies, I would argue, challenge the practice of targeting audiences in these essentialising and homogenising ways. They mean trouble for the larger, more established LGBT film festivals because several groups relevant to the festival structure are pushed out of their comfort zones: 'mainstream' audiences, sponsors and programmers. At a time when funding is especially hard to come by, festivals are not likely to change their programming profiles. Thus, we can only hope that at the 50th anniversary of the Stonewall riots, in 2019, LGBT film festival programming will be as 'revolutionary' as Frameline and other festivals want to make us believe when promoting the 'power of film'.[8]

Works Cited

Armatage, Kay (2009) 'Toronto Women & Film International 1973', in Dina Iordanova with Ragan Rhyne (eds) *Film Festival Yearbook 1: The Festival Circuit*. St Andrews: St Andrews Film Studies with College Gate Press, 82-98.

Barlow, Melinda (2003) 'Feminism 101: The New York Women's Video Festival, 1972-1980', *Camera Obscura*, 18, 3, 3-38.

The Big Queer Film Festival List (2011). On-line. Available HTTP: http://www. queerfilmfestivals.org (30 May 2011).

Fung, Richard (1999) 'Programming the Public', *GLQ: A Journal of Lesbian and Gay Studies*, 5, 1, 89-93.

Gorfinkel, Elena (2006) 'Wet Dreams: Erotic Film Festivals of the Early 1970s and the Utopian Sexual Public Sphere', *Framework*, 47, 2, 59-86.

Howes, Lauren (2009) 'A Complicated Queerness', in Dorothée von Diepenbroick and Skadi Loist (eds) *Bildschön: 20 Jahre Lesbisch Schwule Filmtage Hamburg | Picturesque: 20 Years of Hamburg International Queer Film Festival*. Hamburg: Männerschwarm, 130-3.

June, Jamie L. (2004) 'Defining Queer: The Criteria and Selection Process for Programming Queer Film Festivals', *CultureWork*, 8, 2. On-line. Available HTTP: http://aad.uoregon.edu/culturework/culturework26.html (7 December 2008).

Klippel, Heike (2008) '"The Art of Programming"', in Heike Klippel (ed.) *'The Art of Programming': Film, Programm und Kontext*. Münster: LIT, 7-17.

Loist, Skadi (2008) 'Frameline XXX: Thirty Years of Revolutionary Film: Der Kampf um queere Repräsentationen in der Geschichte des San Francisco International LGBT Film Festival' | 'The Fight for Queer Representations in the History of the San Francisco International LGBT Film Festival', in Ulla Wischermann and Tanja Thomas (eds) *Medien – Diversität – Ungleichheit: Zur medialen Konstruktion sozialer Differenz | Media – Diversity – Inequality: About the Media Construction of Social Difference*. Wiesbaden: VS Verlag für Sozialwissenschaften, 163-81.

Querbild e.V. (ed.) (2008) *19. Lesbisch Schwule Filmtage Hamburg: 21-26.10.2008*. [International Queer Film Festival catalogue.]

Rastegar, Roya (2009) 'The De-Fusion of Good Intentions: Outfest's Fusion Film Festival', *GLQ: A Journal of Lesbian and Gay Studies*, 15, 3, 481-97.

Rhyne, Ragan (2007) 'Pink Dollars: Gay and Lesbian Film Festivals and the Economy of Visibility', unpublished PhD thesis, New York University.

Rich, B. Ruby (1992) 'New Queer Cinema', *Sight & Sound*, 2, 5, 30-5.

Schaffer, Johanna (2004) 'Sichtbarkeit = politische Macht? Über die visuelle Verknappung von Handlungsfähigkeit' | 'Visibility = Political Power? About the Visual Shortening of Agency', in Urte Helduser, Daniela Marx, Tanja Paulitz and Katharina Pühl (eds) *Under Construction? Konstruktivistische Perspektiven in feministischer Theorie und Forschungspraxis | Under Construction? Constructionist Perspectives in Feminist Theory and Research Practice*. Frankfurt/Main: Campus, 208-22.

Searle, Samantha (1996) 'Film and Video Festivals: Queer Politics and Exhibition', *Meanjin*, 55, 1, 47-59.

Siegel, Marc (1997) 'Spilling out onto Castro Street', *Jump Cut: A Review of Contemporary Media*, 41, 131-6. On-line. Available HTTP: http://www. ejumpcut.org/archive/onlinessays/JC41folder/OnCastroStreet.html (30 August 2010).

Stryker, Susan (1996) 'A Cinema of One's Own: A Brief History of the San Francisco International Lesbian & Gay Film Festival', in Jenni Olson (ed.) *The Ultimate Guide to Lesbian & Gay Film and Video*. New York: Serpent's Tail, 364-70.

Zielinski, Ger (2008) 'Furtive, Steady Glances: On the Emergence and Cultural Politics of Lesbian & Gay Film Festivals', unpublished PhD thesis, McGill University, Montreal.

____ (2009) 'Queer Film Festivals', in John C. Hawley and Emmanuel S. Nelson (eds) *LGBTQ America Today: An Encyclopedia*. Westport, CT: Greenwood Press, 980-4.

Zielinski, Ger and Stephen Kent Jusick (2010) 'Ger Zielinski in Conversation with Stephen Kent Jusick, Executive Director of MIX Festival of Queer Experimental Film and Video', *Fuse*, 16-22.

Notes

[1] In the U.S. and Canada, women's film and video festivals had already begun by the early 1970s, as the examples from New York and Toronto attest (Barlow 2003; Armatage 2009).

[2] For a study of erotic film festivals, see Gorfinkel 2006.

[3] Film critic and academic B. Ruby Rich coined the term 'New Queer Cinema' after several queer films gained critical attention and won awards at film festivals such as Sundance, Berlin, and Toronto in 1991 and 1992.

[4] I don't want to discount the fact that these festivals are largely dependent on ticket sales and will therefore program more 'mainstream' selections in bigger venues than other programs that are deemed of interest to fewer audience members. However, LGBT/queer festivals should not forget their original goal to challenge mainstream notions of representation and community.

[5] The programme note for 'A Complicated Queerness,' with a list of the films screened, is available on-line at: http://www.lsf-hamburg.de/modules/mod_timetable/programm_popup.php?id_programm=292&date=Sonntag,%2026.%20Oktober&time=17:30 (accessed 31 August 2010).

[6] The English programme description, as well as the list of films included in 'Girl's Room,' is available on-line at: http://www.lsf-

hamburg.de/modules/mod_timetable/programm_popup.php?id_
programm=267&date=Sonntag,%2026.%20Oktober&time=15:00
(accessed 31 August 2010).

[7]   The mission statement can be found on-line at: http://www.frameline.
org/about/ (accessed 30 August 2010).

[8]   Frameline's tag line for the 30th festival in 2006 was 'Thirty Years of
Revolutionary Film'; for the 33rd festival in 2009, Frameline featured a
logo announcing the 'Power of Film'. Past festival programmes can be
searched at: http://www.frameline.org/festival/archive.aspx (accessed
31 August 2010).

Chapter 11

It's 'Oscar' Time in Asia!

The Rise and Demise of the

Asia-Pacific Film Festival, 1954-1972

Sangjoon Lee

On 17 December 2009, the 53rd Asia-Pacific Film Festival (APFF) was held, after a two-year hiatus, in Kaohsiung, the largest city in southern Taiwan. Taiwan's Ministry of Culture supported the festival to lend a hand to the southern region, where a typhoon had devastated the economy only a few months before, and to bring tourists back to this harbour city. Celebrities such as Jackie Chan, Andy Lau, Chi-ling Lin, and John Woo attended the occasion and raised money for charity. To revive the event's faded standing, the festival committee invited Dieter Kosslick, director of the Berlin International Film Festival since 2001, to supervise the official competition section. However, despite the Taiwanese government's support, the 53rd gathering attracted much less attention from the outside world than its more scintillating competitors — the Busan International Film Festival[1] and the Shanghai International Film Festival, which itself had eclipsed the Hong Kong International Film Festival, owner of the competitive edge in the 1980s and 1990s. Indeed, the APFF's presence in the region has been diminishing since the 1980s and, in the new millennium, the festival carries little clout in Asia's thriving film culture and industry. Nevertheless, as the region's first international film organisation, APFF was for at least two decades the single most important annual cinema event in Asia. Its parent organisation, the Federation of Motion Picture Producers in Asia-Pacific (FPA), played a vital role in invigorating the region's cinema network: co-producing films, exchanging stars, providing location shooting incentives, sharing the latest technical inventions and offering a forum for gauging the local state of filmmaking.

Despite its historical implications (the first festival was held in 1954), APFF has been overlooked, omitted, or simply forgotten in the chronicle of Asian cinema. While preparing for the festival's 50th anniversary in 2005, Dr Rais Yatim, Malaysia's Minister of Culture, lamented the paucity of primary materials available. He wrote that 'no one man or entity keeps in store the 50-year struggle and the success of the APFF' (APFF 2005: 2). Likewise, film festival studies in Asia, particularly of the pre-1990s period, have yielded few results and, except for Hong Kong-based film historian Shuk-ting Yau's brief, pioneering article (2003), the APFF has not yet received the appropriate scrutiny. The APFF does not comfortably fit within the rigid borders of national cinema. Indeed, it and other equally important festivals in Asia during the Cold War era were seldom bound to a single nation. They were mostly regionally constructed entities, closely tied to non-governmental organisations or the cultural policies of post-war U.S. hegemony.

Throughout its first 15 years, I argue, APFF was a political film festival in its own right. It had emerged in the exceedingly transformative post-war Asian sphere, which was apparently under U.S. dominion. As the years went by, however, the festival's geopolitical identity was converted from a U.S.-led cultural apparatus to a showcase of developing states. On top of that, the exploitation of markets and capital by regional cinema moguls during the 1960s ultimately yielded a golden age of motion picture studios. In the following pages, I trace the early years of the APFF from this perspective: how it was initiated, to what extent it interacted with regional politics, who the key players were and why its significance rapidly receded in the early 1970s.

It All Began with *Rashomon*

The festival's parent organisation, the FPA, was established in 1953 by the will of a Japanese film executive, Masaichi Nagata, president of Daiei Studio in Japan. His meetings with film executives in Indonesia, Hong Kong, the Philippines and Malaysia resulted in the formation of the FPA on 18 November. As film historian Poshek Fu points out, its aim was, at least on face value, 'to become the Asian equivalent of the Cannes and Venice Film Festivals, a prestigious event at which filmmakers competed and made business deals' (2008: 11). Within a year, the organisation's first event — then named the Southeast Asian Film Festival — was held in Tokyo's prestigious Kaikan with an inaugural address delivered by Takejiro Otani, president of Shochiku Studio. Unlike other nation-bound film festivals, this one was to be hosted neither in a single city nor a single country; instead, it adopted a peripatetic system under which no member country was allowed to accommodate the festival in

11.1. Akira Kurosawa's *Rashomon* won the grand prize at the 1951 Venice film festival and inspired filmmaking in other Asian nations. © Unknown

two consecutive years. At the FPA's third festival, Alexander Grantham, governor of Hong Kong, gave the host's welcome speech at the opening reception. Interestingly enough, he remarked that the festival 'teaches me some geography, for I had never realised before that Japan was part of Southeast Asia!' (*Report* 1956: 34). Whether or not this comment influenced the decision, the festival was renamed the Asian Film Festival after the Hong Kong event.

As the most influential film executive in Asia at the time, Nagata was well known for his Machiavellian business instincts. He began his career as a studio guide at Nikkatsu Studio and rose to become the president of Daiei Studio in a mere two decades. Nagata's sway over Asia was based on the success of Akira Kurosawa's *Rashomon*, a Daiei Studio product that won a grand prize at the 1951 Venice International Film Festival.

175

The ramifications of this honour at the time were far greater than we can realise now. It was, in fact, a sensation. Film critic Curtis Harrington, reviewing the Venice festival and its surprising grand prize winner, wrote:

> Such a discovery was the memorable event of last year's Venice Film Festival; from Japan, a country whose film production has been largely ignored by the Western world for many years, came the brilliant *Rashomon*, a film that, thus called to the attention of the world by winning the grand prize in competition with the best of American, French, and Italian films, has since been playing successfully in all the capitals of the world. (1952: 32)

A year later, in March 1952, *Rashomon* won the award for Best Foreign Language Film at that year's Oscars, which excited all of Asia. Indeed, at the 1956 festival in Hong Kong mentioned previously, Wan-tho Loke, president of Motion Picture and General Investments (MP&GI), gave Nagata the name, 'Mr. Motion Picture' of Southeast Asia (Report 1956: 38). *Rashomon*'s triumph influenced numerous regional film executives, directors and policymakers in Asia (figure 11.1). Hyeon-chan Ho, a renowned film critic in South Korea, claimed that Korean cinema 'should go to Venice and win the prize as Japan did a decade ago [...] to be recognised and receive awards, Korean cinema should put forward our local colour in tandem with an Asiatic "theme" that could appeal to Westerners' (1965: 65). With a similar result in mind, Shaw Brothers had dispatched a large number of delegates to the 1960 Cannes International Film Festival with the studio's *Ching nu yu hun* (*The Enchanting Shadow*, Han-hsiang Li, 1960, Hong Kong), the most expensive costume film ever produced by the studio.

Run Run Shaw aimed to expand his studio's limited market — Hong Kong and Malaysia — and sell films to the outside world. From *Rashomon*'s example, he well understood the weight of European film festivals and how a single film could change an industry. In line with Ho's proposal for South Korean cinema, Shaw's strategy was to place an accent on Asian themes — music, costumes, dance, and production design as well as the historical background of medieval China, preferably the Ming Dynasty. However, *The Enchanting Shadow* failed to attract significant attention either from festival participants or Euro-American distributors. Shaw came home empty-handed, but his efforts continued nonetheless.[2]

In post-war Asia, *Rashomon* and its producer, Nagata, gained respect and jealousy simultaneously from other nations. Japanese cinema, with the help of its victories from diverse international film festivals, promptly recaptured its dominion in the region. No longer subject to the American occupation authority's cultural policies or government censorship, the content of Japan's cinema diversified. Genres that had previously been taboo — such as *jidaigeki* (period film) and war pictures — received an enthusiastic reception from Japan's new-generation audiences (Kitamura 2010: 177-80). Nikkatsu Studio, after a long hiatus, re-entered the market in March 1953, and competition among the major studios — Toho, Shochiku, Daiei, Toei, Shin Toho, and Nikkatsu — became fierce (Schilling 2007: 12-29). Nagata's Southeast Asian tour in 1953 should therefore be situated in the context of the Japanese film industry's recovery of its pre-war condition, and the overall optimism of Japan's top film executives, particularly Nagata, whose industry supremacy had reached its zenith around that time. The establishment of the FPA was a collective aspiration of the Japanese film industry, a means for creating an Asian market through a cultural event.

Since the unexpected success of *Rashomon*, the number of Japanese film exports had increased tremendously, and motion pictures had risen to a prominent position among various export articles (Anon. 1954: 6). To help mitigate the nation's trade deficit, the Japanese film industry was encouraged to export more films to new destinations, including Southeast Asian countries and, if possible, India. Although the stated aims and objectives of the FPA were 'to promote the motion picture industry in the countries or territories of Southeast Asia [...] thereby contributing to the development of friendly relations among the participating nations' (*Report* 1956: 7), the Japanese film industry's ultimate goal was to expand and secure the market for its products. Representatives of South Korea — where Japanese cultural products had been prohibited since 1945 — were not invited to the inaugural meeting of the FPA, as the new country was not Japan's trade partner. Taiwan, on the other hand — another former colony, but relatively open to Japanese cultural products — participated from the beginning. South Korea eventually joined the FPA in 1956. Its belated arrival is particularly important at this point in the discussion, as the presence of South Korea transformed the organisation completely. In this period, the APFF entered a new phase: namely, the Cold War film festival.

The Cold War Film Festival

South Korea's participants in the FPA cooperated with and were supported by The Asia Foundation (TAF), a private non-profit organisation incorporated in the state of California. TAF was, in fact, fully funded by various arms of the U.S. government, particularly the Central Intelligence Agency (CIA).[3] In the immediate post-war period, TAF and other agencies supported many in the Asian cultural elite, including film personnel. Kuo-sin Chang, a Hong Kong delegate, committee treasurer of APFF and president of Asia Pictures, was an ardent pro-U.S. figure who founded the *Asia Press* with financial backing from the U.S. government by way of TAF and the Free Asia Association. In addition to Chang, Kwan-soo Kim, president of the Korean Motion Picture Association, Manuel de Leon of the Philippines' LVN Pictures, and the Indonesian film industry were all receiving grants or material support from American organisations. Tony Judt suggests that U.S. foreign cultural programmes 'employed 13,000 people and cost US$129 million' by 1953 (2005: 223). Although most of this expenditure went to the intellectual elites of Western Europe, Asia had emerged as a new front in the Cold War with the birth of the People's Republic of China (PRC) in 1949. Therefore, despite the Japanese film industry's somewhat different expectations, the FPA and its annual festival were increasingly subsumed in the cultural battle between two post-war powers, the U.S. and the Soviet Union.

Marijke de Valck delineates several rationales for film festivals: politics, ideology, and restoring the national film industry (Berlin), off-season tourism (Venice and Cannes), and rebuilding run-down cities (Karlovy Vary and Rotterdam) (2008: 14). Applying her categorisation, APFF can be grouped with Berlin as a 'political-purpose institution' and progeny of Cold War politics. According to Heide Fehrenbach, American authorities contributed financially for at least the first five years of the Berlin festival, although U.S. involvement was never officially disclosed (1995: 236). As one might expect, the festival therefore became a political front that explicitly placed its political and ideological messages in the spotlight. APFF fits comfortably under the rubric of political institution for the first few years of its existence. It can be distinguished from Berlin in a fundamental way, however, because the U.S. government was not directly involved. In place of the U.S., Japan led the organisation and, curiously, it was not U.S. authorities but individual participants who voluntarily made the festival an ideological battlefield. Nagata, as president of the FPA, proclaimed in 1956:

We can say proudly, without any other ulterior motives of a political and ideological background, but only through self-reliance, we have overcome insurmountable difficulties in maintaining this project and we are now here to hold the 3rd annual film festival. (*Report* 1956: 11)

What Nagata meant by 'political and ideological background' was the conflict between capitalism and communism. APFF would remain a politics-free event as long as its films came only from 'free Asia.' In that sense, ironically, the festival represents a remarkable political and ideological entity. Indonesian delegates Djamaludin Malik and Usmar Ismail proposed to include North Korea and the PRC at the first meeting in Tokyo, and this remained a contentious subject during the first and second forums of the festival in 1954 and 1955, respectively. Indonesia's proposal was rejected by other member countries, particularly Japan, Taiwan, and South Korea. Kwan-soo Kim, a South Korean delegate, stated in a local newspaper that the aim and purpose of FPA was to 'protect "free Asia" from the invasion of the communist force throughout the cinema' (Anon. 1956). An anti-communist consensus, particularly in South Korea and Taiwan, was sustained under military regimes. For example, the 1966 APFF, held in Seoul, ended in scandal when Satsuo Yamamoto, a socialist-inclined Japanese director, won the best director award for *Shonin no isu* (*The Burglar Story*, Japan, 1965). All of the South Korean festival jurors, including committee chair Sang-ok Shin, were summoned to court and investigated for violation of an anti-communist law. The jurors were interrogated by the National Intelligence Service and told that the committee should have rejected the film completely and deported the 'communist' director Yamamoto (An 2006: 424). This rather absurd incident clearly shows how the region's politics and ideological beliefs influenced regional film culture, even in the international cultural arena.

In light of such incidents, the APFF might be considered a vulnerable institution, and its identity has indeed changed several times due to the instability of the region's political atmosphere. With the significant waning of the Cold War in Asia, and a recession in the Japanese film industry at the beginning of the 1960s, the APFF was gradually transformed. The most conspicuous change arrived in the form of state intrusion, especially from South Korea and Taiwan, two developing nations. But along with such state intervention, the map of the regional film industry changed. Run Run Shaw might have been the least politically engaged producer in the FPA, but his Shaw Brothers

Studio probably benefitted the most from the APFF. During the 1960s, Shaw Brothers used the APFF both to promote its annual releases and as a conciliation site for co-productions, firmly seizing control of the industry.

It's 'Oscar' Time in Asia! Shaw Brothers Rule the APFF

Shaw Brothers, in Hong Kong film historian Kar Law's words, 'utilized festival awards to bolster the company's reputation in Southeast Asia' (2005: 167). Focussing on the role of Daiei and Shaw Brothers, Shuk-ting Yau claims that the history of the festival, especially between 1954 and 1969, demonstrates how 'Shaws established its close ties with Japan's Big Five, and replaced them as the leading studio in Asia' (2003: 279). In 1959, *Nan Guo Dian Ying* (*Southern Screen*) — Shaw Brothers' monthly magazine, which publicised the studio's stars, business plans, and films — proclaimed: 'It's "Oscar" time in the Asian movie field!' (Anon. 1959a: 15). In that year, the APFF was held in Kuala Lumpur, the capital of Malaysia. Thanks to the Shaw Malaya studio, three out of Malaysia's five festival entries were de facto Shaw Brothers' products. What's more, the studio either owned or was affiliated with over 100 theatres and numerous amusement parks in the country. The festival invited films from eight member countries — Taiwan, Hong Kong, South Korea, Indonesia, Japan, the Philippines, Singapore, and Malaysia — and Shaw Brothers' films were entered by three of them (Hong Kong, Singapore, and Malaysia). In the end, the studio's films won 13 awards, including best picture and best director for *Jiang shan mei ren* (*The Kingdom and the Beauty*, Hong Kong, 1959), directed by Han-hsiang Li (Anon. 1959b: 5).

The APFF performed two functions for Shaw Brothers. It helped demonstrate the company's status in the region and was useful in penetrating new territories, since award-winning films could be distributed and released with the festival label. The APFF's 'best picture' label demonstrably boosted sales, and nearly all APFF-awarded films proved to be highly profitable — at least in the Southeast Asian market. Thus, Run Run Shaw was a passionate supporter of the APFF throughout the early period. As the studio matured, Shaw gained more confidence. In 1960, a Shaw Brothers film won the festival's best picture award for the second year in a row: *Hou men* (*Back Door*, Hong Kong, 1960). Like the 1959 winner, it was directed by Han-hsiang Li. In 1961, Shaw noted that 'Japan and Hong Kong are both leaders in Asian cinema. With Japan's profound relationship with Southeast Asia and the similarities we share in our cultural backgrounds [...] we will have to seek total collaboration

11.2. In 1962, the Asia-Pacific Film Festival was held in Seoul, the first international cultural event hosted by South Korea. © Asia-Pacific Film Festival

with our Japanese counterpart' (Yau 2003: 282). However, regional politics and the film industry's rapid transformations soon changed the nature of the festival once again.

For most film executives in Asia's underdeveloped and newly independent countries, 'modernising the industry' and 'rationalising the system' were the catchphrases of the time. In the late 1950s, most Asian film entrepreneurs faced political instability, rising nationalist sentiment — which was often paired with the fear of communism — and foreign currency regulations that made it difficult to purchase or borrow raw film stock or modern filming equipment from America. Indonesian representatives Malik and Ismail closed their studios in 1957 due to persistent conflict with the government, while the Philippine film industry fell into recession. Kuo-sin Chang and his Asian Pictures stopped producing films in 1958, after the U.S. government withdrew support for his studio. As a result, Southeast Asia became under-represented at the APFF, which became an arena for what we now call East Asia. Shaw Brothers, as one might expect, turned its attention to East Asia, particularly to Taiwan but also to some extent South Korea, as well as the most attractive market, Japan. In this light, the Seoul gathering in 1962 is the most representative festival of the decade (figure 11.2). Its events show how politics and international relations affected the APFF and how film industry moguls in three countries collaborated, competed, and traded with each other.

The Rise of South Korea and Taiwan in the APFF

South Korea held its first APFF in May 1962. It was the first international cultural event that the new country, under the regime of a military government, had ever hosted. Every cultural and political sector in South Korea was expected to contribute. Nearly every day, national newspapers heralded the latest updates about the festival, where Koreans would 'proudly introduce our bright new country to the world'(Anon. 1962a). To celebrate the one-year anniversary of the coup d'état led by Park Chung Hee in 1961, the festival was scheduled to be held from 12 to 16 May. Although Hong Kong and Japan complained that Cannes also was to be held in May, the festival committee stuck with those dates, since the grand finale would be a celebration of the 16 May revolution. In April, the festival committee announced the full schedule. All participants were to visit the national army cemetery, Panmunjom, and the military academy. Park, the new president, would attend the closing ceremony to present the highest award, the best picture prize (Anon. 1962b). As evidence of the unpredictable direction of regional political transformation, however, Indonesia withdrew, becoming involved with the PRC and North Korea in discussions for a new Asian film festival that would include the countries outside of the FPA. Thailand also withdrew. Thus, Seoul hosted only five other member countries: Japan, Hong Kong, the Philippines, Singapore/ Malaysia, and Taiwan, which together sent approximately 80 delegates, directors, and performers along with 25 feature films.

The 1962 APFF was an important turning point for most of its regional participants, as well as for the festival itself, as an international sociopolitical and cultural entity. The Park government had initiated a five-year plan for economic development in 1961, and all political, economic and cultural sectors in South Korea, including the film industry, had dedicated themselves to the new nation's economic development. During the same period, the Shaw family relocated their motion picture business from Malaysia and Singapore to Hong Kong; the completion of the new Clearwater Studio, known as a 'movie town', also occurred in 1961. Shaw Brothers wanted to boost its volume of epic films, which had been popular in Southeast Asia's Mandarin-speaking communities, but Hong Kong, a tiny island, was simply not suitable for shooting those grand-scale genre films. Working the 1962 festival like a business meeting, Run Run Shaw contacted Taiwan's Central Motion Picture Corporation (CMPC), Japan's Daiei and Toho studios and South Korea's Shin Films for co-production agreements.

Recognising that the Seoul festival would be a watershed for Japan's economic and political re-normalisation with the South Korean government, Japanese cultural delegates were determined to show 'good will' to Korean civilians. In fact, Japan dispatched the largest number of delegates, 33, of all the member countries (Anon. 1962c). Just before the festival opened, Nagata announced that his company had decided to import a South Korean film, *Seong Chun-hyang* (*Chunhyang*), Sang-ok Shin's 1961 production, and would release it in six major Japanese cities.

At the festival itself, another Sang-ok Shin film, *Sarangbang sonnimgwa eomeoni* (*My Mother and Her Guest*, 1961) won the best picture prize. Park Chung Hee handed the trophy to Shin, owner of Shin Films, the country's most powerful studio at the time. The unexpected triumph of *My Mother and Her Guest* caused a nationwide sensation. It was the first time that a South Korean film had won the best picture award at the APFF. At this pivotal moment in the nation's film industry, South Korea became a keen festival enthusiast.

Two years later, in 1964, Taipei hosted the APFF for the first time. The Taiwanese film industry had blossomed in the 1960s. The state-owned CMPC's new executive, Henry Gong Hong, was the de facto initiator of a film genre called 'healthy realism', a type of melodrama 'with a strong civic message of conscientiousness, charity, hygiene, and environmentalism' (Yeh 2006: 161). *Ke nu* (*Oyster Girl*, Hsing Lee and Chia Li, Taiwan, 1964) and *Yang ya ren jia* (*Beautiful Duckling*, Hsing Lee, Taiwan, 1965) are two signature examples of healthy realism. *Oyster Girl* grabbed the best picture award at the Taipei festival, where Henry Gong Hong was chief of the jury.[4] Indonesia and Thailand were again absent, and the APFF had become more or less an East Asian film showcase. From 1964 onward, the region's two developing states — South Korea and Taiwan — and its regional media capital, Hong Kong, dominated the festival. As

Han-hsiang Li, a notable director of Mandarin-language cinema during the 1960s and a founder of Guolian Studio, reminisced,

> To be perfectly honest, many awards at the festival were dished out under the special manoeuvrings of producers, who were doing a lot of PR, taking people for meals, etc. The ulterior motive for organising a festival was to cement connections and help each other sell films. That was exactly how the particular festival was formed, under the arrangement of Daiei's representative Masaichi Nagata, Run Run Shaw, Korean director Sang-ok Shin and several prominent producers of the Philippines. (Ng 2007: 143)

By the late 1960s, the intensity of the Cold War in Asia had abated, and the American-led Asia-Pacific system had stabilised. The Japanese economy, as Washington had planned, had been a success story since the late 1950s, but the Japanese film industry was incurably wounded by the rising popularity of television. With its glorious studio era in the past, Japanese cinema suffered from a decline in national audience and the mass influx of Hollywood cinema. As a result, Japan's participation in the APFF was mostly passive, even while it maintained the presidency until the end of the 1960s. During that same period, most Southeast Asian countries expressed discontent with the FPA and APFF. After South Korea's second hosting, in 1966, when Shaw Brothers' *Lan yu hei* (*The Blue and the Black*, Ching Doe, Hong Kong, 1966) won the best picture award, and South Korea, Taiwan, and Hong Kong shared most of the other major awards, Southeast Asian countries began to consider creating their own event. With the inauguration of the Association of Southeast Asian Nations (ASEAN) in 1967, Indonesia, Malaysia, the Philippines and Thailand initiated an ASEAN sub-committee on film. That group staged the first Southeast Asian Film Festival in 1972. In 1974, Indonesia led the establishment of the ASEAN Motion Picture Producers Association (*Third Meeting* 1974).

Epilogue

By the early 1970s, Asian cinema again faced a time of transition. Daiei, the most powerful and influential motion picture studio in Asia during the 1950s, declared bankruptcy in 1971. Nagata, who had initiated the FPA, left the studio the following year. With Nagata's retirement and Daiei's impoverishment, Japan withdrew from the FPA committee completely in 1972. In that same year, the APFF was held in Seoul as a non-competition event. Japan sent only film prints, and no industry personnel attended. During the festival, Hong Kong, Taiwanese, and even some South Korean producers and executives seriously considered cancelling the festival, as no regional industry moguls were left except Shaw. However, APFF survived and has been maintained since then, although its initial promise and influence are gone.

At this point, film festivals in Asia entered a new phase. In 1978, with support from the Government Information Office, Taiwan launched its own 'Pan-Chinese' film competition, the Golden Harvest Awards. And a year earlier, the Hong Kong International Film Festival became, in Stephen Teo's words, Asia's first film festival 'devoted not to the commercial interests of the industry but to cinema as film culture and art' (2009: 109).

After Hong Kong's notable success as a showcase of Asian cinema, Japan initiated its own prestigious international film festival, led by the Ministry of Economy, Trade and Industry (METI). The ministry had been preparing for Tsukuba Expo, Japan's third world's fair after Expo '70 in Osaka and Expo '75 in Okinawa. To take advantage of potential synergies, the Tokyo International Film Festival was planned for 1985. Although Nagata passed away a few months before the festival, film industry moguls took charge of the festival committee, just as they had for the APFF in the 1950s. The collective intention of government and industry, however, was fundamentally different from what it had been in the past. From its inception, Tokyo aimed to project itself as an international film festival comparable to Cannes and Venice, and not necessarily limited to Asian cinema. In spite of its promising start, however, Tokyo failed to establish itself as a world-class event. Its status rapidly faded after the entrance of Busan in 1996.

Considering these more recent events, a history of the APFF remains important to understanding the current film festival phenomenon in Asia. From its roots as the Southeast Asian Film Festival, the Asia-Pacific Film Festival maintained a flexible identity — reacting, contradicting, negotiating, and transforming in accordance with regional politics.

Works Cited

An, Byeong-sub (1956) 'Asian Film Festival Scandal', *Shin Donga*, August, 30-2.
Anon. (1956) *Kyeonghyang Sinmun*, June 19.
___ (1959a) '"Oscar" Time in Asia: Sixth Asian Film Festival', *Southern Screen*, May, 15.

___ (1959b) 'Glittering Sixth Asian Film Festival', *Southern Screen*, June, 5.

___ (1960) 'The Colorful Cannes Film Festival', *Southern Screen*, June, 30-3.

___ (1962a) *Seoul Sinmun*, 10 January.

___ (1962b) *Donga Ilbo*, 10 May.

___ (1962c) *Nippon Times*, 15 May.

___ (1963) 'Shaw Brothers into World Market', *Southern Screen*, July, 3-4.

Asia-Pacific Film Festival 50th Anniversary Catalogue (2005). Kuala Lumpur, Malaysia: Ministry of Culture.

de Valck, Marijke (2007) *Film Festivals: From European Geopolitics to Global Cinephilia*. Amsterdam: Amsterdam University Press.

Fehrenbach, Heide (1995) *Cinema in Democratizing Germany: Reconstructing National Identity After Hitler*. Chapel Hill and London: University of North Carolina Press.

Fu, Poshek (2008) 'The Shaw Brothers Diasporic Cinema', in Poshek Fu (ed.) *China Forever: The Shaw Brothers and Diasporic Cinema*. Champaign, IL: University of Illinois Press, 1-26.

Harrington, Curtis (1952) 'Film Festival at Cannes', *The Quarterly of Film, Radio and Television*, 7, 1, 32-47.

Ho, Hyeon-chan (1965) 'Korean Cinema on the Road to the Venice', *Silver Screen*, August, 65.

Judt, Tony (2005) *Postwar: A History of Europe Since 1945*. New York: Penguin Books.

Kitamura, Hiroshi (2010) *Screening Enlightenment: Hollywood and the Cultural Reconstruction of Defeated Japan*. Ithaca: Cornell University Press.

Law, Kar and Frank Bren (2005) *Hong Kong Cinema: A Cross Cultural View*. Lanham: Scarecrow Press.

Ng, Grace (2007) 'Li Han Hsiang's *Long Men Zhen*', in Wong Ain-Ling (ed.) *Li Han-Hsiang, Storyteller*. Hong Kong: Hong Kong Film Archive, 138-57.

Report on the Third Annual Film Festival of Southeast Asia (1956). Hong Kong: The Executive Committee.

Schilling, Mark (2007) *No Borders, No Limits: Nikkatsu Action Cinema*. Farleigh, UK: FAB Press.

Stern, Sol (1967) 'A Short Account of International Student Politics and the Cold War with Particular Reference to the NSA, CIA, etc.', *Ramparts 5*, 9, 29-39.

Teo, Stephen (2009) 'Asian Film Festivals and their Diminishing Glitter Domes: An Appraisal of PIFF, SIFF and HKIFF', in Richard Porton (ed.) *Dekalog 3: On Film Festivals*. London: Wallflower Press, 109-21.

Third Meeting of the ASEAN Sub-Committee on Film: Official Report (November 1974). Jakarta, Indonesia.

Turner, Wallace (1967) 'Asia Foundation got CIA Funds', *The New York Times*, 22 March, 17.

Yau, Shuk-ting Kinnia (2003) 'Shaws' Japanese Collaboration and Competition as Seen Through the Asian Film Festival Evolution', in Wong Ain-ling (ed.) *The Shaw Screen: A Preliminary Study*. Hong Kong: Hong Kong Film Archive, 279-91.

Yeh, Yueh-yu Emilie (2006) 'Taiwan: Popular Cinema's Disappearing Act', in Anne Tereska Ciecko (ed.) *Contemporary Asian Cinema: Popular Culture in a Global Frame*. New York: Berg Press, 156-68.

Notes

1   On 24 February 2011, the Pusan International Film Festival officially changed its name to the Busan International Film Festival (BIFF). The move came a decade after the host city changed its name under new romanisation standards implemented in 2000.

2   It was not until 1963 that Run Run Shaw's endeavours finally succeeded. *Wu zetian* (*Empress Wu*, Han-hsiang Li, Hong Kong, 1963) won the cinematography award at Cannes in 1963 (Anon. 1960, 1963).

3   The Asia Foundation's CIA connections were not publicly acknowledged until 1967, when the truth was unveiled by a former CIA agent and printed by the leftist magazine *Ramparts* and, subsequently, *The New York Times* (Turner, 1967; Stern, 1967).

4   Wan-tho Loke, president of Cathay Organization (including MP&GI), and a rival of the Shaw family, was killed in a calamitous plane crash during the festival. Taiwan's Fang Long, a director at Taiwan Studio, along with other directors and executives from the Philippines, were killed as well. This tragic accident changed the regional film industry. The diminishment of MP&GI's film production department contributed to Shaw Brothers' domination in the region.

Chapter 12

Programming African Cinema at the New York African Film Festival

Mahen Bonetti

Africa was making American headlines in the 1980s: in the news, on special television segments, in documentaries. But when American audiences turned on their TV sets in the 1980s, most often it was not African 'world musicians' (as the genre had recently been termed) who appeared on screen; nor was it Spike Lee, who had just splashed into Hollywood and was helping to popularise conversations about 'African-American' (again, a new term at the time) culture, identity, and roots. Instead, when it came to Africa, Americans were bombarded with images of malnourished African children, suffering from famine in the Horn of Africa. They saw AIDS and war. Yes, these were realities of Africa at the time, and devastating ones at that. But the depiction was so one-sided. As a proud young African living in New York, I was disturbed to realise that there were few, if any, African voices present in these depictions of our continent, or the ensuing conversations.

I became totally obsessed with the dichotomy between the Africa that I experienced during my youth, and the Africa that I saw in the American media. I felt angry, frustrated and most of all ashamed. I urgently needed to find a way to show my daughter, my friends and the people of New York City the Africa in which I grew up — to give them a more multifaceted depiction of the continent that shaped me into the person I had become. I believed wholeheartedly that audiences were much smarter than the media took them to be, and that many people must have been looking for alternative representations of Africa. And what representations there could be! Africa, though suffering through the issues we saw on TV, was at the same time the source of much of our cultural nourishment in North America. Of course, we can all trace the unique sounds of American musical genres such as jazz, R&B, rock and hip-hop to their obvious African ancestry; but there was much more waiting to be introduced to the mainstream. The cultural context seemed ripe for presenting Africa in a new light. I turned my thoughts to developing African cultural events.

During this time, distributor Dan Talbot was introducing African cinema to American audiences, along with other foreign films. Africa's unique contributions to the art of filmmaking were largely overlooked at the time, but still there was a limited number of screenings. The few that I was able to see — at the New York Film Festival (NYFF) and at the Thalia Theater — stuck with me. I did not immediately make the connection that cinema was the medium where Africans could challenge the pre-existing notions of Africa — where they could speak for themselves instead of being dictated to — but still, I was intrigued.

It was the Locarno Film Festival, however, that really inspired the creation of the New York African Film Festival (NYAFF). I was in Locarno in the summer of 1989. I went to a presentation of *Sex, Lies, and Videotape* (Steven Soderbergh, U.S., 1989) and as I was flipping through the festival programme, I saw the headline, 'Thirty Years of African Cinema'. Imagine! I had no idea that there had been such a body of work coming out of my own continent. Suddenly, I realised what amazing potential there was in African cinema. We come from an oral tradition, and you find storytelling everywhere in Africa. With cinema, I realised, the narrators were speaking from first-hand experience. We were telling our own stories. If this cinema was substantial enough to comprise a programme within a festival, perhaps it could also sustain a festival all its own in New York... I quickly tracked down the woman who had organised the Africa programme at Locarno (Silvia Voser, who also produced Djibril Diop Mambéty's films), who gave me advice and a few good contacts. The ball was rolling.

There had been a few other programmes of African cinema in the 1980s and 1990s, but it is really the Pan-African Film Festival of Ouagadougou (FESPACO), the world's largest festival of African cinema, that has most influenced the New York African Film Festival. Our relationship with FESPACO began in 1993, when I travelled to Ouagadougou to drum up some interest in NYAFF and to invite filmmakers to attend. At first, I felt that the filmmakers at FESPACO perhaps did not know what to make of me — an ambitious young woman, completely unknown to the participants, not from a Francophone country (I am from Sierra Leone), not even from a country with a film industry — but it was at FESPACO that I began forging relationships with the key players of African cinema, including the legendary director Ousmane Sembène. NYAFF's relationship with FESPACO progressed quickly from there; four years later, I was chosen as a member of the jury for feature films at

FESPACO 1997.

All of this, in a nutshell, is how the New York African Film Festival came into being. African Film Festival, Inc. (AFF) — the organisation of which I am founder and executive director, which presents the NYAFF every year — held an inaugural festival of contemporary and classic African films in 1993, in collaboration with the Film Society of Lincoln Center (FSLC). The push for initial support of the festival was challenging: there was very little evidence to support my conviction that there was an audience in the U.S. for African film and that there were enough films being produced on the continent to sustain such a film festival.

Fortunately, we were able to prove that there were works to screen and audiences to attract. The 1993 New York African Film Festival proved to be a landmark event that established an innovative way to present African films and cultivate new audiences. Prior to the first NYAFF, African cinema was relegated to art house presentations for niche audiences. As such, general audiences had limited access to it. Yet the U.S. has one of the largest populations of people of African descent in the world — how could these people remain left out? NYAFF specifically targeted local black audiences, taking what I call an 'African courtyard' approach: we approached community leaders and gatekeepers of black communities throughout the New York area, gave our greetings and told them of our programme, and requested that they help us reach their communities, to make sure they felt welcome in our programme. We also specifically targeted local media outlets that actually reach these communities. We were the first to actively engage local black audiences, particularly those who were not a part of the art house scene — and we continue to do this every year. I should mention that through all of our initial struggles to get NYAFF on its feet, Richard Peña of the Film Society of Lincoln Center was always very encouraging; he gave me confidence to push forward. He and FSLC still give us incredible support.

In 1993, there was no precedent for a U.S. film festival focussed entirely on African cinema, so there were limited examples against which to measure our first festival. We were able to look to a retrospective that MoMA had done on Ousmane Sembène in 1973, and certainly there were African filmmakers like Sembène and Mambéty represented in New Directors New Films and the seminal NYFF at Lincoln Center. For the most part, though, we were working with a vision, but not a template, for what we hoped to accomplish: the most extensive celebration of African filmmaking ever held in New York. We presented the first festival under the banner theme 'Modern Days, Ancient Nights: Thirty Years of African

Filmmaking'. The festival included three panel discussions: one on the films of Sembène; one on the dialogue between African and African-American filmmakers; and a more general panel on contemporary African cinema. We exhibited paintings and sculptures from 10 countries at the Frieda and Roy Furman Gallery at the Walter Reade Theater, Lincoln Center, which set a precedent for pairing fine arts with film, one that we continue today. Our audiences that first year were almost 50 per cent black — and these were not only the 'usual suspects,' the academics and artists. We had audiences from communities throughout the city, from all sorts of backgrounds and socioeconomic levels and walks of life. This, of course, was a revelation to the few distributors of African film that existed at the time, none of which had previously had faith that such audiences existed at all. It helped to shift the commonly held assumption that African film, as a foreign genre, was something intended for niche audiences formed mostly of art house cinéphiles and academics. The festival made the front page of *The New York Times'* Arts and Leisure section — with a beautiful, half-page still image from *Yeelen* (*Brightness*, Souleymane Cissé, Mali/Burkina Faso/France/West Germany/UK, 1987).

With its quick success, NYAFF became a biennial event. As more and more high-quality films were coming out of Africa and the African diaspora, and audiences were growing in New York, we expanded our programming to include year-round screenings. In 1999 we began presenting NYAFF as an annual event. Today, it is one of the largest and most popular film festivals dedicated to African film and video in the U.S. The festival has also responded to the increasing demand from American and international audiences for films that experiment with storytelling techniques and African themes, that synthesise African and Western aesthetics. An excellent example is Jean-Pierre Bekolo's film *Les saignantes* (*The Bloodiest*, France/Cameroon, 2005), a superbly photographed, stylishly edited sci-fi-action-horror hybrid that follows two young femmes fatales as they set out to rid a futuristic country of its corrupt and sex-obsessed male leaders. *Les saignantes* had its New York première at the NYAFF in 2005.

Now, almost two decades after its inception, NYAFF has become an essential part of the American cultural and media landscape, where there are still too few opportunities to view African media (figure 12.1). It is a hub for African filmmakers seeking distribution in the U.S., lovers of film from the African diaspora, American independent film houses and television networks and people of all ages who use African film as a window onto African culture. We do our work each year in celebration of new stories emerging from the continent, with the hope that we can redress the marginalisation of African diaspora film in this country. By presenting cutting-edge films and videos from the continent and its diaspora, NYAFF demonstrates to American audiences that African culture is not a static entity, but part of the vibrant and sophisticated global marketplace of ideas and products. Once again, I recall the work of veteran filmmaker Djibril Diop Mambéty: although influenced particularly by the French new wave, Mambéty brought a distinct African sensibility to his films. His classic 1973 drama *Touki Bouki* (Senegal), considered by many to be among the greatest of African films, transcends any label or categorisation, just as Mambéty himself is renowned not only as an African filmmaker, but as an independent, creative-minded director with a global reach — one of the most innovative filmmakers of his generation.

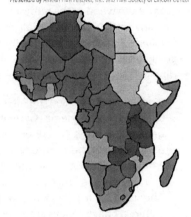

12.1. The New York African Film Festival celebrates the great continental diversity of African cinema. © New York African Film Festival

Much of the success NYAFF has experienced has been due to the growing demystification of African cinema. Traditionally, American audiences simply have not had much exposure to films made by Africans and, because of this, such audiences often are not accustomed to the themes, subjects, aesthetics, and narrative styles that are a part of many of the films coming out of Africa. This unfamiliarity has relegated African cinema to existence as an obscure, art-house-oriented cinema. On top of that, even under the umbrella of art house film, African cinema is often seen in an extremely essentialised manner and treated as a genre within itself, as opposed to cinema that spans a range of genres and appeals to a diverse audience with different interests and tastes.

In fact, there is great debate among filmmakers from Africa and the diaspora about whether the terms 'African cinema' and 'African filmmaker' convey any useful meaning at all. In AFF's publication *Through African Eyes, Volume 2: Dialogues with the Directors*, Mama Keïta — a filmmaker originally from Senegal, with Guinean and Vietnamese roots, currently residing in France — summarises the issue well:

> It is unusual for one to refer to European cinema. One talks of French cinema, German cinema, and Spanish new generation, but it is very odd to identify Almodóvar or any other director from Europe as a 'European cineaste'. And yet, one eliminates all the differences between Malian and Senegalese, Burkinabé and Chadian, Mauritanian and Angolan [...] It is all Africa without differentiating among cultures. I have always stood up to say, 'I am not an African filmmaker, I am a filmmaker'. (2010: 53)

Congolese filmmaker Zeka Laplaine further adds:

> They say the director gives his nationality to his film. For what it is worth, I am African and I am a filmmaker, but I do not like to be called an African filmmaker. It makes no sense. I am a Congolese filmmaker or simply a filmmaker. The phrase 'African filmmaker' is diminishing. This label is not based on any justifiable specificity. Are we all alike? Do we all do the same things? Do we all see the world in the same way and have the same background? No! Do we generally make films with modest resources? Perhaps, but that is not a choice. (2010: 53)

Some argue that it would be more appropriate to label African films according to region, or colonial roots (based on language spoken). Angolan filmmaker Zézé Gamboa suggests a breakdown:

> I would say that there are at least five basic kinds of writing in African cinema. When you go to a movie theater, you can tell if the film is from North, West, Central, Southern, or Lusophone Africa just by looking at the timing and the rhythm of the film [...] The oral tradition is almost the same across the continent, but in terms of structure, Lusophone

scripts in general are more urban, and that forces you to have a faster speed and rhythm than if you were in the village. For instance, if you look at the madness of the traffic here in Luanda, if you want to shoot, you almost don't have to move the camera, and it will still show the chaos and that kind of detail. This differentiates Lusophone cinema from West Africa 'Calebasse' cinema, which is more rural and takes place in the villages. In South Africa the cinema also evolves a lot around the city and urban violence. (2010: 43)

The difficulty in categorising all films produced (or directed? or with local content?) in Africa (or in Africa and the African diaspora?) as 'African films' is further compounded by the emergence — some would say, explosion — of the popular movie industry throughout the continent. The clear leader, of course, is Nollywood, the Nigerian popular film industry, which has become the third largest producer of films in the world (in terms of quantity produced each year), behind only Hollywood and Bollywood. Most Nollywood films, however popular they may be in Nigeria and other parts of Africa, are low-budget, and often of rather low technical quality — leading them to be left out of the international festival circuit, and often to be considered an entity distinct from the general notion of 'African film'. Nevertheless, some Nollywood films have received immense critical acclaim, including *Araromire* (*The Figurine*, Kunle Afolayan, 2010, Nigeria), which NYAFF presented in 2010. And there are other similar, though substantially smaller (and often still struggling) popular film industries throughout the continent; for example, Riverwood in Kenya, and the heretofore-unnamed Ghanaian popular movie scene. There are even those who speak of the potential for 'Sollywood' in Sierra Leone!

Then, there are filmmakers who use Nollywood aesthetics to produce incisive experimental films; in 2011, NYAFF presented Zina Saro-Wiwa's *Phyllis* (2011, Nigeria), a low-budget silent film that explores the gothic possibilities of Nollywood through the story of a psychic vampire who lives in Lagos. Another fascinating experimental hybrid is Teco Benson and Jakob Boeskov's short, *Dr. Cruel* (2010, Nigeria), whose world première took place at NYAFF in 2010. This tongue-in-cheek Scandinavian-Nigerian-American co-production follows the interrogation of a white oil executive in a hideout somewhere in Nigeria. *Dr. Cruel* is an exceptional example of the influence Nollywood is having worldwide, as opposed to the oft-cited influence of world cinemas on African film. Its distinct visual and narrative appropriation of Nigerian cinema (not to mention its unique distribution model, which unfortunately is beyond the scope of this essay) draws both foreign filmmakers and foreign audiences to the form.

Undeniably, African cinema is complex, rich, and diverse beyond the labels and assumptions attached to it by Western critics and audiences. However, we programmers must also take some blame. The misunderstanding of African cinema has, in part, been perpetuated by programmers. There is oftentimes a tendency for us to fall into the trap of perceiving certain films as emblematic of what we consider to be African cinema; in other words, of essentialising the continent, and presenting what is predictable, or even stereotypical. It is true that African filmmakers are known for using Africa's rich cultural fabric to weave timeless stories that can be passed on for generations: African storytellers have been highly esteemed since long before the invention of cameras, and their craft often was central to the daily lives of their communities. As others have noted, the griot cultures that grew out of — and are so specific to — African societies have deeply influenced cinematic language in Africa. However, the form that a contemporary griot takes, and the form of his or her stories, is something that has been continually evolving since the first African films were produced more than 50 years ago.

Since programmers are responsible for presenting most screenings of African cinema in the U.S. and throughout the world, what people know of this cinema comes for the most part from programmers' exposure to early pioneers such as Sembène, Mohammed Lakhdar-Hamina, Ababacar Samb-Makharam, Mustapha Alassane, and Souleymane Cissé. It is fitting that these masters of African cinema be revered, and that their works continue to be accessible to wide audiences; however, by programming African film based on the classics, programmers run the risk of excluding works that do not fit into this most basic model of African cinema.

This can be dangerous: audiences that see only films that fit the classic model lack exposure to the incredible breadth of narratives and approaches that exist within African cinema. This can profoundly affect an audience's understanding not only of the genre, but of the subject matter — which is particularly risky when the subject matter concerns a continent whose representation is so often controlled not from within, but by outsiders. For example, it is not uncommon for African filmmakers to tell stories that recall the precolonial times of African societies. However, more often than not, those people with little familiarity or exposure to African cinema tend to think that these precolonial trajectories epitomise

African filmmaking. The images that they repeatedly see, while more realistic and, in my opinion, more respectable than those of mainstream American media, inform their understandings of the entire body of film from the whole of Africa and, as an extension, their understanding of the continent and its people.

Thus, many African filmmakers now see it as their personal duty to diversify these images and approaches by politicising the modern history of Africa and its peoples, and also by using cinema not merely for mass consumption, but to help bolster the development of postcolonial African cultures and consciousnesses. They also stress their solidarity with progressive filmmakers in other parts of the world.

The emerging generation of African filmmakers has moved even further, using narrative, technical and aesthetic approaches to create films in a multitude of genres and very diverse styles, which challenge notions of African cinema and the people to whom it gives voice. In the words of Souleymane Cissé: 'African filmmakers' first task is to show that people here are human beings and to help people discover the African values that can be of service to others. The following generation will branch out into other aspects of film' (Thackway 2003: 39). Indeed, it has. We still see traces of early influences from the French New Wave, Italian Neo-Realism, Brazilian Cinema Novo, the theatre of Bertolt Brecht etc.; but this new generation is also bringing something entirely fresh to the tradition of African cinema. In addition, with steady increases in migration, access to new technology, and wider flows of communication and information sharing, African cinema currently finds itself continuing to push the envelope not simply through narrative structure but also through film style.

Among the brightest of the younger generation's stars is Wanuri Kahiu, a young Kenyan filmmaker who brings a new level of innovation both to her production and her storytelling. Her first film, *From a Whisper* (Kenya, 2009), is a film about the bombing of the U.S. embassy in Nairobi in 1998, which sources real footage from security cameras and weaves it into a beautifully narrated fictional story. The film had its U.S. première at the 2009 NYAFF. For her next film, *Pumzi* (South Africa/ Kenya, 2009), Kahiu used the set of the Hollywood blockbuster *District 9* (Neill Blomkamp, U.S./New Zealand/Canada/South Africa, 2009) to make a futuristic sci-fi short, which depicts Africa as the final frontier after humans have depleted their natural resources. But Kahiu is only one of many emerging filmmakers — along with Daouda Coulibaly, Zina Saro-Wiwa, and Rungano Nyoni — pushing African cinema toward what is certainly an even brighter future.

Both veteran and emerging filmmakers who have witnessed the legacy of war and subsequent migration are using film to address issues that are, in some cases, dramatically reshaping the face of the African continent. Current African films such as *Thembi* (Jo Menell, South Africa, 2010), *Conversations on a Sunday Afternoon* (Khalo Matabane, South Africa, 2006), and *Solo andata — Il viaggio di un Tuareg* (*One Way — A Tuareg Journey*, Fabio Caramaschi, Italy/Niger, 2010) are exploring personal narratives of displacement, experiences of xenophobia, homophobia, and individual discoveries. These films also act as allegories for Africa's postcolonial development and quest for true independence. In countries such as South Africa, where independence and subsequent national identity are merely one generation old, we see an explosion of films that personalise voyages in search of reconciliation and understanding: *Congo My Foot* by Okpene Ojang, Kyle O'Donoghue, and Dylan Valley (South Africa/Congo, 2008); *Triomf* by Michael Raeburn (South Africa/France/UK, 2008); *The Prodigal Son* by Kurt Orderson (South Africa, 2008); and others.

Clearly, African cinema is not a genre to be easily defined — if it is a genre at all. For this reason, it is up to us, the programmers, to move beyond the familiar and comfortable and steadily pay more attention to emerging directors who are exploring different ways of storytelling. This is important not only to ensure that our programmes stay current, but also to properly honour and convey the tradition of innovation set forth by those who pioneered African cinema, as well as the emerging generation that carries this tradition into the future.

NYAFF addresses the challenges of programming African cinema in a few key ways. For one, we provide as much exposure to African cinema as we can. Through partnerships with schools, government agencies, national and international institutions and community-based organisations (including our longstanding relationships with the United Nations, UNESCO, the Film Society of Lincoln Center, the Brooklyn Academy of Music, the French Institute/Alliance Française, FESPACO, the International Center for Photography, and the Schomburg Center for Research in Harlem, to name a few), AFF provides year-round programming. In addition to the annual New York African Film Festival, we also present a free outdoor summer series, a national travelling series, an in-school educational programme, and regular community-based screenings. Many of our screenings are accompanied by panel discussions featuring renowned critics, artists, and scholars, question and answer sessions with filmmakers, lectures and workshops. The panel discussion at NYAFF 2011, entitled 'African Diaspora: The Genesis', explored the voluntary and forced migration of African people, transatlantic slave routes, and the significant contributions of the African diaspora to host societies. These panel discussions feature prominent scholars, artists and critics (past panellists have included veteran filmmaker Harry Belafonte and rising Kenyan director Wanuri Kahiu, for example). Furthermore, we enhance our film screenings with interactive elements, such as African dance and drum workshops with master teachers, arts and crafts workshops and samplings of African cuisine. In doing so, we seek to encourage audiences to become more than observers: to become actively engaged participants, invested in the films themselves, but also in the subjects they address and the voices they represent.

The films we programme are, of course, key to our mission. As we work to expand public perception of what constitutes Africa and African film, NYAFF exhibits the breadth of African cinema by presenting films of as many genres and countries of origin as possible. These diverse films are united by the festival's theme, which changes each year to reflect an issue or event of international importance. For example, in 2000, NYAFF was presented under the theme 'African Women in the Media: From Griot to Filmmaker', which showcased the work of eight female directors, including the first black African woman filmmaker, Safi Faye. Spanning various subjects and styles, the films in the series addressed issues concerning African women with startling honesty, humour and emotion. It expressed an overarching message that African women have been and continue to be a powerful and vital source of artistic expression in cinema. In 2004, we programmed 'Let's Talk about Sex', a series that explored Africa's emerging dialogue on sexuality and gender identity. In 2007, we spotlighted Seke Somolu of Nigeria, Teboho Mahlatsi of South Africa, and Brahim Fretah of Morocco in a programme titled 'Young Rebels', which featured emerging directors who continue to create national cinema languages with global themes. Also featured that year was a mid-career retrospective of Fanta Regina Nacro from Burkina Faso. In 2009, as part of the focus on 'Africa in Transition', we spotlighted three up-and-coming Kenyan filmmakers — Lupita Nyong'o, Judy Kibinge and Wanuri Kahiu — who represent a growing female presence in African film, while paying homage to veteran filmmakers Jean-Marie Téno and Mahamat-Saleh Haroun.

Looking forward, as the African continent continues to experience the displacement of populations by transnational economic forces, war and environmental degradation, many Africans must forge new transitional cultural identities, often abroad or in increasingly overpopulated cities. Thus, a new African cinema is being created as an important forum to address shifting cultural identities, human rights and social justice. There is a growing willingness of African media-makers to tackle controversial contemporary subjects, from female genital cutting and HIV/AIDS to land reform. Turning away from African cinema's early focus on colonialism, young filmmakers — many of them women — are exploring new themes, genres, and previously taboo subjects with radically original sensibilities. One of Africa's brightest emerging directors, Osvalde Lewat-Hallade, makes films, as she describes, 'whose subject matter makes you think, and that challenge the established thought patterns' (*Through African Eyes* 2010: 119). She tackles tough subjects with an incisive, yet sensitive documentary approach: *Une affaire de nègres* (*Black Business*, Cameroon, 2009) tells the story of Cameroonian families who are victims of government disappearances, and who are still seeking to find out what happened to their loved ones; *Un amour pendant la guerre* (*A Love During the War*, Congo/Cameroon, 2006) tackles the senseless killings and brutal rapes that have become hallmarks of the on-going conflict in the Democratic Republic of the Congo.

Over the past 20 years, the success of NYAFF continually reminds the public that there is an incredible body of work coming out of Africa and the African diaspora. Fifty years in the making, African cinema is now a conduit through which a crucial inter- and intra-national conversation is taking place; therefore, its visibility in the mainstream is now, more than ever, paramount to the health of the global society. It is my hope that, as African cinema continues to grow and thrive and as demand for African films continues to build in the international community, programmers throughout the U.S. and around the world will take responsibility not only for presenting African cinema, but also for contributing to the vitality of this vibrant conversation. Through film, Africa has found a new voice.

Works Cited

Thackway, Melissa (2003) *Africa Shoots Back: Alternative Perspectives in Sub-Saharan Francophone African Film*. Bloomington: Indiana University Press.

Through African Eyes, Volume 2: Dialogues with the Directors (2010). New York: African Film Festival.

Chapter 13

The Spirit of the Hiroshima International Animation Festival, 1985-2010

Sayoko Kinoshita

Just like many other festivals, the Hiroshima International Animation Festival was established after a very difficult gestation period. Here, then, is the story of what happened.

In 1972, for the first time, my partner Renzo Kinoshita and I learned how to submit our own work to an international film festival abroad. We entered our nine-minute animation, *Made in Japan*, into the New York International Animation Film Festival. There, we were fortunate to receive the grand prize, and we returned to Japan with the belief that we could now live successful lives as independent animation filmmakers. But soon reality struck. In Japan, during the 1970s, this was not to be. We were sorely disappointed. Then, we hit upon a new idea: we should not just make films. We ought to start an innovative movement to promote animation. A film festival could display the diversity of animation art as well as its attractiveness to many professional people — producers, sponsors, commercial agencies, distributors, journalists, curators — as well as the general public.

We set our minds to creating an international animation festival in our country. For 12 years we travelled all over Japan looking for sponsors. It was very challenging for us to explain the cultural significance and artistic profundity of animation, especially to people who seemed dedicated mainly to the pursuit of profit. At that time, in the early 1970s, animation was generally recognised only as TV entertainment for children. From the very beginning, we had to explain that animation offers a broad spectrum of expression. However, because we wanted to gain recognition in Japan for animation as an art form, we plunged ahead, determined to launch the first animation festival in Asia.

Our relationship with the city of Hiroshima goes back to 1978, when Renzo and I decided to depict the atomic bomb disaster through animation. We visited the city in early August to do research and collect material. Renzo and I wanted to experience the same kind of atmosphere that existed when the atomic bomb was dropped — the very hot summer morning, the burning sunshine, the flowing river, the sky, the air. We also visited the Hiroshima Peace Memorial Museum to uncover documentary material for our film. But it was from survivors that we learned about the grim reality of the atomic bombing; that it was a hell on earth, that it was difficult to recount and not something that can be described easily by an entertainment medium like manga anime.

Renzo and I felt as if we had been pelted with stones and we returned to Tokyo heartbroken. We felt a deep regret for visiting Hiroshima near the time of the Peace Memorial Ceremony of 6 August. We sensed that we had offended the survivors. At the same time, our encounters only further convinced us of the importance of making our Hiroshima film. We worked desperately. We thought it was our mission as independent animation filmmakers to make it. The production funds came from our own savings, earned by making commercials and TV programmes. It was a big gamble we were taking. If the people of Hiroshima did not accept our film, we would not be able to release it to the public, and the funds that we invested — equivalent to the cost of a house — would all be lost. At last, when the film was completed, holding our breath, we sent it to our friend in Hiroshima who worked in educational film distribution, asking him to preview it. We waited for the reactions of people in Hiroshima. No response. One week went by. Two weeks. Three weeks. We were afraid to ask our friend what was happening. One month passed.

Then, suddenly, newspapers and TV reporters, magazine writers and all kinds of mass media representatives flooded into our studio in Tokyo. They praised our work highly. When our friend had taken out his 16mm projector to preview some other works with his colleagues, he'd noticed our film print on the shelf, forgotten. So, he screened our work for the first time, and was so surprised and impressed that he immediately held a press conference. That 10-minute animated documentary, *Pica Don* (1978), without any dialogue, revealed the power of animation.

Our friend appreciated the fact that we had made an animated film about Hiroshima. Sometime later, when he kindly asked if there was anything he could do for us in return, we told him that there were many more inspirational animation films in the world and that it was our dream to hold an animation festival in order to introduce these wonderful works to Japan. He said he would help us appeal to key citizens and city officials to create such a festival in Hiroshima. And he energetically began introducing us to many important people there. Who, you might ask, is this helpful friend? His name is Shotaro Tanabe. Over the years, he has continued to play a significant role in our festival's progress. In fact, he appeared in a wheelchair at the closing ceremony of the 2010 Hiroshima festival, presented the Audience Prize and received loud applause from the public.

In the early 1980s, as we plugged along, trying to put our festival together, the Japanese animation community started to mock, calling us 'Unrealistic dreamers'. Thus, we decided to leave Japan. Renzo began to explore the possibility of working in the U.S. In autumn 1983, Renzo was in New York preparing for our move. Just a few days before he was to return to Tokyo to take me to New York, I received a telephone call from the city of Hiroshima that would totally change our future. An official asked if I could really organise an international animation festival in Hiroshima if the city would give its approval. A few days later, another Hiroshima official visited our studio. I described three different types of festival we could mount, depending on available budget. I told Renzo the news when he returned to Tokyo on 26 December but, as usual, we thought it was another long shot. We had experienced similar scenarios before. However, it was perhaps because my heart was filled with the anticipation of moving to New York that I also had a feeling that this time our dream might — just might — come true.

The new year came. Another Hiroshima city official visited us in early January 1984. And, wonder of wonders, we were invited to submit our formal request to establish an international animation festival, and also to meet the mayor, who had already determined to accept our plan. In April, the Hiroshima City Council officially adopted a resolution to hold a festival biennially, starting in August 1985, as a project commemorating the 40th anniversary of the atomic bombing of Hiroshima.

Renzo had been a board member of the Association Internationale du Film d'Animation (ASIFA) since 1979. He had also established a national branch, ASIFA-Japan, in 1981. Thus, we set up our festival under an agreement that ASIFA-Japan, as representative of the animation industry, would be responsible for programming and for running the festival. The city of Hiroshima would be responsible for fundraising and administrative assistance.

In 1985, there were not many international festivals dedicated to animation. ASIFA endorsed four: one held in France (Annecy International

Animated Film Festival), one in Yugoslavia (Zagreb World Festival of Animated Film), one in Bulgaria (Varna World Festival of Animated Film), and another in Canada (Ottawa International Animation Festival).

During the 12 years of our struggle to create a festival in Japan, many animation filmmakers and professionals heard about our efforts and offered us encouragement. All ASIFA board members and many animation people from around the world congratulated us on the establishment of the festival. For many years, Renzo had been making reports to ASIFA about the progress of our preparations as well as about our festival policy. Thus, at the ASIFA board meeting during the 1984 Zagreb festival, a resolution was taken unanimously to approve the Hiroshima International Animation Festival as the first ASIFA-endorsed festival in Asia, on condition that the festival should be organised according to the rules and regulations of ASIFA-endorsed competitive international festivals. It was exceptional to receive such approval from the get-go. The mayor of Hiroshima served as the festival president, Renzo as the festival producer, and I as the festival director. Because everything had to be started from scratch, Renzo and I tried to ensure all the practical and policy issues were clearly defined, considering them groundwork for the future.

The city of Hiroshima and ASIFA clearly shared the same goal; that is, to contribute to the achievement of perpetual peace through cross-cultural exchange and the promotion of animation. However, in spite of Hiroshima being famous for its Peace Memorial Ceremony, there arose significant conflicts in organising a festival as the city's first international project; for example, between art and bureaucracy, between international viewpoints and local practices, and between men and the appointment of a woman as leader. As an outsider who had no previous connection with Hiroshima, I needed a strong will to execute leadership of the festival. In various ways, it was still a conservative time. And it was an old-fashioned time, when even fax machines were not yet popular. We relied mainly on postal letters to communicate with filmmakers abroad, or we sent telexes and telegrams when we were in a hurry. Because many animation people from around the world supported me, I was confident of success. Still, it is no exaggeration to say that I had to be ready to risk my professional life in order to establish a high-quality festival that would benefit, above all, the filmmakers themselves.

Many Japanese animators were both happy and excited about the news of the festival. Yet, there were also some people who remained sceptical spectators. When we announced that Paul Grimault (France)

13.1. Audiences flock to the entrance for the first edition of the Hiroshima festival in 1985, the culmination of years of hard work by founders Sayoko and Renzo Kinoshita. © Hiroshima International Animation Festival

would attend as the honorary president, and when the selection committee actually started to work, everyone became more cooperative. We received 451 entries for our first festival, Hiroshima 1985. With the participation of Jules Engel (U.S.) as one of the committee members, we were able to have competition programmes of an extremely high quality, which included films from a variety of genres, from experimental artistic works to commercials and mass entertainment forms. I am proud to say that our competition programmes have been consistently outstanding ever since that first edition (figure 13.1).

At Hiroshima 1985, Raoul Servais (Belgium), Bratislav Pojar (Czechoslovakia), Ishu Patel (Canada), Wang Shu Chen (China), Robi Roncarelli (U.S.), Shigeo Fukuda (Japan), and Yoji Kuri (Japan) attended as the international jury members. Osamu Tezuka's *Broken Down Film* (Japan, 1985) won the grand prize and Richard Condie's *The Big Snit* (Canada, 1985) received the Hiroshima prize. Also, Alvy Ray Smith's *The Adventures of André and Wally B.* (U.S.,1984) won the special prize and marked the arrival of computer animation on a large scale.

Everyone recognised the success of the first edition. However, its results were not exclusively positive. The second edition, Hiroshima 1987, was at the mercy of people who believed that the festival was organised with a huge budget and planned to take advantage for their own personal profit. Renzo and I worked hard to protect the festival from unethical behaviour. Fortunately the festival ended up being a success after all and I still have positive memories of it. With Karel Zeman (Czechoslovakia) as the honorary president, the international jury was made up of Yuri Norstein (Russia), Bruno Bozzetto (Italy), Paul Driessen (Canada), Te Wei (China), Nicole Salomon (France), and Osamu Tezuka (Japan). *L'homme qui plantait des arbres* (*The Man Who Planted Trees*, Canada, 1987) by Frédéric Back won the grand prize, and John Lasseter's *Luxo Jr.* (U.S. ,1986) won the first prize for films shorter than five minutes.

During the 1987 festival, John Halas, the ASIFA honorary president, and Nicole Salomon, the ASIFA general secretary at that time, addressed their policy over the control of the festival. They explained the problem in front of the Japanese animation community, announcing clearly that ASIFA would withdraw its endorsement if they did not offer support, trust, and respect to Renzo and Sayoko.

The third edition was scheduled to be held in 1990. Because many animation festivals were held in odd years, Hiroshima, a newcomer, decided to move to even years. It was convenient for us too because the city of Hiroshima planned to organise a major 'Sea and Island Expo' in 1989. Renzo and I were quite exhausted. The conspiracies and challenges to our leadership during the previous years had been wearing. We were grateful to have some time to rest, and we even felt that others could take over the festival if they wanted to do so. But once it became more widely known that our festival had a very small budget, only those interested in the position of festival director as an honorary position stayed involved. Incredibly, one suggested that the programmes could simply be the same as Annecy's, while another said that I should help him organise the festival as a secretary without any power.

Because our festival was established after a very difficult gestation period — 12 years of work by Renzo and myself — I could not just leave it. Instead, I devoted my energy to teaching others how to organise a film festival. Once our opponents recognised the hard work required of a festival director, they gradually began to doubt whether they could organise the third edition themselves. Finally, in February 1990, they gave up. Following the official resolution taken by ASIFA-Japan, I returned as the director of Hiroshima 1990, with Renzo as producer, only six months before the festival was due to begin. Immediately, I encouraged the call for entries and informed ASIFA about our return. Many messages of congratulation arrived via telegram, fax and telex. Although there were only 27 entries by the time we rejoined the festival in February, many more works soon started to arrive from all over the world.

We welcomed Bob Godfrey (UK) as the honorary president of Hiroshima 1990. The international jury consisted of Eduard Nazarov (Russia), Alison de Vere (UK), Fusako Yusaki (Japan), Bob Stenhouse (New Zealand), Tadanori Yokoo (Japan) and John Lasseter (U.S.). The grand prize was awarded to *Korova* (*Cow*, Russia, 1989) directed by Alexander Petrov. This great film, conveying a message about true and selfless love, has guided me in my life since then. Many people involved in the festival's organisation recognised that if the third edition had not been held successfully, the festival would not still be running today. Because of the two-year break, the quality of the competition programmes was very high, as was the number of participants. Thus, I think that the hardships we experienced were of benefit in the long run. Also, I came to realise that, if you continue working under a firm philosophy and with a good spirit, there will always be good friends to support you.

Today, many participants from around the globe warmly praise our festival team. Our staff is my treasure. They always do their best, working very hard on any given task. They do not work only for their wages, but also for the joy of making the festival a success. During each festival, I am also very pleased that many former staff members return to work voluntarily backstage. Together with our team, I appreciate the wonderful films submitted by filmmakers from all over the world. It is my sincere wish to introduce them to global audiences.

Now, I would like to describe our selection committee, because its work is so important in laying a firm foundation for each festival. The selection committee of the Hiroshima festival consists of five animation experts from different countries, balanced by region. The committee meets for two weeks in May, from early morning till evening — sometimes until midnight. Committee members must have a wide knowledge of animation. In addition, they must have a great deal of stamina and energy, both physical and mental, in order to get through the rigorous screening process. From nearly 2000 entries (1937 entries in 2010), we ask them to select works for four competition programmes — 450 minutes in total. As a result, usually, only around 60-70 works are selected for competition. Since the sixth edition in 1996, all entries are judged equally and impartially without any categorisation, just by quality. The name of the director and country of each work are not shared with the committee.

Of course, some members meet for the first time while working on the committee, and some members experience the selection process for the first time. Thus, the initial meeting of the selection committee can be held in a nervous atmosphere. This is how it works. As the festival director, I attend all the screenings and meetings, to assure that selection flows smoothly. I never express my opinion concerning the films, but trust the work of our selection committee. I concentrate on creating a good working environment and atmosphere for the committee to carry out its task, free of worries. At the first meeting, I lay out several important points. I ask the committee members not to judge by comparing different entries, but to evaluate each entry separately by its own artistic criteria, respecting their first impressions. This way, hopefully, members will not make an error of judgement, either on the first entry they see or when they are very tired. Their artistic values have been fostered over many years and won't waver so easily. Also, I ask our selection committee members to talk only about the good points of each film. A work with many good points will rise to the top. Should they talk about the weak points, they may start to feel stress and more time will be required for discussion, which will exhaust them. Talking only about good points is the best selection method I acquired over many years of experience.

In addition, together with the festival office, I ensure that all the screenings begin promptly, so that committee members can work efficiently. It is important to budget time for short breaks, meals, shopping, and even some exercise. And it is essential that members spend an enjoyable time at dinner, so that they gather the strength for the next day. Still, because it is natural for many committee members to grow nervous when thinking about judging nearly 2000 entries in two weeks, I have a story which I always tell at the beginning.

'Once upon a time, there was a young woman who married into a farm. One day, her mother-in-law took her to a vast wheat field, all ripened in yellow as far as she could see on the horizon. And, handing her a scythe, her mother-in-law asked her to start harvesting. The young woman was shocked by the endless field and stood immobilised. Then, her mother-in-law said, "Don't think too much and just harvest the wheat at your own feet". As she continued working, the young woman noticed one day that all the wheat had been harvested'.

After the story, I tell the selection committee to just focus on the film in front of them. I also mention that every time the committee completes its job, I feel like seeing another 300 films. Because each animation work is unique, inspirational and full of originality, I never lose interest in the art of animation. Every day, I am pleased to find new questions, laughter

13.2. Now one of the major animation festivals in the world, the Hiroshima festival welcomed large audiences to its main hall in 2010. © Hiroshima International Animation Festival

and surprises by appreciating these films, one right after another.

The Hiroshima festival is held for five days in August, at Aster Plaza. The city's cultural complex has three theatrical halls: a large hall with 1200 seats, a medium hall with 500 seats and a small one with 200 seats (figure 13.2). All programmes, including competition and special programmes, as well as seminars, symposiums, exhibitions, workshops and press conferences are held at Aster Plaza. In addition to the competition programmes for films under 30 minutes, we also hold more than 50 official special programmes, such as 'Best of the World', 'Stars of Students', 'Animation for Children', 'Japanese Animation Today' and 'Animation from the World', as well as retrospectives of masters, special programmes dedicated to individual countries and so on.

Since 2006, we have organised the unique 'Educational Film Market' to seek out new young talents and to serve as a liaison among students, schools and animation-related companies. We also have spaces for free presentations and screenings for participants: 'Frame In', a 60-seat space for students, and 'Nexus Point', a 50-seat space for professional filmmakers and producers. 'Frame In' is also used for Q&A sessions with filmmakers who need more time after the official programme concludes in the main hall.

However, our festival is about more than just animation. We also offer various programmes so that attendees may experience different aspects of Japanese culture, such as tea ceremonies, Chinese calligraphy, trying on kimonos, tours of sake factories, home visits and so forth. For example, we always have a picnic on the third day of the festival at Miyajima (a world heritage site), or a barbecue on a beach. Every night after the competition screenings we host parties. The opening party and closing party are by invitation only, but there are other parties held by 'Lappy Club', the festival's friendship club, or by ASIFA. Anyone is welcome to come to these parties to enjoy food and drink and to socialise. The aim of the Hiroshima festival is to pursue world peace through international cultural exchange and to enhance mutual understanding through the art of animation. I hope participants will not just enjoy the animation but also meet others at our festival who will animate their spirits and make them feel more alive.

Twenty-seven years have passed since the first festival was held in 1985. We say that 'persistence is power'; however, in order to continue moving forward, we need various kinds of power. We need love, trust, appreciation, vigour, devotion, courage and more. Even today, not everything is going well, and we are still fighting to cope with various difficulties. Sometimes I feel like a boxer who is also fighting herself.

I was very pleased to host the 13th edition in August 2010 and to celebrate the festival's 25th anniversary together. During the past quarter century, I was fortunate to meet with many important people who taught me many essential points for living. Each person kindly taught me to hold fast to my strong beliefs and convictions.

ASIFA, established with an eye toward world peace by several animation masters who survived hardship during the First and Second World Wars, celebrated its 50th anniversary in 2010. ASIFA has a wonderful history of filmmakers exchanging friendship and supporting one another, even during the Cold War. The Hiroshima festival has always respected the spirit of the founders of ASIFA. Hiroshima 2010 opened with the film *Neighbours* (Canada, 1952) directed by Norman McLaren, the first president of ASIFA. Raoul Servais (Belgium) served as the honorary president, and the international jury members consisted of Vivien Halas (UK), Anri Koulev (Bulgaria), Alexei Alekseev (Russia), Gerrit van Dijk (The Netherlands), Michaela Pavlatova (Czech Republic) and Seiichi Hayashi (Japan). The grand prize went to *Sinna Mann* (*Angry Man*, 2009, Norway) by Anita Killi (figure 13.3). Because Hiroshima is one of the qualifying film festivals for an Academy Award, *Angry Man* was also submitted for Oscar competition.

13.3. Anita Killi (left) receives the grand prize at the 2010 Hiroshima festival for *Sinna Mann* (*Angry Man*, Norway, 2009), from Vivien Halas, the chairperson of the jury. © Hiroshima International Animation Festival

Thirty-eight years ago, there was an attractive world of independent animation, which inspired in me a strong enthusiasm for creating an animation film festival in Japan. Today, the situation has changed in various ways. It has become easier to make animation digitally. Animation education has become more widely offered, and many talented filmmakers are emerging. There is also an increasing number of amateur filmmakers, so-called 'Sunday animators', and the sophistication of the audience has improved. Animation festivals, both large and small, are held nearly every day somewhere in the world. However, in spite of all these improvements, I regret that animation artists still find it difficult to support themselves. In the past, filmmakers received more income from 35mm and 16mm films, as prints had the value of scarcity, and were purchased by schools, libraries and museums at higher prices. It has now become very convenient to make DVD copies, but the DVDs themselves sell for less. Moreover, people tend to treat the same animation work with less respect when it is stored on a DVD. In the case of books, the difference between comic books and deluxe editions is immediately apparent, but it is more difficult in the case of animation. New problems arise with the new times.

Moving images are still less than 120 years old, and we are still in chaos, above all due to dramatic developments in technology. Animation is widely recognised today as an effective medium, and it has become indispensable in the 'content industry', as well as in our daily lives. The entertainment industry has grown enormously, and it is expected to expand more with the development of new technologies, the internet and other visual media. On the other hand, people also crave something more significant, essential and philosophical than just entertainment. We need artists to make films just because they want to, without thinking of profit or popularity. When we see outstanding animation shorts in film festivals, we appreciate the existence of fine art in a true sense, art that is created by using animation with originality.

I believe it is very important to encourage and support others living pure artistic lives, believing that their work will be understood and recognised in the future, just as Vincent van Gogh did. I feel I still have a mission to carry out for the sake of filmmakers. As festival director, I think it is most important to remember the hearts and spirits of artists when organising a festival. Thus, for instance, it is very important to write letters to the filmmakers whose works are not selected for competition. Understanding the disappointment of these filmmakers, I look over my notes on each work. I sometimes add a short handwritten message. Also, I return all entries unless the filmmakers ask us not to. These are basic things to do as a festival director, but I try to carry out these tasks with care, with all my heart, hoping that better days will come for us all.

I have been very fortunate to meet many master filmmakers — Paul Grimault, Norman McLaren, Ivan Ivanov-Vano, Karel Zeman, John Halas, Jules Engel, Faith Hubley, Steven Bosustow, June Foray, Bill Littlejohn, and many, many others — who taught me by example to have infinite hope and courage. If you saw the films we showed at Hiroshima 2010, I am sure you would understand that our activity is worthwhile and that we can share hope together. By looking into the world of animation art, you discover something new, or a new way of thinking. Here you can find all kinds of art forms and cultures created by human beings, as well as artists who live their lives earnestly. Even when making gag animation, they are serious about making people laugh!

I feel that the 27 years of the Hiroshima festival have passed so quickly. I feel time whizzing by faster and faster, especially since Renzo left us in 1997. Nevertheless, I would like to keep on carrying out our original intention. In order to remind myself of the spirit of those early days, I would like to quote my message published in the official catalogue of Hiroshima 1985:

It has been our dream for a long time to hold an International Animation Festival in Asia, and I think it is epoch-making that this dream has come true, especially as an official festival endorsed by ASIFA. I am very grateful to all people who kindly supported us in this goal. Animation is an art that brings together every kind of cultural endeavour created by mankind including music, fine art, literature, history, philosophy, science, natural science, imagination, etc., pursuing human kindness. Animation means giving life to the lifeless and it is not taking away lives from the living. Thus, enjoying animation is exactly the world of 'love and peace'. I believe the fact that the city of Hiroshima established the first International Animation Festival in Asia, as one of the projects commemorating the 40th anniversary of atomic bombing, will contribute enormously for our future. It is because I strongly believe that culture will serve as a great power to achieve true world peace and also, I believe that animation is a cultural form worthy to prove this. For this aim, I think it is most important to continue this festival for ten years and twenty years. Only then, we will know whether this festival was a success or not. I would like to express my sincere gratitude to you for your kind support to our festival. Thank you very much.

Today, as we plan for the next edition, my thoughts remain the same.

Festivals Cited

Abu Dhabi Film Festival, http://www.abudhabifilmfestival.ae
AFI FEST, http://www.afi.com/afifest
Amiens International Film Festival, http://www.filmfestamiens.
org/?lang=en
Anima Mundi, http://www.animamundi.com.br/en/home
Animation Now!, http://www.trojmiasto.pl/animation-now
Animator International Festival of Animated Film, http://www.animator-
festival.com/index.php?lang=EN
Annecy International Animated Film Festival, http://www.annecy.org/
home
Asia-Pacific Film Festival, http://www.apff.com.tw
Ballerina Ballroom Cinema of Dreams, http://www.cinemaofdreams.
co.uk
Bangkok International Film Festival, http://www.bangkokfilm.org
Beeld voor Beeld: Documentary Film Festival on Cultural Diversity,
http://www.beeldvoorbeeld.nl/2en/fs.html
Bergman Week, http://bergmancenter.se/en/bergman-week
Berlin International Film Festival, http://www.berlinale.de/en/
HomePage.html
Buenos Aires International Festival of Independent Cinema, http://
www.bafici.gov.ar/home/web/es/index.html
Bursa Silk Road Film Festival, http://www.silkroadfilmfestival.com
Busan International Film Festival, http://www.biff.kr
Cairo International Film Festival, http://www.cairofilmfest.org/Pages/
SliderEn.aspx
Cannes International Film Festival, http://www.festival-cannes.com/
en.html
Carthage Film Festival, http://www.jccarthage.org/index_eng.php#
Central Park Film Festival, http://www.centralpark.com/guide/activities/
movies.html
Chicago International Film Festival, http://www.chicagofilmfestival.com
Cinanima, http://www.cinanima.pt/apresentacao_en.html
Cinéma du Réel International Documentary Film Festival, http://www.
cinemadureel.org/?lang=en
Cork Film Festival, http://www.corkfilmfest.org
Cracow Film Festival, http://www.kff.com.pl/en
Denver Film Festival, http://www.denverfilm.org/festival

Documentarist — Istanbul Documentary Days, http://www.
documentarist.org
Dubai International Film Festival, http://www.dubaifilmfest.com:80/
index.php/en
Edinburgh International Film Festival, http://www.edfilmfest.org.uk
Etiuda&Anima, http://en.etiudaandanima.com
Fajr International Film Festival, http://www.fajrfestival.ir
Fantasy Filmfest, website unknown
Fantasy World Film Festival, http://www.fwifft.com
Festival dei Popoli International Documentary Film Festival, http://www.
festivaldeipopoli.org
Festival on Wheels, http://www.festivalonwheels.org
15 Second Film Festival, http://www.15secondfilmfestival.com
Film Harvest, http://http://film.iksv.org/en
Filmex, no website
Filminute, http://www.filminute.com/2010
Flaherty Film Seminar, http://www.flahertyseminar.org
Flash Forward Film Festival, http://www.flashforwardconference.com
Flying Broom International Women's Film Festival, http://www.
ucansupurge.org
Frameline: San Francisco International LGBT Film Festival, http://www.
frameline.org/festival
French/American Film Workshop, no website
Golden Harvest Awards, http://www.ctfa.org.tw/en_golden.htm
Göttingen International Ethnographic Film Festival, http://www.gieff.de
Guadalajara International Film Festival, http://www.
guadalajaracinemafest.com/english/index.php
Handmade Puppet Dreams, http://www.handmadepuppetdreams.com/
home.html
Havana Film Festival, http://www.habanafilmfestival.com
Hiroshima International Animation Festival, http://hiroanim.org
Hisar Short Film Competition, http://www.hisarfilm.boun.edu.tr
Holland Animation Film Festival, http://www.haff.nl/en
Hong Kong International Film Festival, http://www.hkiff.org.hk/en/
index.php
identities Queer Film Festival, http://www.identities.at/en/the-festival
!f Istanbul AFM International Independent Film Festival; http://2011.
ifistanbul.com/en
International Adana Golden Boll Film Festival, http://www.
altinkozafestivali.org.tr/en

International Antalya Golden Orange Film Festival, http://www.aksav.
org.tr/en

International Architecture and Urban Film Festival, http://www.
archfilmfest.org/eng

International Documentary Film Festival Amsterdam, http://www.idfa.
nl/nl.aspx

International Film Festival Marrakech, http://en.festivalmarrakech.info

International Film Festival Rotterdam, http://www.filmfestivalrotterdam.
com/en

International Istanbul Film Festival, http://film.iksv.org/en

International 1001 Documentary Film Festival, http://
www.1001belgesel.net/eng

International Short Film Festival Oberhausen, http://www.kurzfilmtage.
de/en/57th-international-short-film-festival-oberhausen.html

International Surrealist Film Festival, website unknown

Istanbul Animation Film Festival, http://www.iafistanbul.com/index_
en.php

Istanbul International Meeting of History and Cinema, http://www.
sinematarih.tursak.org.tr/main.htm

Istanbul Photography and Cinema Amateurs Club Short Film Days,
http://www.ifsak.org.tr/index.php

Jerusalem Film Festival, http://www.jff.org.il/?cl=en

Karlovy Vary International Film Festival, http://www.kviff.com/en/news

Kaunos Golden Lion Film Festival, http://www.muglakulturturizm.gov.
tr/arp/koycegiz.html

Lesbisch Schwule Filmtage Hamburg | International Queer Film Festival,
http://www.lsf-hamburg.de/english-info.html

Lisbon International Documentary Film Festival, http://www.doclisboa.
org

Locarno Film Festival, http://www.pardo.ch/jahia/Jahia/home/lang/en

Mar del Plata International Film Festival, http://www.
mardelplatafilmfest.com/25/prg/index_en.php

Margaret Mead Film and Video Festival, http://www.amnh.org/
programs/mead

Melbourne International Animation Festival, http://www.miaf.net

Midnight Sun Film Festival, http://www.msfilmfestival.fi/fpage.
php?lang=1

Mill Valley Film Festival, http://www.mvff.com

MIX: New York Queer Experimental Film Festival, http://www.mixnyc.org

New Directors New Films, http://newdirectors.org

NewFest: The New York LGBT Film Festival, http://newfest.org/
wordpress
New York African Film Festival, http://africanfilmny.org
New York Film Festival, http://www.filmlinc.com/pages/new-york-film-
festival
New York International Animation Film Festival, website unknown
NSI Online Short Film Festival, http://www.nsi-canada.ca/film_festival.
aspx
Ottawa International Animation Festival, http://www.animationfestival.
ca
Pan-African Film Festival of Ouagadougou, http://www.fespaco-bf.net
Pesaro Film Festival, http://www.pesarofilmfest.it
Polish Festival of Auteurs in Animation, http://www.ofafa.pl/pages/
index.php?p=news
Pordenone Silent Film Festival, http://www.cinetecadelfriuli.org/gcm
Providence Children's Film Festival, http://www.
providencechildrensfilmfestival.org
Provincetown International Film Festival, http://www.ptownfilmfest.org
Re-Animacja, http://www.reanimacjafestival.com/2007/en
San Francisco International Film Festival, http://www.sffs.org/sf-intl-
film-festival.aspx
Seattle International Film Festival, http://www.siff.net/index.aspx
Shanghai International Film Festival, http://www.siff.com
SilverDocs: American Film Institute/Discovery Channel Documentary
Festival, http://silverdocs.com
60Seconds, http://www.60sec.org/English.html
Southeast Asian Film Festival, website unknown
Sundance Film Festival, http://www.sundance.org/festival
Telluride Film Festival, http://www.telluridefilmfestival.org
Thessaloniki International Film Festival, http://www.filmfestival.gr/
default.aspx?lang=en-US
Tokyo International Film Festival, http://www.tiff-jp.net/en
Toronto International Film Festival, http://www.tiff.net/thefestival
Tribeca Film Festival, http://www.tribecafilm.com/festival
Tricky Women, http://www.trickywomen.at
25 FPS, http://25fps.hr/2011
Varna World Festival of Animated Film, http://www.varnafest.org
Venice International Film Festival, http://www.labiennale.org/en/
cinema/festival
Verzaubert/Liebe Filme Festival, http://www.liebefilme.com

White River Indie Films, http://www.wrif.org
World Film Festival, http://www.ffm-montreal.org/en_index.html
Zagreb World Festival of Animated Film, http://www.animafest.hr/en

Works Cited

Aftab, Kaleem (2008) 'Due North: The Ballerina Ballroom Cinema of Dreams', *The Independent*, 23 July. On-line. Available HTTP: http://www.independent.co.uk/arts-entertainment/films/features/due-north-the-ballerina-ballroom-cinema-of-dreams-874666.html (27 May 2011).

Alpan, Cem (ed.) (2011) *30: 20 Directors from 30 Years of the Istanbul Film Festival*. Istanbul: Istanbul Foundation for Culture and Arts.

An, Byeong-sub (1956) 'Asian Film Festival Scandal', *Shin Donga*, August, 30-2.

Anon. (1956) *Kyeonghyang Sinmun*, June 19.

___ (1959a) '"Oscar" Time in Asia: Sixth Asian Film Festival', *Southern Screen*, May, 15.

___ (1959b) 'Glittering Sixth Asian Film Festival', *Southern Screen*, June, 5.

___ (1960) 'The Colorful Cannes Film Festival', *Southern Screen*, June, 30-3.

___ (1962a) *Seoul Sinmun*, 10 January.

___ (1962b) *Donga Ilbo*, 10 May.

___ (1962c) *Nippon Times*, 15 May.

___ (1963) 'Shaw Brothers into World Market', *Southern Screen*, July, 3-4.

___ (2005) 'The Best of the Fests', *Screen International*, 18-24 February, 15.

___ (2006) *Anlar: Uluslararası Istanbul Film Festivali'nin 25 yılı | Moments: 25 Years of International Istanbul Film Festival*. Istanbul: İstanbul Kültür Sanat Vakfı.

Armatage, Kay (2009) 'Toronto Women & Film International 1973', in Dina Iordanova with Ragan Rhyne (eds) *Film Festival Yearbook 1: The Festival Circuit*. St Andrews: St Andrews Film Studies with College Gate Press, 82-98.

Asia-Pacific Film Festival 50th Anniversary Catalogue (2005). Kuala Lumpur, Malaysia: Ministry of Culture.

Augé, Marc (1995) *Non-Places: Introduction to an Anthropology of Supermodernity*, trans. J. Howe. London: Verso.

Bailey, Cameron (2009) 'The Festival as Dinner Party', *Schnitt: Das Filmmagzin*, 54, 2, 41.

Barlow, Melinda (2003) 'Feminism 101: The New York Women's Video Festival, 1972-1980', *Camera Obscura*, 18, 3, 3-38.

Bendazzi, Giannalberto (2007) 'Defining Animation—A Proposal', *Cartoons: The Journal of Animation*, 2, 26-9.

Benjamin, Walter (1968 [1936]) 'The Work of Art in the Age of Mechanical Reproduction', *Illuminations*. New York: Harcourt Brace Jovanovich, 217-52.

Benson, Sheila (1998) 'The Mill Valley Film Festival's First Twenty Years', in *Variety International Film Guide*. New York: A.S. Barnes, 353-62.

The Big Queer Film Festival List (2011). On-line. Available HTTP: http://www.queerfilmfestivals.org (30 May 2011).

Bordwell, David (2011) 'Never the Twain Shall Meet: Why Can't Cinephiles and Academics Get Along', *Film Comment*, 47, 3, 38-41.

Bourdieu, Pierre (1979) *Distinction: A Social Critique of the Judgement of Taste*. London: Routledge.

Bouwman, Melissa (1997) 'Animation on the Web', *Frame by Frame, a Quarterly Publication of ASIFA/Central*, Summer, 6-7. On-line. Available HTTP: http://www.asifa.org/newsletter/bowman.php (24 August 2010).

Calloway, Larry (2006) 'The 33rd Telluride Film Festival and the Sudden End of the Pence Era'. On-line. Available HTTP: http://larrycalloway.com/tride-2006 (25 May 2011).

Clarkson, Wensley (1995) *Quentin Tarantino: Shooting from the Hip*. London: Piatkus Books.

Comolli, Jean-Louis and Jean Narboni (1969) 'Cinéma/Idéologie/Critique', *Cahiers du cinéma*, October, 216, 11-15.

Cousins, Mark (2006) 'Widescreen: On Film Festivals', *Prospect*, December. On-line. Available HTTP: http://www.prospectmagazine.co.uk/2006/12/7970-widescreen (25 May 2011).

Cowie, Peter (2010) *The Berlinale, The Festival*. Berlin: Bertz + Fischer.

Czach, Liz (2004) 'Film Festivals, Programming, and the Building of a National Cinema', *The Moving Image*, 4, 1, 76-88.

de Barbaro, Jakub (2002) 'The New Motion Picture Medium', *2+3D*, 4, 69.

de Valck, Marijke (2006) *Film Festivals: History and Theory of a European Phenomenon that Became a Global Network*, published PhD thesis, University of Amsterdam.

____ (2007) *Film Festivals: From European Geopolitics to Global Cinephilia*. Amsterdam: Amsterdam University Press.

____ (2008) '"Screening" the Future of Film Festivals: A Long Tale of Convergence and Digitization', *Film International*, 6, 4, 15–23.

____ (2010) 'De rol van filmfestivals in het YouTube-tijdperk' | 'The Role of Film Festivals in the YouTube Age', *Boekman*, 83, 54-66.

de Valck, Marijke and Skadi Loist (2009) 'Film Festival Studies: An Overview of a Burgeoning Field', in Dina Iordanova with Ragan Rhyne (eds) *Film Festival Yearbook 1: The Festival Circuit*. St Andrews: St Andrews Film Studies with College Gate Press, 179-215.

____ (2010) 'Thematic Annotated Bibliography of Film Festival Research - Update: 2009', in Dina Iordanova with Ruby Cheung (eds) *Film Festival Yearbook 2: Film Festivals and Imagined Communities*. St Andrews: St Andrews Film Studies, 220-58. On-line. Available HTTP: http://www. filmfestivalresearch.org or directly at www1.uni-hamburg.de/Medien/ berichte/arbeiten/0091_08.html (22 January 2010).

Dönmez-Colin, Gönül (2008) *Turkish Cinema: Identity, Distance and Belonging*. Reaktionbooks: London.

____ (2010a) Interview with Hülya Uçansu, 15 April, International Istanbul Film Festival.

____ (2010b) Interview with Tayfun Pirselimoğlu, 9 August, Locarno Film Festival.

Ebert, Roger (1987) *Two Weeks in the Midday Sun: A Cannes Notebook*. Kansas City, MO: Andrews and McMeel.

Edera, Bruno (1997) 'Animation Festivals: A Brief History', *Animation World Magazine* January, 1. On-line. Available HTTP: http://www.awn.com/ mag/issue1.10/articles/edera.eng1.10.html (24 August 2010).

Elsaesser, Thomas (2005) *European Cinema: Face to Face with Hollywood*. Amsterdam: Amsterdam University Press.

Elton, Zoë (2011) Interview with Sheila Benson, 27 April, Mill Valley, CA.

English, James (2005) *The Economy of Prestige: Prizes, Awards and the Circulation of Cultural Value*. Cambridge: Harvard University Press.

Fehrenbach, Heide (1995) *Cinema in Democratizing Germany: Reconstructing National Identity After Hitler*. Chapel Hill and London: University of North Carolina Press.

Fu, Poshek (2008) 'The Shaw Brothers Diasporic Cinema', in Poshek Fu (ed.) *China Forever: The Shaw Brothers and Diasporic Cinema*. Champaign, IL: University of Illinois Press, 1-26.

Fung, Richard (1999) 'Programming the Public', *GLQ: A Journal of Lesbian and Gay Studies*, 5, 1, 89-93.

Gorfinkel, Elena (2006) 'Wet Dreams: Erotic Film Festivals of the Early 1970s and the Utopian Sexual Public Sphere', *Framework*, 47, 2, 59-86.

Harbord, Janet (2009) 'Film Festivals-Time-Event', in Dina Iordanova with Ragan Rhyne (eds) *Film Festival Yearbook 1: The Festival Circuit*. St Andrews: St Andrews Film Studies with College Gate Press, 40-6.

Harrington, Curtis (1952) 'Film Festival at Cannes', *The Quarterly of Film, Radio and Television*, 7, 1, 32-47.

Heijs, Jan and Frans Westra (1996) *Que Le Tigre Danse, Huub Bals een biografie | May the Tiger Dance: A Biography of Huub Bals*. Amsterdam: Otto Cramwinckel.

Ho, Hyeon-chan (1965) 'Korean Cinema on the Road to the Venice', *Silver Screen*, August, 65.

Howes, Lauren (2009) 'A Complicated Queerness', in Dorothée von Diepenbroick and Skadi Loist (eds) *Bildschön: 20 Jahre Lesbisch Schwule Filmtage Hamburg | Picturesque: 20 Years of Hamburg International Queer Film Festival*. Hamburg: Männerschwarm, 130-3.

Iordanova, Dina with Ragan Rhyne (eds) (2009) *Film Festival Yearbook 1: The Festival Circuit*. St Andrews: St Andrews Film Studies with College Gate Press.

Iordanova, Dina with Ruby Cheung (eds) (2010) *Film Festival Yearbook 2: Film Festivals and Imagined Communities*. St Andrews: St Andrews Film Studies.

_____ (2011) *Film Festival Yearbook 3: Film Festivals and East Asia*. St Andrews: St Andrews Film Books.

Judt, Tony (2005) *Postwar: A History of Europe Since 1945*. New York: Penguin Books.

June, Jamie L. (2004) 'Defining Queer: The Criteria and Selection Process for Programming Queer Film Festivals', *CultureWork*, 8, 2. On-line. Available HTTP: http://aad.uoregon.edu/culturework/culturework26.html (7 December 2008).

Kael, Pauline (1963) 'Circles and Squares', *Film Quarterly*, 16, 3, 12-26.

_____ (1964) 'Are Movies Going to Pieces?', *The Atlantic Monthly*, 214, 6, 61-81.

Kehr, Dave (2011) 'Donald Krim, Film Distributor, Dies at 65', *The New York Times*, 22 May. On-line. Available HTTP: http://www.nytimes.com/2011/05/23/movies/donald-krim-film-distributor-dies-at-65.html?_r=1&emc=eta1 (24 May 2011).

Kitamura, Hiroshi (2010) *Screening Enlightenment: Hollywood and the Cultural Reconstruction of Defeated Japan*. Ithaca: Cornell University Press.

Klippel, Heike (2008) '"The Art of Programming"', in Heike Klippel (ed.) *'The Art of Programming': Film, Programm und Kontext*. Münster: LIT, 7-17.

Knight, Arthur (1957) *The Liveliest Art*. New York: MacMillan.

Kwai, Wise (2010) *Thai Film Journal*. On-line. Available HTTP: http://thaifilmjournal.blogspot.com/2010/10/bangkok-international-film-festival.html?utm_source=feedburner&utm_medium=feed&utm_campaign=Feed%3A+WiseKwaisThaiFilmJournal+%28Wise+Kwai%27s+Thai+Film+Journal%29 (5 May 2011).

Law, Kar and Frank Bren (2005) *Hong Kong Cinema: A Cross Cultural View*. Lanham: Scarecrow Press.

Lloyd, Matthew (2009) *How the Movie Brats Took Over Edinburgh: The Impact of Cinephilia on Edinburgh International Film Festival, 1968-1980*. St Andrews: St Andrews Film Studies.

Loist, Skadi (2008) 'Frameline XXX: Thirty Years of Revolutionary Film: Der Kampf um queere Repräsentationen in der Geschichte des San Francisco International LGBT Film Festival' | 'The Fight for Queer Representations in the History of the San Francisco International LGBT Film Festival', in Ulla Wischermann and Tanja Thomas (eds) *Medien – Diversität – Ungleichheit: Zur medialen Konstruktion sozialer Differenz | Media – Diversity – Inequality: About the Media Construction of Social Difference*. Wiesbaden: VS Verlag für Sozialwissenschaften, 163-81.

Mazower, Mark (2005) *Salonica, City of Ghosts: Christians, Muslims and Jews, 1430-1950*. New York: Alfred A. Knopf.

Mill Valley Film Festival Catalogue (2010). Mill Valley: California Film Institute.

Ng, Grace (2007) 'Li Han Hsiang's *Long Men Zhen*', in Wong Ain-Ling (ed.) *Li Han-Hsiang, Storyteller*. Hong Kong: Hong Kong Film Archive, 138-57.

Nornes, Abé Markus (2011) 'Asian Film Festivals, Translation and the International Film Festival Short Circuit', in Dina Iordanova with Ruby Cheung (eds) *Film Festival Yearbook 3: Film Festivals and East Asia*. St Andrews: St Andrews Film Studies, 37-9.

Özgüç, Agah (1991) 'Antalya Film Festivali ya da Bir Festivalin Perde Arkası' | 'Antalya Film Festival or Behind the Curtain of a Festival', *Antrakt* (November), 77-85.

Peranson, Mark (2009) 'First You Get the Power, Then You Get the Money: Two Models of Film Festivals', in Richard Porton (ed.) *Dekalog 3: On Film Festivals*. London: Wallflower, 23-37.

Porton, Richard (ed.) (2009) *Dekalog 3: On Film Festivals*, London: Wallflower.

Porton, Richard (2009) 'A Director on the Festival Circuit: An Interview with Atom Egoyan', in Richard Porton (ed.) *Dekalog 3: On Film Festivals*. London: Wallflower, 169-81.

Querbild e.V. (ed.) (2008) *19. Lesbisch Schwule Filmtage Hamburg: 21-26.10.2008*. [International Queer Film Festival catalogue.]

Quintín (2009) 'The Festival Galaxy', in Richard Porton (ed.) *Dekalog 3: On Film Festivals*. London: Wallflower, 38-52.

Ramey, Kathryn (2010) 'Economics of the Film Avant-Garde: Networks and Strategies in the Circulation of Films, Ideas, and People', *Jump Cut: A Review of Contemporary Media*, Summer, 52. On-line. Available HTTP: http://www.ejumpcut.org/currentissue/rameyExperimentalFilm/index.html (24 August 2010).

Rastegar, Roya (2009) 'The De-Fusion of Good Intentions: Outfest's Fusion Film Festival', *GLQ: A Journal of Lesbian and Gay Studies*, 15, 3, 481-97.

Report on the Third Annual Film Festival of Southeast Asia (1956). Hong Kong: The Executive Committee.

Rhyne, Ragan (2007) 'Pink Dollars: Gay and Lesbian Film Festivals and the Economy of Visibility', unpublished PhD thesis, New York University.

Rich, B. Ruby (1992) 'New Queer Cinema', *Sight & Sound*, 2, 5, 30-5.

Ruoff, Jeffrey (1994) 'On the Trail of the Native's Point of View: The Göttingen International Ethnographic Film Festival', *CVA Newsletter*, 2, 15-18.

____ (1996) 'Reminiscences of a Journey to the Flaherty Film Seminar', *Wide Angle*, 17, 1-4, 66-9.

____ (2008) 'Ten Nights in Tunisia: Les Journées Cinématographiques de Carthage', *Film International*, 6, 4, 43-51.

____ (2011) 'The Gulf War, the Iraq War, and Nouri Bouzid's Cinema of Defeat: *It's Scheherazade We're Killing* (1993) and *Making Of* (2006)', *South Central Review*, 28, 1, 18-35.

Schaffer, Johanna (2004) 'Sichtbarkeit = politische Macht? Über die visuelle Verknappung von Handlungsfähigkeit' | 'Visibility = Political Power? About the Visual Shortening of Agency', in Urte Helduser, Daniela Marx, Tanja Paulitz and Katharina Pühl (eds) *Under Construction? Konstruktivistische Perspektiven in feministischer Theorie und Forschungspraxis | Under Construction? Constructionist Perspectives in Feminist Theory and Research Practice*. Frankfurt/Main: Campus, 208-22.

Schilling, Mark (2007) *No Borders, No Limits: Nikkatsu Action Cinema*. Farleigh, UK: FAB Press.

Schröder, Nicholaus (ed.) (2000) *Zwischen Barrikade und Elfenbeinturm: Zur Geschichte des unabhängigen Kinos. 30 Jahre Internationales Forum des Jungen Films | Between Barricade and Ivory Tower: On the History of Independent Cinema. 30 Years of the International Forum of New Cinema*. Freunde der Deutschen Kinemathek. Berlin: Henschel.

Searle, Samantha (1996) 'Film and Video Festivals: Queer Politics and Exhibition', *Meanjin*, 55, 1, 47-59.

Siegel, Marc (1997) 'Spilling out onto Castro Street', *Jump Cut: A Review of Contemporary Media*, 41, 131-6. On-line. Available HTTP: http://www.ejumpcut.org/archive/onlinessays/JC41folder/OnCastroStreet.html (30 August 2010).

Stern, Sol (1967) 'A Short Account of International Student Politics and the Cold War with Particular Reference to the NSA, CIA, etc.', *Ramparts* 5, 9, 29-39.

Stringer, Julian (2001) 'Global Cities and International Film Festival Economy', in Mark Shiel and Tony Fitzmaurice (eds) *Cinema and the City: Film and Urban Societies in a Global Context*. Oxford: Blackwell, 134-44.

___ (2003) 'Regarding Film Festivals', unpublished PhD thesis, University of Indiana-Bloomington.

Stryker, Susan (1996) 'A Cinema of One's Own: A Brief History of the San Francisco International Lesbian & Gay Film Festival', in Jenni Olson (ed.) *The Ultimate Guide to Lesbian & Gay Film and Video*. New York: Serpent's Tail, 364-70.

Teo, Stephen (2009) 'Asian Film Festivals and their Diminishing Glitter Domes: An Appraisal of PIFF, SIFF and HKIFF', in Richard Porton (ed.) *Dekalog 3: On Film Festivals*. London: Wallflower Press, 109-21.

Thackway, Melissa (2003) *Africa Shoots Back: Alternative Perspectives in Sub-Saharan Francophone African Film*. Bloomington: Indiana University Press.

Third Meeting of the ASEAN Sub-Committee on Film: Official Report (November 1974). Jakarta, Indonesia.

Through African Eyes, Volume 2: Dialogues with the Directors (2010). New York: African Film Festival.

Turan, Kenneth (2002) *Sundance to Sarajevo: Film Festivals and the World They Made*. Berkeley, CA: University of California Press.

Turner, Wallace (1967) 'Asia Foundation got CIA Funds', *The New York Times*, 22 March, 17.

Wijnberg, Nachoem W. and Gerda Gemser (2000) 'Adding Value to Innovation: Impressionism and the Transformation of the Selection System in Visual Arts', *Organization Science*, 11, 3, 323-9.

Xanthopoulos, Lefteris (ed.) (1999) *Pavlos Zannas*. Athens: Thessaloniki International Film Festival.

Yau, Shuk-ting Kinnia (2003) 'Shaws' Japanese Collaboration and Competition as Seen Through the Asian Film Festival Evolution', in Wong Ain-ling (ed.) *The Shaw Screen: A Preliminary Study*. Hong Kong: Hong Kong Film Archive, 279-91.

Yeh, Yueh-yu Emilie (2006) 'Taiwan: Popular Cinema's Disappearing Act', in Anne Tereska Ciecko (ed.) *Contemporary Asian Cinema: Popular Culture in a Global Frame*. New York: Berg Press, 156-68.

Zielinski, Ger (2008) 'Furtive, Steady Glances: On the Emergence and Cultural Politics of Lesbian & Gay Film Festivals', unpublished PhD thesis, McGill University, Montreal.

___ (2009) 'Queer Film Festivals', in John C. Hawley and Emmanuel S. Nelson (eds) *LGBTQ America Today: An Encyclopedia*. Westport, CT: Greenwood Press, 980-84.

Zielinski, Ger and Stephen Kent Jusick (2010) 'Ger Zielinski in Conversation with Stephen Kent Jusick, Executive Director of MIX Festival of Queer Experimental Film and Video', *Fuse*, 16-22.

INDEX

Page numbers in italics refer to illustrations.

St Andrews Film Studies
International Advisory Board

Professor Dudley Andrew, Yale University, U.S.

Professor Alberto Elena, Universidad Carlos III de Madrid, Spain

Jean-Michel Frodon, Projection Publique and Sciences Po, Paris, France

Professor Faye Ginsburg, New York University, U.S.

Professor Andrew Higson, University of York, UK

Dr Adrian Martin, Monash University, Australia

Dr Richard Porton, *Cineaste*, New York, U.S.

Professor B. Ruby Rich, University of California, Santa Cruz, U.S.

Lightning Source UK Ltd.
Milton Keynes UK
UKOW041926180512

192851UK00001B/8/P